How States Respond to Crisis

The UNU World Institute for Development Economics Research (UNU-WIDER) was established by the United Nations University as its first research and training centre and started work in Helsinki, Finland, in 1985. The mandate of the institute is to undertake applied research and policy analysis on structural changes affecting developing and transitional economies, to provide a forum for the advocacy of policies leading to robust, equitable, and environmentally sustainable growth, and to promote capacity strengthening and training in the field of economic and social policy-making. Its work is carried out by staff researchers and visiting scholars in Helsinki and via networks of collaborating scholars and institutions around the world.

United Nations University World Institute for
Development Economics Research—UNU-WIDER
Katajanokanlaituri 6B, 00160 Helsinki,
Finland
www.wider.unu.edu

How States Respond to Crisis

Pandemic Governance Across the Global South

Edited by

RACHEL M. GISSELQUIST
ANDREA VACCARO

UNU WIDER

A study prepared by the United Nations University World Institute for Development Economics Research-(UNU-WIDER)

OXFORD
UNIVERSITY PRESS

OXFORD
UNIVERSITY PRESS

Great Clarendon Street, Oxford, OX2 6DP,
United Kingdom

Oxford University Press is a department of the University of Oxford.
It furthers the University's objective of excellence in research, scholarship,
and education by publishing worldwide. Oxford is a registered trade mark of
Oxford University Press in the UK and in certain other countries

World Institute for Development Economics Research of the United Nations University (UNU-WIDER),
Katajanokanlaituri 6 B, 00160 Helsinki, Finland

Published in the United States of America by Oxford University Press198 Madison Avenue,
New York, NY 10016, United States of America

British Library Cataloguing in Publication Data
Data available

Library of Congress Control Number: 2024951242

ISBN 9780198907206

DOI: 10.1093/9780198907237.001.0001

Printed and bound by
CPI Group (UK) Ltd, Croydon, CR0 4YY

Foreword

We expect the state to matter and act responsibly in times of crisis, but why is it that the quality and resilience of the state matters greatly? The COVID-19 pandemic which burst onto the global scene in 2020 provided Petri-dish conditions for our researchers and partners to analyse outcomes within national contexts with a focus on the Global South. A puzzling, counterintuitive picture emerged from the early research work—supposedly strong state institutions and effective public services appeared to struggle to cope with the unprecedented shock, whereas many Global South countries with supposedly weak and dysfunctional state institutions were, or seemed to be, better prepared for the pandemic.

Experts have argued that the lessons learned from recent epidemics—such as Ebola and Zika in Africa and MERS and SARS in Asia—contributed to more effective responses by Global South countries. And given that COVID-19 is particularly dangerous for the elderly, low-income countries, which tend to have comparatively weak state institutions, may have the advantage of having younger populations.

However, multiple studies have also found that the data on COVID-19 in the Global South may be biased towards showing a rosier picture than reality. Indeed, the state's ability to collect, process, and report information heavily influences the accuracy of data on health and mortality outcomes. Poorer countries with weak public sector institutions tend to have limited data collection and reporting capacities, hence they could appear to perform relatively well according to official statistics simply because the data is inaccurate.

This body of work speaks to our question of why the state matters in times of great crisis through comparative study of how diverse states responded to the pandemic. I sincerely thank the editors, Rachel M. Gisselquist and Andrea Vaccaro, for their careful architecture of the research work which nests within the larger UNU-WIDER project 'The State and Statebuilding in the Global South—International and Local Interactions'. And I thank the chapter authors for their intriguing contributions to the work. Readers are greatly encouraged to delve into this collection which provides a fascinating narrative on the politics and actions, or lack thereof, of states as they grappled with the largest global health crisis in living memory.

UNU-WIDER gratefully acknowledges the support and financial contribution to its work programme by the Institute's core donors of the governments of Finland and Sweden. Without this vital funding, our research and policy advisory work would be impossible.

Kunal Sen
Director of UNU-WIDER
Helsinki
March 2024

Acknowledgements

We have incurred many debts in the writing and compilation of this edited volume. We thank first the chapter authors for their excellent scholarship and active engagement. We are especially grateful for their contributions as the core work of this volume was done during the months and years when the pandemic posed so many challenges for daily life and work. Early versions of each of the chapters were presented and discussed at an online contributors' workshop in November 2021. Authors have since skilfully revised their chapters several times, taking into account feedback from us and others.

We began collaborating on research on COVID-19 and the state in 2020, in the early months of the pandemic. We are grateful to our colleagues at UNU-WIDER, the University of Oxford, the University of Insubria, and Sapienza University of Rome for their engagement with and support of this work. We thank in particular Kunal Sen as Director of UNU-WIDER for his strong encouragement of research in this area. We presented an early version of our cross-country analysis at the annual meeting of the International Studies Association in April 2021 and benefited from a lively online panel discussion and excellent comments from Amy Patterson as discussant. Anustup Kundu and Durgesh Solanki collaborated and provided research support to Rachel in related work. In addition, this volume has benefited from the parallel development of another volume on pandemic governance, focused at the subnational level across Indian states, co-edited by Rachel, Anustup Kundu, and Kunal Sen. Special thanks also go to David Gisselquist and Omar McDoom for their feedback on and engagement with our research, as well as to multiple anonymous referees.

The volume has been supported under UNU-WIDER's 2019–2024 work programme as part of the project 'The State and Statebuilding in the Global South—International and Local Interactions'. We gratefully acknowledge the financial contributions provided in support of this programme by the core donors of the governments of Finland and Sweden. We are thankful for the support provided to the 'States' project by the team at UNU-WIDER—in particular, Iina Kuuttila, Tim Shipp, Teresa Undurraga, and Janis Vehmaan-Kreula.

Huge thanks go to Lorraine Telfer-Taivainen for her expert editorial guidance and management of the publications process on the UNU-WIDER side, as well as to Siméon Rapin for strong editorial support. We are thankful to Oxford University Press and especially to Adam Swallow for his enthusiasm for the volume and for guiding it skilfully from review to publication.

The views expressed in this volume are those of the authors. The conclusions we draw in Chapter 1 reflect our views as editors and are not necessarily those of the individual contributors.

Rachel M. Gisselquist
Andrea Vaccaro
Helsinki and Oxford
March 2024

Contents

PART IV. LATIN AMERICA

List of Figures

List of Tables

List of Abbreviations

Africa CDC	Africa Centres for Disease Control
ASEAN	Association of Southeast Asian Nations
CCM	Chama Cha Mapinduzi
CFR	case fatality rate
CHADEMA	Chama cha Demokrasia na Maendeleo
CHE	catastrophic health expenditure
CHPS	Community-based Health Planning and Services
CODEO	Coalition of Domestic Election Observers
CSO	civil society organization
DIE	Deutsches Institut für Entwicklungspolitik (German Development Institute)
DOH	Department of Health
EC	Electoral Commission
ECLA	Economic Commission for Latin America
EmOC	emergency obstetric care
EOC	Emergency Operation Centre
EU	European Union
FSLN	Sandinista National Liberation Front
GDP	gross domestic product
GHS	Ghana Health Service
GHSI	Global Health Security Index
IACHR	Inter-American Commission on Human Rights
IATF-EID	Inter-Agency Task Force for the Management of Emerging Infectious Diseases
ICU	intensive care unit
IDB	International Development Bank
IMF	International Monetary Fund
INE	Instituto Nacional de Estadística (National Institute of Statistics)
MAS	Movimiento al Socialismo (Movement towards Socialism)
MEF	Ministry of Economy and Finance
MINSA	Nicaraguan Health Ministry
MMR	maternal mortality ratio
MoH	Ministry of Health
NAS	National Ambulance Service
NDSD	National Disease Surveillance Department
NGO	non-governmental organization
NPHI	National Public Health Institute
NSC	National Steering Committee

PAHO	Pan American Health Organization
PAPI	Provincial Governance and Public Administration Performance Index
PHEMC	Public Health Emergency Management Committee
PO-RALG	President's Office—Regional Authority and Local Government
PPE	personal protective equipment
PpR	Presupuestos por Resultados (Budgeting for Results Programme)
OxCGRT	Oxford Covid-19 Government Response Tracker
SAPs	structural adjustment policies
SDGs	Sustainable Development Goals
SIS	Seguro Integral de Salud
SWS	Social Weather Stations
TANU	Tanganyika African National Union
TEC	Tanzanian Episcopal Conference
TSE	Tribunal Supremo Electoral (Supreme Electoral Tribunal)
UN	United Nations
UNU-WIDER	United Nations University World Institute for Development Economics Research
WAHO	West African Health Organization
WHO	World Health Organization

List of Contributors

Kofi Takyi Asante is a senior research fellow at the Institute of Statistical, Social and Economic Research at the University of Ghana. His research over the years has focused on exploring the emergence, transformations, and contemporary character of the Ghanaian state, as well as the implication of these political economy trends on citizenship and civic engagement. His publications have appeared in *African Economic History*, *Studies in Ethnicity and Nationalism*, *International Journal of Politics, Culture, and Society*, and *World Development Perspectives*, among others.

Carew Boulding is a professor of political science and Director of the Program on International Development at the University of Colorado Boulder. Her research investigates political participation in democracies. She has worked on non-governmental organizations (NGOs) and credit-claiming, the impact of participatory budgeting on wellbeing, political competition and social spending, voter turnout in Bolivia and Brazil, civil society and support for democratic political systems, and attitudes of indigenous people towards the government in Bolivia. She has published two well-received books and articles in top political science journals.

Duc Anh Dang is Vice President, Central Institute for Economic Management (CIEM), Ministry of Planning and Investment, Vietnam. He has dedicated much of his time to public policy in Vietnam. His current research specializes in the macroeconomy, trade, labour market, and economic development in Association of Southeast Asian Nations (ASEAN) countries, especially Vietnam. His research has been published in *Journal of Comparative Economics*, *Journal of Development Studies*, *Food Policy*, and *Energy Policy*, among others.

Camila Gianella Malca received a PhD in psychology from the University of Bergen. She holds an MSc from Charité-Universitätsmedizin Berlin and a degree in psychology from the Pontificia Universidad Católica del Perú, where she is currently an assistant professor at the Department of Social Sciences and director of the Master in Political Sciences and International Relations. Her research interests include the right to health, analysis of health systems and policies, sexual and reproductive rights and health, and socio-legal mobilization.

Rachel M. Gisselquist is Professor in Governance and Development, and Director of the Governance and Social Development Resource Centre (GSDRC), University of Birmingham (UK). She is also a non-resident senior research fellow with UNU-WIDER, where she was based 2011–2024. Previously, she was a research director at Harvard University, where she co-authored the first several editions of the Ibrahim Index of African Governance, now a standard reference on governance. Her research examines issues of inequality, ethnic politics, state-building, foreign aid, governance, and democracy. She holds a PhD in Political Science from the Massachusetts Institute of Technology and an MPP from Harvard.

Calla Hummel (they/them) is an assistant professor of political science at the University of British Columbia. Their research examines why and how groups lobby their governments, focusing on issues of health, civil rights, and employment in the Americas. Their work has been published in top political science and public health outlets such as *Lancet Global Health, BMJ Global Health, The British Journal of Political Science, Comparative Political Studies*, and more. Their book, *Why Informal Workers Organize*, was published in 2021 by Oxford University Press and won the 2023 William Riker Award for the Best Book in Political Economy.

Mateo Jarquín is assistant professor of history and director of the programme in War, Diplomacy, and Society at Chapman University in Southern California. His scholarship analyses historical connections between revolutions, democracy, and international relations in Latin America. He is the author of *The Sandinista Revolution: A Global Latin American History* (University of North Carolina Press, 2024). Additionally, he writes regularly about contemporary Central American politics. Originally from Nicaragua, he holds a BA from Grinnell College and a PhD from Harvard University.

Jami Nelson-Nuñez is an associate professor of political science at the University of New Mexico. She works on the politics of service delivery in decentralized settings with a focus on water politics. Her research explores key development actors, especially NGOs and mayors, and the challenges they face in providing services critical to combating poverty. In particular, she explores the policy areas of water, sanitation, and energy provision. Her research has been published in top political science and development journals.

Amy S. Patterson is Carl Gustav Biehl Professor of International Affairs and Professor of Politics at the University of the South. She has authored or co-authored six books, including *Dependent Agency in the Global Health Regime* (2017), *Africa and Global Health Governance* (2018), and *Africa's Urban Youth: Challenging Marginalization, Claiming Citizenship* (2023). A two-time Fulbright Scholar, her work has appeared in African studies and public health journals. Her most recent project examines the politics of mental health in Africa. She teaches courses on development, African politics, and global health governance, directs community-engaged learning projects, and has led semester-abroad programmes to Ghana.

Julio C. Teehankee is a professor of political science and international studies at the Department of International Studies, De La Salle University, Manila. His research is on issues of popular participation, governance, democratization, and contested institutions in East and Southeast Asia. He has published extensively on the topics of elections, party politics, and political dynasties.

Anh Tran is a professor at the Paul O'Neill School of Public and Environmental Affairs, Indiana University, specializing in the governance issues of developing countries. His current research focuses on performance management and leadership in public organizations. His articles have appeared in *American Political Science Review, Journal of Financial Economics, Journal of Law and Economics, Journal of Public Economics, Journal of Politics, American Economic Journal: Applied Policy*, and other leading academic journals.

Andrea Vaccaro is a postdoctoral research fellow at the Blavatnik School of Government, University of Oxford, and an associate member of St Antony's College. Previously, he was a visiting researcher at UNU-WIDER and a postdoctoral researcher at the University of Insubria. His research interests lie at the crossroads between comparative politics and global development. Recently, he has worked on the interplay between the state, political regimes, and development, as well as international aid, COVID-19 responses, and measurement and indicators. He received his PhD from Sapienza University of Rome.

V. Ximena Velasco Guachalla is an assistant professor in the Department of Government at the University of Essex, United Kingdom. Her research interests include the link between contentious mobilization, demand making, and weak institutional contexts, as well as the relationship between protest participation, attitudes towards the political system, and democratic backsliding.

PART I
INTRODUCTION

1
What COVID-19 Can Tell Us about the State
A Global Look at the First Year of the Pandemic

Rachel M. Gisselquist and Andrea Vaccaro

1.1 Introduction

We expect the state to matter in times of crisis—for more 'capable' or 'stronger' states to better provide for and protect their populations. But how is it, precisely, that the quality of the state matters? This volume speaks to this question through comparative study of how diverse states in the Global South responded to the COVID-19 pandemic, the largest global crisis in recent memory. Bringing together insights from quantitative cross-country analysis and seven detailed country case studies, this volume analyses the ways in which the quality of the state—in terms of its capacity, authority, and legitimacy—affected national policy responses and pandemic health outcomes. Overall, while the significance of state capacity to deliver public services in effective pandemic response is clear, so too is striking variation in responses and health outcomes among states at similar levels of capacity. State legitimacy and authority shed light on this variation, linked in particular to the degree to which governments' responses were evidence-based versus politically driven, and the tenor of citizen compliance with and government enforcement of public health regulations. This chapter both introduces the volume and presents its core findings.

It is widely accepted that effective state institutions matter in a country's ability to respond to crises. Yet, in the first year of the COVID-19 pandemic, wealthy countries with strong state institutions were heavily affected by surging numbers of infections and deaths, while many poorer countries with comparatively weaker and less effective state institutions like Colombia, Nigeria, and Senegal (Mormina and Nsofor 2020) were praised for their policy responses. In other words, a counterintuitive picture seemed to emerge from the first pandemic year as countries with supposedly strong state institutions and effective public services struggled to cope with an unprecedented shock to their national health systems.

Rachel M. Gisselquist and Andrea Vaccaro, *What COVID-19 Can Tell Us about the State*. In: *How States Respond to Crisis*. Edited by: Rachel M. Gisselquist and Andrea Vaccaro, Oxford University Press. © UNU-WIDER (2025).
DOI: 10.1093/9780198907237.003.0001

This is surprising because countries with well-functioning public sector institutions should be better equipped to respond promptly and successfully to crises like the COVID-19 pandemic.

Experts have put forward several arguments to explain why many Global South countries were—or appeared to be—better prepared for the pandemic. For instance, it has been argued that the lessons learned from recent experiences with other infectious diseases such as Ebola in Africa (Impouma et al. 2021; Mobula et al. 2020) and MERS and SARS in Asia (Koyama 2021; Stasavage 2020) contributed to more effective policy responses. Africa's lower COVID-19 death toll has been explained also in terms of factors such as the rapid implementation of a set of coordinated responses across the continent by the Africa Centres for Disease Control and Prevention (Maeda and Nkengasong 2021) and more favourable climate conditions (Nguimkeu and Tadadjeu 2021). Moreover, given that COVID-19 has been particularly dangerous for the elderly (Yanez, Weiss, Romand, and Treggiari 2020), low-income countries, which tend to have comparatively weak state institutions, may have been advantaged by structurally younger populations (Evans and Werker 2020).

That being said, multiple studies have also argued that data on COVID-19 in Global South countries may be biased towards showing a better picture than reality. Indeed, the state's ability to collect, process, and report information directly influences the accuracy of data on pandemic outcomes (Knutsen and Kolvani 2022). Poor countries with weak or underfunded public sector institutions tend to have limited data collection, processing, and reporting capacities, so their good performance according to official statistics could be driven by inaccurate numbers. Official statistics on COVID-19 underestimated the true toll of the pandemic even in wealthy countries because not everyone can be tested and the sensitivity of tests is not perfect (Wu et al. 2020). Testing rates were relatively low, for instance, in many African countries (Nordling 2020), and infrastructural, technical, and economic factors severely impeded widespread testing in conflict-affected countries such as Yemen (Dhabaan, Al-Soneidar, and Al-Hebshi 2020). Many cross-country studies of the pandemic acknowledge such weaknesses in the data, but have nevertheless used them in analysis in the absence of any better information.

In Gisselquist and Vaccaro (2022), we offered another explanation for the puzzle. Drawing on the available cross-country data to study the relationship between the quality of the state—measured using multiple standard indicators—and COVID-19 response and health impact during the early stages of the pandemic, we found that the puzzling relationship shown in simple *correlations* is in fact misleading. Yes, poorer countries with less effective state institutions report fewer COVID-19 cases and deaths than rich countries with more effective institutions, but when we look beyond correlations and conduct analysis controlling for key confounding factors (such as testing capacity, elderly population, and national income), the relationship between indicators of the state and pandemic outcomes is much as conventional wisdom and theory predict. That is, countries with more robust state institutions—with higher ratings in terms of state capacity, authority, and legitimacy, according to standard metrics—indeed appear to have been more successful in responding to the pandemic and curbing the health impact. As explained more in detail in section 1.4, this analysis informed the design of this volume, underscoring the value of in-depth country case studies alongside analysis of cross-country data in building a better understanding of the complex relationship between the state and pandemic response.

In this volume, we draw on core findings from our quantitative analysis of the cross-country data, alongside detailed country case studies covering seven carefully selected countries of the Global South: Bolivia, Ghana, Nicaragua, Peru, the Philippines, Tanzania, and Vietnam. Much more has been written on Global North contexts, so this Global South focus addresses an important gap in the literature. In so doing, this volume offers new empirical insight into what happened during the first year of the pandemic, from the first infections to November 2020 when the era of mass vaccinations began.[1] While states' responses to COVID-19, and COVID-19 health outcomes, have continued to evolve, this early pandemic period offers an important snapshot of early reactions and preparedness, crucial to understanding the functioning of states in crisis. During this early pandemic period, all countries had to respond in some way to the same unprecedented global shock and all had similarly highly incomplete knowledge about COVID-19's transmission and prevention, as well as about the scope and nature of the shock they faced.

This volume shows clearly that *state capacity* matters. In the cross-country analysis, higher state capacity is among the strongest predictors of more effective pandemic response. Global South countries tend to have lower state capacity than Global North countries, according to standard metrics. At the same time, the cross-country data—and the case studies in this volume—also show striking variation in response and outcomes across states with similar levels of capacity. As the case studies in this volume suggest, lower state capacity implied greater challenges in the formulation and implementation of effective policy responses, but governments across countries met (or did not meet) these challenges in different ways.

State legitimacy sheds strong light on such variation. In particular, the studies in this volume suggest, the legitimacy of state institutions can help us to understand the degree to which governments' responses were more evidence-based versus more politically driven. In responding to COVID-19, governments of all types seemed to be influenced by a variety of factors in their response—including

[1] In November 2020, Bahrain started to vaccinate selected population groups as the first country in the world (Hale et al. 2021a) and Pfizer-BioNTech applied for permission for emergency use of their vaccine, leading to its mass rollout worldwide.

political pressures and incentives. But governments operating in states without strong legitimacy and capacity seemed to have fewer constraints in implementing politically motivated responses. In a conjunction of weak popular support and poor administrative competence, it might have been easier for governments to enact policies aimed more at keeping themselves in power than at providing for the broader public good. Studies in this volume of Nicaragua and Tanzania in particular show deliberate and successful government strategies to minimize the seriousness of the pandemic in part by manipulating information on infections and deaths. This in turn complicated an effective, evidence-based pandemic response. Further, the legitimacy of state institutions, the studies in this volume show, is intricately linked with the legitimacy of the government in power—indeed, it can be difficult to disentangle the two in countries with low to moderate state capacity.

State authority also sheds light on the diversity of pandemic responses and outcomes across lower-capacity settings. In particular, it can be seen to influence the nature of government pandemic policies and their enforcement, as well as citizen compliance with public health regulations.

This introductory chapter has three key objectives. First, it sets out a general framework for studying the relationship between the state and pandemic response and outcomes. Second, it discusses the selection of the seven case studies in this volume and provides a comparative overview of the state–pandemic nexus in these countries. Third, it summarizes the core conclusions and themes of this volume, bringing together the findings of the case studies with those of the cross-country analysis.

1.2 Why should the state matter?

The state is typically understood in the literature as 'a human community that (successfully) claims the monopoly of the legitimate use of physical force within a given territory' (Weber 1946: 78). While there is less scholarly consensus on the core dimensions of the state, three aspects have been useful in understanding variations across states in recent studies on the state and state-building: authority, capacity, and legitimacy (Andersen, Møller, and Skaaning 2014; Bratton and Chang 2006; Carbone and Memoli 2015; Carment and Samy 2019a, 2019b; Grävingholt, Ziaja, and Kreibaum 2015; Tikuisis, Carment, Samy, and 2015; Ziaja, Grävingholt, and Kreibaum 2019). Authority refers to the control of violence and enforcement of rules, capacity to the provision of public services and basic administration, and legitimacy to the acceptance of the rule by society (Grävingholt et al. 2015). We build on that tri-dimensional distinction here.

Conventional wisdom holds that strong and well-functioning state institutions play a key role in the ability of the state to reach its policy objectives. By contrast, weak and fragile states are often trapped with poverty, conflict, and the incapacity to implement desired policies (Carment and Samy 2019a). 'State effectiveness' thus is expected to matter for a variety of development outcomes. Global commitment to building 'effective' state institutions is underscored in the Sustainable Development Goals (SDG 16).

Theoretical considerations suggest that higher authority, capacity, and legitimacy are all associated with better pandemic outcomes and responses, although via distinct mechanisms (Gisselquist and Vaccaro 2022). High-authority countries should be more effective at enforcing COVID-19-related restrictions such as quarantine and stay-at-home requirements; high-capacity countries should be better prepared to respond to COVID-19 by having adequate pandemic response plans and preventative infrastructure; and high-legitimacy countries should be advantaged in ensuring voluntary compliance of the population with rules and support of public activities. However, even if distinct theoretical mechanisms can be identified, the empirical literature on the state and COVID-19—with the exception of Gisselquist and Vaccaro (2022)—has not considered these core dimensions of the state separately.

Past studies underscore that weak states are not well equipped for successful crisis response. More effective states are better prepared to deal with natural disasters like earthquakes, cyclones, and floods (Ahlbom Persson and Povitkina 2017; Kahn 2005; Keefer, Neumayer, and Plümper 2011; Sjöstedt and Povitkina 2017). Moreover, they appear to provide better public goods (Asadullah, Savoia, and Sen 2020; D'Arcy and Nistotskaya 2017) and produce better public health outcomes (Cingolani, Thomsson, and de Crombrugghe 2015; Holmberg and Rothstein 2011). We would expect similar patterns to emerge in the state's relationship with the COVID-19 crisis.

Early in the pandemic, prominent political scientists indeed argued that effective state institutions are crucial for successful pandemic responses (Ang 2020; Fukuyama 2020). Yet, cross-country evidence on the state–pandemic nexus was inconclusive. Some analyses were consistent with the argument that effective state institutions matter for better pandemic outcomes. For instance, Liang, Tseng, Ho, and Wu (2020) and Serikbayeva, Abdulla, and Oskenbayev (2021) find that higher government effectiveness is related to better pandemic outcomes, Knutsen and Kolvani (2022) show that countries with higher state capacity had lower excess mortality during COVID-19, and González-Bustamante's (2021) study on South American countries suggests that state capacity is a key factor for adopting quicker policy responses. Other studies, however, suggested contradictory findings. For instance, Redlin (2022) argues that better-governed countries adopted weaker responses, and both Cronert (2022) and Toshkov, Carroll, and Yesilkagit (2022) find that countries with weak capacity more rapidly adopted some specific policy measures such as school closures. Empirical evidence indicates that timely and strong response measures were crucial to curbing the transmission of COVID-19 (e.g. Fuller et al. 2021; Hale et al. 2021b).

Our earlier study (Gisselquist and Vaccaro 2022) bridges these contrasting interpretations by demonstrating that results on the state–pandemic nexus are contingent on controlling for other relevant factors. Countries with more effective state institutions were in general better prepared to handle the COVID-19 crisis—when confounding factors are held constant. Furthermore, we found that the relationship varies across state authority, capacity, and legitimacy. High-authority and in particular high-capacity countries had better health outcomes than low-authority and low-capacity countries in the first year of the pandemic, whereas we found no statistically significant relationship between legitimacy and COVID-19 health outcomes (Figure 1.1).

That said, tracing a link from the quality of the state to policy response to health outcomes is not straightforward in the cross-country data. Using available data on the stringency of pandemic containment and economic support measures compiled by the Oxford Covid-19 Government Response Tracker (OxCGRT) dataset (Hale et al. 2021a), we found evidence of a link between policy responses and legitimacy, but no clear relationship between policy responses and capacity and authority. As Figure 1.2 illustrates, higher legitimacy is related to less stringent containment policies, whereas authority and capacity do not seem to matter for the strength of adopted policy interventions.

1.3 Data-related challenges in a global cross-country approach

Stepping back from these findings, what about the data quality concerns mentioned earlier? Problematic statistics (for Global South countries in particular) clearly complicate our understanding of the global relationship between COVID-19 and the state.

Consider briefly the cross-country data on COVID-19 health outcomes and state authority, capacity, and legitimacy. The puzzle presented at the start of this chapter is illustrated in Figure 1.3: on average, weak states had better health outcomes than more effective states during the first year of the pandemic. Countries with more recorded COVID-19 cases per million people had in general higher authority (Pearson's $r = 0.25$), capacity ($r = 0.57$), and legitimacy ($r = 0.30$). The relationship is similar for COVID-19 deaths ($r = 0.14$, $r = 0.44$, and $r = 0.31$, respectively). When confounding factors are *not* taken into account, weaker states—especially in terms of capacity—had overall better health outcomes.

Yet if we, for one, measure COVID-19 health outcomes with an indicator of all-cause excess mortality for selected countries, the relationship between the disease and the three core dimensions of the state looks quite the opposite. As Figure 1.4

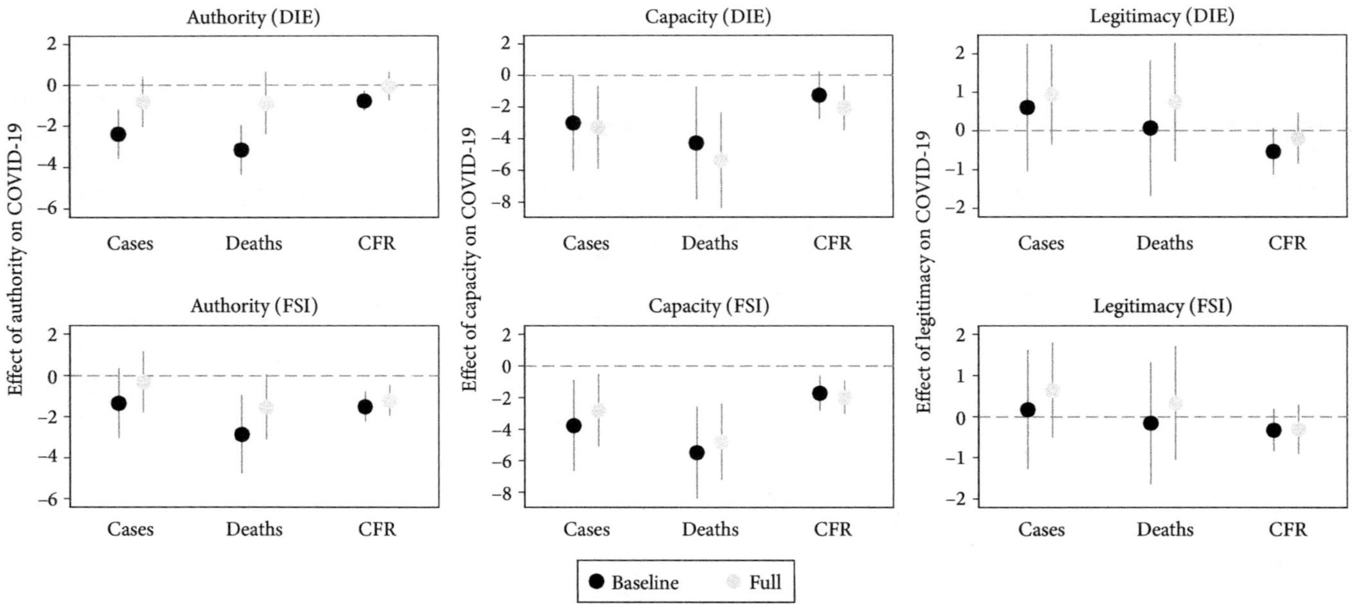

Figure 1.1 Relationship of state authority, state capacity, and state legitimacy with COVID-19 cases, deaths, and case fatality rate (CFR).

Source and note: The authors, based on Gisselquist and Vaccaro (2022). See Gisselquist and Vaccaro (2022) for further information on the regression models, included variables, and data sources.

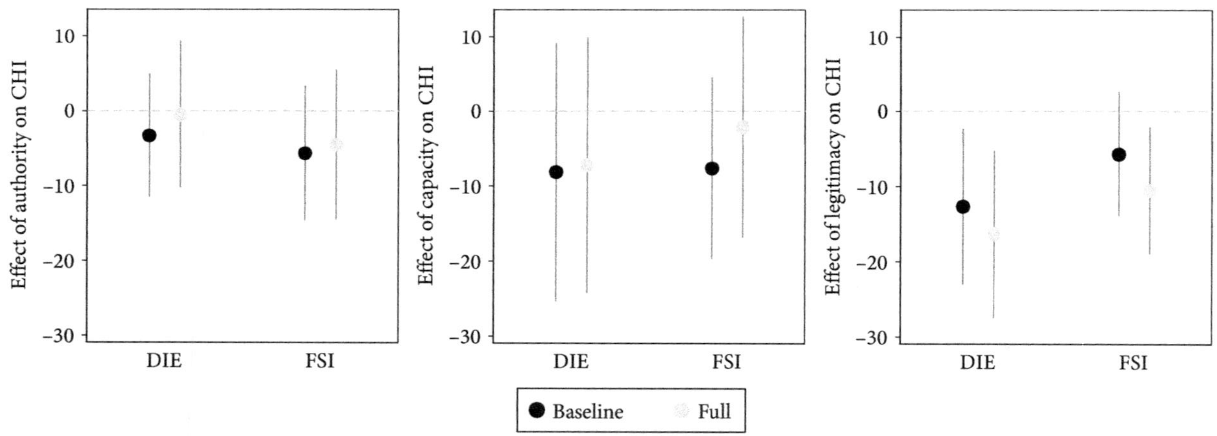

Figure 1.2 Relationship of state authority, state capacity, and state legitimacy with stringency of COVID-19-related containment and health index (CHI).

Source and note: The authors, based on Gisselquist and Vaccaro (2022). See Gisselquist and Vaccaro (2022) for further information on the regression models, included variables, and data sources.

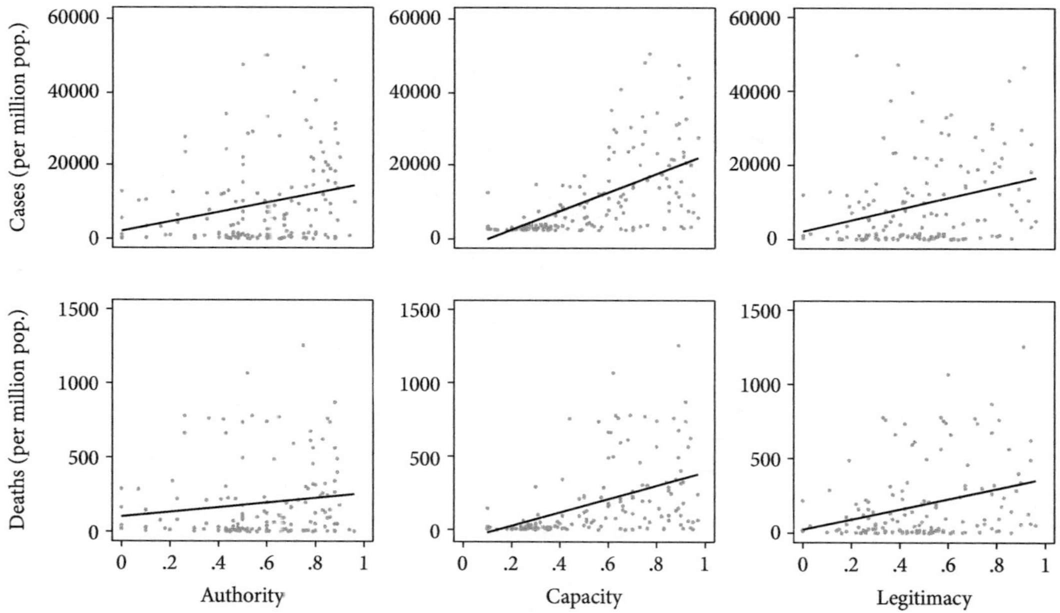

Figure 1.3 COVID-19 cases, deaths, and the ccre dimensions of the state.

Source and note: The authors, based on data from the European Centre for Disease Prevention and Control (ECDC 2020) and Ziaja et al. (2019). Data on COVID-19 cases and deaths refer to cumulative values as of 15 November 2020. Data on the state refer to 2015.

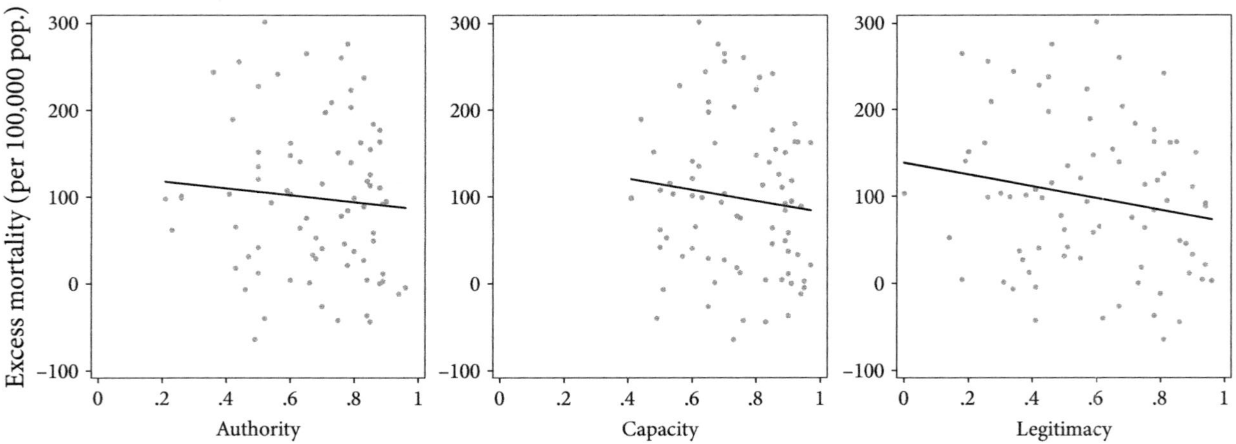

Figure 1.4 Excess mortality and the core dimensions of the state.

Source and note: The authors, based on data from Karlinsky and Kobak (2021) and Ziaja et al. (2019). Data on excess mortality refer to estimates for 2020. Data on the state refer to 2015.

shows, albeit weakly, states with higher excess deaths had on average lower authority ($r = -0.09$), capacity ($r = -0.11$), and legitimacy ($r = -0.18$) in the first year of COVID-19.

It has been argued that excess mortality data provide a more accurate picture of COVID-19 health outcomes than estimates on cases and deaths (Beaney et al. 2020; Knutsen and Kolvani 2022). However, excess mortality data do not exist for many Global South countries. Indeed, they are not available for low-authority and low-capacity states; they are available only for countries with a level of capacity higher than 0.40 and a level of authority higher than 0.20 (on a scale from 0 to 1).[2] This should not be surprising as reliable numbers on mortality in general are needed for the construction of excess mortality estimates and states with low capacity tend to have low statistical capacity as well. Differences in the correlations suggested in Figure 1.3 versus Figure 1.4 could therefore be driven by data coverage, data quality, or both. Regardless, it is clear that drawing strong conclusions from cross-country data is tricky, so insights from case studies become invaluable. This is especially true when we are interested in countries that are not even represented in available cross-country statistics. For these countries, only in-depth case studies can provide evidence-based insight.

Three specific data-related challenges can be mitigated by a case study approach to the state–pandemic nexus. The first relates to indicators of COVID-19 health outcomes. As discussed above, excess mortality data are not available for many weaker states. While we do have country-level data on COVID-19 cases and deaths for almost all countries in the world, we also can be sure that some cases and deaths went unreported. Underreporting is likely to be contingent on factors such as testing rates and the possibility to seek medical care, which vary across countries. It is then essential to take any potential confounding factors into account. While the 'impact' of these factors can be controlled for through different statistical approaches such as regression analysis—as we do in Gisselquist and Vaccaro (2022)—data on these confounding factors are not available for many poor countries. The bottom line seems to be then that specific contextual evidence is required to assess the accuracy of cross-country figures and to better understand the relationship between COVID-19 and the state, especially in the Global South.

A second challenge relates to data on government responses to the pandemic. There are a lot of data available on pandemic responses around the world, but not all questions can be answered with these data. For instance, the most widely used and comprehensive dataset on COVID-19 government responses—the OxCGRT dataset—is designed to capture information on the enactment of official policies; like most policy-tracking datasets, it does not focus on how well they are implemented or enforced, or the extent of compliance with them (Hale et al. 2021a).

[2] These values of capacity and authority are based on data from Ziaja et al. (2019) and refer to the year 2015.

Simply put, some countries might enact stringent containment policies but do not have the capability to enforce them—especially if voluntary compliance is, for some reason, low. Detailed case studies then are needed to shed light on the entirely plausible mismatches between formal policies and implementation, enforcement, and compliance in practice.

A third key challenge concerns data on the state and its dimensions. A flourishing body of scholarship on the measurement of the state shows that scholars do not fully agree on its core dimensions or how to measure them. Different approaches emphasize different aspects, and the usefulness of a given conceptualization and measure of the state can vary with the context analysed (Vaccaro 2023). As the level of analysis increases, the degree of generalization also increases, and so a broad cross-country approach cannot consider all potentially relevant contextual variation in the state. Detailed case studies make possible fuller consideration of contextual diversities and thus increase the possibility of better reflecting the state's complexity.

1.4 Delving deeper into selected country experiences in the Global South

In addition to mitigating data challenges, case studies are also useful in probing the unexplained heterogeneity in findings identified in previous large-n studies and providing deeper insight into causal relationships. Indeed, as Hertog (2021: 5) observes, 'most statistical models in political science cannot make reliable point predictions about causal effects in individual cases, even if the model itself is estimated with a high degree of precision'.

Yet, which countries should case studies cover? According to a 'nested approach' (Lieberman 2005), results from cross-country analysis can be helpful in informing the selection of case studies. Following the recommendations of the broader methodological literature dealing with how to select case studies based on regression results and the use of such cases in theory development (e.g. Lieberman 2005; Møller and Skaaning 2017; Seawright 2016; Seawright and Gerring 2008; Hertog 2021), we use Gisselquist and Vaccaro's (2022) regression estimates to identify countries that can be particularly informative on the state–pandemic nexus.

We identify a mix of 'deviant' and 'typical cases'. Typical cases are those with small residuals in a regression and are useful in providing both confirmation and disconfirmation of hypothesized mechanisms, whereas deviant cases are those with large residuals and are useful in generating new explanations for an outcome or in disconfirming a theoretical argument (Seawright and Gerring 2008). While Lieberman (2005) recommends selecting both typical and deviant cases, Seawright (2016: 512) argues that selecting typical cases is not a good idea 'when the goal is to discover more about the relationship in question than what can be captured by regression'. As we are mainly interested in delving deeper into the state–pandemic nexus, but also in assessing the robustness of past macro-level findings, we select mainly deviant but also typical cases.

In selecting the case studies of this volume, to increase comparability across cases, we also considered other factors that significantly explain variation in COVID-19 outcomes as identified in our previous work. Our regression results indicate that the level of per capita income was associated with pandemic outcomes, and we focus on Global South countries, thus excluding high-income countries. Geographic proximity was another important determinant of pandemic outcomes, thus we selected several sets of neighbouring countries across three world regions. While the selected country cases are analysed more in-depth in the next chapters of this volume, we provide here an initial discussion of these cases in relation to available cross-country indicators of interest.

In sum, we selected seven countries—six lower-middle and one upper-middle income economy[3]—across three world regions: Bolivia, Ghana, Nicaragua, Peru (upper-middle income), the Philippines, Tanzania, and Vietnam. Two chapters focus on experiences from sub-Saharan Africa, two from Southeast Asia, and three from Latin America.

Table 1.1 presents a summary of the key cross-country indicators on the state–pandemic nexus for these seven countries. Cases (per million inhabitants), deaths (per million inhabitants), and tests (per 1,000 inhabitants) are total, cumulative official numbers as of 15 November 2020. The first two indicators are published by the European Centre for Disease Prevention and Control (ECDC 2020), while testing data (noted when available) are taken from Our World in Data (OWID 2020). Case fatality rate (CFR) is then calculated as the ratio between cases and deaths. Excess mortality per 100,000 people (when available) is an estimate of 2020 from Karlinsky and Kobak (2021). Measures of the state refer to the year 2015 and are taken from Ziaja et al. (2019). Government response data refers to average levels from the first reported infection for each country until 15 November 2020 and are taken from the OxCGRT dataset (Hale et al. 2021a).

Among the deviant cases, Peru had the world's second highest per-capita death toll (1,066.88 per million people), as well as a high number of reported infections (28,354.46 per million people; 141st out of 154) and a high CFR (3.76; 134th out of 149).[4] Excess mortality data draw an even grimmer picture; no country in the world had more excess deaths (301.90 per 100,000 people). Yet, Peru's state institutions do not appear to be particularly weak by standard metrics or its initial policy responses to be pandemic negligent. In fact, in comparison to the other six

[3] As defined by the World Bank's 'Country and Lending Groups' income classification in 2022.

[4] As explained in more detail in the note to Table 1.1, 1st-ranked countries have the most normatively desirable outcomes.

Table 1.1 State institutions, health outcomes, and national policy responses to the COVID-19 pandemic in 2020

Country	COVID-19 health outcomes					State institutions			Policy responses	
	Cases	Deaths	CFR	Excess deaths	Tests	Authority	Capacity	Legitimacy	Containment and health measures	Economic support measures
Bolivia	12265.97 (109/154)	757.39 (141/149)	6.17 (144/149)	189.10 (68/81)	29.54 (71/97)	0.42 (124/152)	0.44 (95/152)	0.58 (48/152)	75.48 (17/149)	32.33 (107/149)
Ghana	1609.70 (63/154)	10.30 (34/149)	0.64 (13/149)		18.34 (78/97)	0.77 (39/152)	0.34 (113/152)	0.58 (48/152)	62.44 (68/149)	17.14 (133/149)
Nicaragua	854.55 (43/154)	23.85 (54/149)	2.79 (114/149)			0.43 (119/152)	0.57 (76/152)	0.53 (59/152)	11.99 (149/149)	0.00 (141/149)
Peru	28354.46 (141/154)	1066.88 (148/149)	3.76 (134/149)	301.90 (81/81)	35.22 (67/97)	0.52 (89/152)	0.62 (66/152)	0.60 (45/152)	80.41 (3/149)	71.95 (17/149)
Philippines	3708.09 (74/154)	71.10 (76/149)	1.92 (75/149)	−6.40 (9/81)	45.56 (64/97)	0.46 (112/152)	0.51 (83/152)	0.34 (107/152)	70.70 (35/149)	32.52 (106/149)
Tanzania	8.52 (2/154)	0.35 (3/149)	4.139 (137/149)			0.53 (87/152)	0.35 (110/152)	0.52 (62/152)	27.41 (146/149)	0.00 (141/149)
Vietnam	13.00 (3/154)	0.36 (4/149)	2.779 (110/149)		12.95 (87/97)	0.79 (32/152)	0.56 (78/152)	0.24 (131/152)	61.56 (73/149)	29.04 (114/149)

Note: Ranks in parentheses; 1st-ranked countries have the most normatively desirable outcomes (e.g. Ghana ranks globally 78th out of 97 countries for testing rates, which means that 77 countries with available data have higher testing rates than Ghana and that the country has the second-lowest testing rate among the countries reported in the table). Stronger containment and health measures are assumed to be more desirable in this ranking.
Source: The authors, based on own calculations as well as data from the European Centre for Disease Prevention and Control (ECDC 2020), Karlinsky and Kobak (2021), Our World in Data (OWID 2020), OxCGRT (Hale et al. 2021a), and Ziaja et al. (2019).

countries covered in this volume, Peru had the highest levels of state capacity (0.62; 66th out of 152) and legitimacy (0.60; 45th out of 152). It had an average level of authority (0.52; 89th out of 152) and enacted some of the strongest containment and health (80.41; 3rd out of 149) and economic support measures (71.95; 17th out of 149) worldwide in the first pandemic year.

Peru's neighbour Bolivia also stood out for doing worse than expected. It was among the countries with the highest number of recorded deaths (757.39 per million), as well as remarkably high excess mortality (189.10 per 100,000; 68th out of 81) in 2020. The number of reported infections (12,265.97 per million; 109th out of 154) was lower (although still high), which is why the country also had one of the world's highest CFRs (6.17; 144th out of 149). However, Bolivia by no means had a weak state. Its levels of authority (0.42), capacity (0.44), and legitimacy (0.58) were close to the scale's middle. In cross-country comparative perspective, Bolivia enacted some of the world's strongest containment and health measures (75.48; 17th out of 149) during the first year of the pandemic, but its economic support policies were broadly moderate (32.33; 107th out of 149).

By contrast, Tanzania's official pandemic statistics tell an optimistic story. According to available figures, Tanzania had the world's second-lowest number of population-adjusted COVID-19 infections (8.52 per million) and third-lowest number of population-adjusted COVID-19 deaths (0.35 per million) in the first pandemic year. These numbers are surprising not only because its CFR (4.13; 137th out of 149) was particularly high but also because it had some of the weakest containment and health policies in the world (27.41; 146th out of 149) and did not enact any economic support policies. As Tanzania did not report testing data, nor is its excess mortality data available, it is not possible to say based on the globally available data whether the rosy picture suggested by official statistics is a consequence of inadequate testing and misreporting—however, Tanzania's low level of capacity (0.35; 110th out of 152) is suggestive. In terms of other aspects of the state, Tanzania's authority (0.53) and legitimacy (0.52) were rated broadly midrange globally in standard metrics.

Like Tanzania, Nicaragua was a world outlier in its pandemic response policies. It did not provide any economic support for its citizens and enacted the laxest containment and health policies in the world. Despite such a lack of response, official statistics indicate that Nicaragua had fewer cases (854.55 per million; 43rd out of 154) and deaths (23.85 per million; 54th out of 149) than most countries in the world. By comparison, its levels of state authority (0.43), capacity (0.57), and legitimacy (0.53) were close to the middle of the scale. As in Tanzania, cross-country analysis raises questions about the accuracy of the reported numbers, and testing data and all-cause excess mortality data are unavailable for use as additional checks.

Another outlier was the Philippines. Although it had a moderate number of COVID-19 cases (3,708.09 per million; 74th out of 154) and deaths

(71.10 per million; 76th out of 149), compared to global averages, no other country in Asia, except India, had a worse per-capita death toll. Interestingly, however, its reported CFR (75th out of 149) was more or less as expected, and excess mortality data (−6.40 per 100,000; 9th out of 81) indicate that the country actually fared successfully in terms of overall health outcomes in 2020. The Philippines conducted more tests (45.56 per 1,000 people; 64th out of 97) than other countries considered in this volume and formulated strong containment and health measures (70.70; 35th in the world). Still, its economic support measures were somewhat weak (32.52; 106th in the world). In terms of dimensions of the state, the Philippines had an average level of capacity (0.51) and lower levels of authority (0.46) and legitimacy (0.34).

Official statistics tell a more positive story of Vietnam's early pandemic experience. During the first year of COVID-19, Vietnam had the world's third-lowest population-adjusted number of infections (13.00 per million) and fourth-lowest population-adjusted number of deaths (0.36 per million). Its comparatively high CFR (2.77; 110th out of 149) and low testing rate (12.95 per 1,000; 87th out of 97) do suggest some possible underreporting. Vietnam had a high level of state authority (0.79), an intermediate level of capacity (0.56), and a low level of legitimacy (0.24). The strength of its containment and health measures was close to the global average (61.56; 73rd out of 149) and its economic support policies were relatively weak (29.04; 114th out of 149).

Finally, Ghana emerged as a relatively typical case in our cross-country analysis; its performance during the first year of the pandemic was predicted well by the regression models. It reported a moderate number of cases (1,609.70 per million; 63rd out of 154), a comparatively low number of deaths (10.30 per million; 34th out of 149), and one of the lowest CFRs (0.64; 13th out of 149) in the world. It had the highest level of state authority (0.77) in sub-Saharan Africa, globally low but regionally high state capacity (0.34), and better than average state legitimacy (0.58). Compared to other countries, it enacted moderately strong containment and health policies (62.44; 68th out of 149) but weak economic support policies (17.14; 133rd out of 149).

1.5 Comparisons based on cross-national analysis

A comparative approach to the above numbers raises some intriguing questions: For instance, both Bolivia and Peru were among the 10 worst-performing countries in the world in terms of COVID-19 deaths. Both countries had a high number of infections, high CFRs, and some of the highest excess mortality figures in the world. Both countries also enacted strong containment and health policies and had more or less the same level of legitimacy. Yet, the two countries have somewhat different levels of authority and capacity, and Peru formulated much more generous economic support policies than Bolivia. Similar pandemic outcomes are not then explained by our measures of the state.

Nicaragua had a relatively similar level of legitimacy compared to Bolivia and Peru, virtually the same level of authority as Bolivia, and a fairly similar level of capacity as Peru. And yet in terms of initial health outcomes, according to official cross-country statistics, Nicaragua coped much better with COVID-19 than Bolivia and Peru. During the first year of the pandemic, Nicaragua appeared to be one of the best performers in Latin America. Perhaps even more interestingly, Nicaragua's policy responses were negligible in terms of containment and health measures and literally non-existent in terms of economic support.

Some of the differences in COVID-19 health outcomes could be explained by variation in testing rates. Nicaragua and Tanzania, however, did not report their testing figures. Generally speaking, all five countries with available testing data carried out only a fraction of the tests carried out in high-income countries, which obviously leaves some doubts as to the accuracy and global comparability of cross-national data on COVID-19 health outcomes.

Tanzania and Vietnam are also interesting to compare. According to official statistics, both countries performed better than predicted in terms of COVID-19 health outcomes and had exceptionally few cases and deaths. Nevertheless, these two countries are significantly different in terms of the three core dimensions of the state. Vietnam had much higher authority and capacity than Tanzania, but also much lower legitimacy. While Tanzania formulated only weak containment and health measures and no economic support measures, Vietnam enacted standard containment and health policies and provided some economic support to its citizens.

The Philippines and Bolivia had broadly similar levels of authority and capacity, and enacted similarly strong containment and health measures and weak economic support measures. But official statistics show that Bolivia had 10 times as many COVID-19 deaths (per million inhabitants) as the Philippines. As the two countries were relatively different in terms of legitimacy, one might be led to think that their diverse pandemic health outcomes could lie in differences in state legitimacy. Nevertheless, such an interpretation would run against the results of our cross-country analysis in Gisselquist and Vaccaro (2022), which does not find empirical evidence of a direct role of legitimacy for variation in COVID-19 health outcomes.

The above comparisons based on cross-country statistics are illustrative rather than exhaustive. Yet, they demonstrate that even if a large-n approach can be informative on the broad linkages of the state–pandemic nexus, a more detailed small-n approach is necessary for fine-grained understanding of the relationship between the state and pandemic governance and outcomes.

1.6 Evidence from the case study chapters

The next part of this volume presents two experiences from sub-Saharan Africa, the region with both the lowest average state capacity and the best pandemic outcomes in the first year, according to standard metrics and official statistics. These chapters deal with the cases of Ghana by Kofi Takyi Asante (Chapter 2) and Tanzania by Amy S. Patterson (Chapter 3). We then turn to Southeast Asia, a region that was particularly praised for its early pandemic performance: Julio C. Teehankee analyses the Philippines case (Chapter 4) and Duc Anh Dang and Anh Tran discuss Vietnam (Chapter 5). The final part of the volume considers experiences in three countries from Latin America—a region with some of the worst health outcomes in the Global South during the early pandemic period according to official statistics: Bolivia by Calla Hummel, V. Ximena Velasco Guachalla, Jami Nelson-Nuñez, and Carew Boulding (Chapter 6); Peru by Camila Gianella (Chapter 7); and Nicaragua by Mateo Jarquín (Chapter 8).

Asante's chapter on Ghana distinguishes between 'core' and 'residual' capacities and demonstrates that a country with relatively weak core capacity can boost its capability to respond to crises such as COVID-19 by drawing on residual capacity created through previous experiences and strengthened through international coordination. These findings imply that cross-country indicators of the state may underestimate the institutional resilience of some countries by not taking into account residual capacity. As general elections were held in the country at the end of the first year of COVID-19, Asante's chapter also discusses some of the challenges that holding elections during a pandemic can represent and how the country navigated these challenges.

Patterson's chapter on Tanzania approaches the link between COVID-19 and the state through a historical perspective that highlights the importance of ideology in pandemic responses. The Tanzanian state adopted one of the most 'relaxed' responses to COVID-19, and Patterson shows that this atypical approach to the pandemic can be explained by the country's socialist and nationalist past, whose legacies have shaped its subsequent paternalistic leadership and bureaucratic state institutions. By illustrating some of the discrepancies between national policies and local-level practices, her chapter also highlights possible tensions between different levels of the state that are complicated to capture in broad national-level indicators on the state.

A somewhat similar paternalistic and despotic approach to pandemic response is evidenced by Teehankee's chapter on the Philippines, which focuses on the actions of Rodrigo Duterte—the country's former (2016–2022) populist strongman president—during the early stages of COVID-19. Teehankee's study sheds light on the relevance of political agents in deploying state capacity and shows that the various dimensions of the state do not necessarily go hand in hand. The findings of the Philippines case study also imply that despite a particularly strong and lengthy lockdown, the health outcomes of the pandemic were poor, and the state did not manage the pandemic well, even if excess mortality data suggest the opposite.

Dang and Tran's chapter on Vietnam—one of the countries that was most praised for its COVID-19 response in the first year of the pandemic—focuses on provincial-level pandemic responses and outcomes. The authors argue that three institutional factors were particularly relevant in explaining variation in Vietnam's generally successful COVID-19 response across its provinces: health system capacity, transparency in local decision-making processes, and local-level participation opportunities. These findings underscore the importance of analysing the relationship between COVID-19 and the state not only at the national level but also subnationally.

Likewise, Hummel et al.'s chapter on Bolivia examines the interplay between COVID-19 and the state with particular attention to the subnational level. The authors argue that while state capacity in itself did not affect the country's pandemic outcomes, the autonomy of subnational governments in formulating localized COVID-19 responses may have played an important role in mitigating the adverse impact of the pandemic. Moreover, Hummel et al.'s findings highlight the role of containment measures and proximity to Brazil, underscoring the importance of geography and strong policy interventions to better pandemic outcomes. Their case study suggests that Bolivia's early pandemic response was relatively effective, in contrast to what is shown in the cross-country figures.

Through focused consideration of maternal health in the early stages of COVID-19, Gianella's chapter explores why Peru—a country with fairly high state capacity according to standard metrics—was unable to successfully manage the pandemic. Gianella uses maternal health as an indicator of the strength of the country's public health system and argues that the neoliberal structural reforms adopted by Peru meant it appeared to have solid health sector capacity and performance in terms of standard global metrics, even while actual public health sector capacity declined. Structural conditions driving health inequities were ignored and obscured by improvements in specific measurable objectives in the name of evidence-based governance. This hollowing-out of capacity, she argues, was a key factor influencing Peru's poor COVID-19 health outcomes and especially maternal healthcare quality during the pandemic. Gianella's study suggests that cross-country indicators of the state and governance may not accurately reflect reality.

Nicaragua was another country that, like Tanzania, downplayed the threat of COVID-19. Jarquín's chapter on Nicaragua explores the causes of such an outlier response to the pandemic. According to Jarquín, we cannot understand Nicaragua's response by looking at state capacity; we need to focus on how political elites think that a pandemic could affect state legitimacy and state authority. By showing that the country's political leaders intentionally underreported infection and death rates, as well as prioritized economic growth and social order over public health, the case of Nicaragua seems to suggest that in some contexts, where state institutions are not particularly robust, political leaders and their agendas can matter more than state effectiveness.

1.7 Comparative themes

Several broad themes emerge from a collective reading of the case studies and cross-country comparisons. The first is the clear importance of state capacity—a finding that aligns with theoretical expectations. In the cross-country analysis, higher state capacity is among the strongest predictors of more effective pandemic response, and the case studies provide a rich illustration of what state capacity weaknesses mean in terms of the ability to formulate and implement effective policy responses. Asante's discussion of the Ghanaian experience introduces an important nuance to discussion of capacity with the concept of 'residual capacity': local capacity 'reserves' accumulated thanks to past experiences with other health emergencies, along with 'external' capacity originating in one country but distributed transnationally in another country via regional and sub-regional coordination, can be deployed to facilitate the state's ability to deliver beyond its own 'core' capacity. Gianella's discussion of the Peruvian case raises an important caution regarding the assessment and characterization of capacity using standard cross-country indicators: Peru's capacity, she finds, looks stronger than it actually is. Decades of structural reforms have effectively cut down capacity in the health sector, contributing to a pandemic response that was not as effective as expected.

While capacity is clearly important, there is also striking variation in response and outcomes across states at broadly similar levels of capacity. Such variation is illustrated in the case studies in this volume. Global South countries as a group tend to have weaker state capacity than Global North countries and none of the countries studied in this volume has high state capacity (all are low to moderate in the standard indicators), but the effectiveness of policy responses varies significantly. Across the countries with similarly 'moderate' state capacity according to standard metrics, we find some of the best and the worst responses and outcomes. On the one hand, the Vietnam chapter documents an effective, evidence-based, and responsive public health effort which helped to minimize pandemic health impact. On the other hand, the chapter on Nicaragua describes a situation of extremely weak response, with the government undertaking no major public health mitigation efforts and actively working to manipulate statistics to minimize perceived pandemic impact.

Nuanced consideration of state legitimacy helps to shed light on such variation. Blunt differences in the cross-country measures are not so revealing, but the case chapters suggest several key points. For one, considering legitimacy and capacity together seems to give some insight into the constraints faced by governments in implementing more politically driven as opposed to more evidence-based responses. Political pressures and incentives influenced all types of governments in their pandemic response, but governments in states lacking both strong legitimacy and strong capacity seemed to have more freedom to implement politically driven responses. In such countries, governments might have felt empowered to use a crisis like the COVID-19 pandemic to pursue their own political goals over the needs of the people they govern—with weak constraints posed by accountability towards citizens or by an effective and autonomous public service.

Further, in comparatively weaker state settings such as those studied in this volume, the legitimacy of state institutions and the legitimacy of the government in power can be so closely tied together that it becomes tricky to distinguish between the two. The chapters on Bolivia, Nicaragua, the Philippines, and Tanzania illustrate this. In Bolivia, Hummel et al. argue, although the government responded swiftly to the pandemic, adopting competent public health measures, the state's capacity constraints, combined with the government's weak legitimacy, posed challenges for the implementation of the response. In the latter three countries, governments in power—indeed, individual heads of government—exerted decisive influence on pandemic response. In Nicaragua and Tanzania, this meant deliberate and successful government strategies to minimize the seriousness of the pandemic, including by manipulating and controlling information about infections and deaths. In the Philippines, Duterte did adopt policies to address the pandemic. But these policies, Teehankee's discussion suggests, were not designed and implemented through well-functioning state institutions but exemplified Duterte's own 'brute force governance' and exertion of broad societal control.

Finally, state authority also sheds light on the diversity of pandemic responses and outcomes across capacity-constrained settings. In particular, it can be seen to influence the tenor of government pandemic policies and their enforcement, as well as citizen compliance with public health regulations. The Vietnamese experience is suggestive here. Among the countries studied in this volume, Vietnam is rated as having the highest state authority. In their chapter, Dang and Tran describe the Vietnamese government's effective response. While their focus is on understanding subnational variation, implicit in this discussion is the ability of the central party-state to project its authority down to the provincial level and an overall high level of public compliance with public health measures.

Table 1.2 provides a brief comparative overview of our seven countries of focus, bringing together the often variant assessments of state capacity, legitimacy, and authority and pandemic response provided by the cross-country data as compared to the case studies.

Table 1.2 A comparative overview

	Capacity	Legitimacy	Authority	Pandemic Response
Ghana	Low core capacity but strong 'residual capacity'	Moderate	High	Comparatively effective
Tanzania	Low	Moderate and 'discursive'	Low/moderate	Weak: no major public health mitigation; weak/non-existent monitoring of infections
Philippines	Moderate in metrics but weaker in reality	Low/moderate	Moderate	Authoritarian: strong and lengthy lockdown; pandemic used to repress. Ambiguous pandemic health impact
Vietnam	Moderate	Low in metrics but stronger in reality, especially at the provincial level	High	Comparatively effective, with variation across provinces
Bolivia	Moderate	Moderate	Moderate	Moderate public health response but pandemic health impact severe
Peru	Moderate in metrics but weaker in reality	Moderate	Moderate	Moderate public health response but pandemic health impact severe
Nicaragua	Moderate	Moderate	Moderate	Weak: poor public health mitigation, manipulation of official statistics so real pandemic health impact unclear

Source: The authors.

1.8 Conclusions

This introductory chapter began with the illustration of a puzzle that has been noticed by many analysts: poor countries with fragile state institutions seemingly performed better than rich countries with strong state institutions in successfully fighting the COVID-19 pandemic early on. We discussed common explanations to this puzzle and highlighted the importance of both accurate data and careful analysis to avoid misleading conclusions. While all cross-country studies on the topic do not point in the same direction, we showed that once a more comprehensive view on the relationship between COVID-19 and the state is taken into account—as in Gisselquist and Vaccaro (2022)—it appears that high-capacity and high-authority countries were in fact better prepared to combat the pandemic and high-legitimacy countries refrained from adopting the most stringent containment policies but implemented stronger economic support measures. As theory predicts, a strong state generally matters for better crisis responses, although there are some significant differences among authority, capacity, and legitimacy—the three core dimensions of the state.

More detailed case studies, however, are essential for delving deeper into the 'facts on the ground' behind cross-country measures and teasing out the precise links between the state and crisis response during the COVID-19 pandemic. This is the core work of the seven case study chapters of this volume. These seven chapters are purposely diverse in terms of methods, disciplinary grounding, and specific arguments—but they are unified in speaking to the same central questions. Each chapter considers the three core dimensions of the state as presented in this chapter, but some emphasize one or two dimensions over others, and some introduce and argue for the relevance of additional aspects of the state.

Collectively, the studies in this volume, alongside the findings from our cross-country analysis, make clear the significance of state capacity to deliver public services in effective pandemic response, alongside considerable differences among states at similar levels of capacity. State legitimacy and authority shed light on these differences, linked in particular to the degree to which governments' responses were grounded in evidence or driven by political motives and to which citizens adhered to public health regulations and authorities enforced them. In the states studied here, the legitimacy of the state apparatus in turn is often deeply intertwined with the legitimacy of the government in power, illustrating a more tenuous, fluid line between government and the state in low- to moderate-capacity settings than we see in classic work on the state based on wealthy countries, and pointing to the need for a fuller understanding of these interlinkages and their implications.

This volume has key insights for flourishing academic discussions on the state, particularly in the Global South, as well as the rich policy discussions on building 'effective, accountable, and inclusive institutions' for development (SDG 16). It underscores the significance of this goal. In terms of future crisis preparedness specifically, it shows how building more detailed knowledge of the determinants and underlying mechanisms of successful and unsuccessful policy responses can shed light on how the state operates in crises and how the quality of the state influences such responses. Sooner or later, states, individually or collectively, will face new crises. Understanding pandemic preparedness can help us to be more prepared. At the same time, this volume underscores the deep linkages between the challenges of building effective states and of fostering legitimate public institutions in an era of global democratic decline.

References

Ahlbom Persson, T., and M. Povitkina (2017). '"Gimme Shelter": The Role of Democracy and Institutional Quality in Disaster Preparedness'. *Political Research Quarterly*, 70(4): 833–847.

Andersen, D., J. Møller, and S.E. Skaaning (2014). 'The State-Democracy Nexus: Conceptual Distinctions, Theoretical Perspectives, and Comparative Approaches'. *Democratization*, 21(7): 1203–1220.

Ang, Y.Y. (2020). 'When COVID-19 Meets Centralized, Personalized Power'. *Nature Human Behaviour*, 4(5): 445–447.

Asadullah, M.N., A. Savoia, and K. Sen (2020). 'Will South Asia Achieve the Sustainable Development Goals by 2030? Learning from the MDGs Experience'. *Social Indicators Research*, 152(1): 165–189.

Beaney, T., J.M. Clarke, V. Jain, A.K. Golestaneh, G. Lyons, D. Salman, and A. Majeed (2020). 'Excess Mortality: The Gold Standard in Measuring the Impact of COVID-19 Worldwide?'. *Journal of the Royal Society of Medicine*, 113(9): 329–334.

Bratton, M., and E.C.C. Chang (2006). 'State Building and Democratization in Sub-Saharan Africa: Forwards, Backwards, or Together?'. *Comparative Political Studies*, 39(9): 1059–1083.

Carbone, G., and V. Memoli (2015). 'Does Democratization Foster State Consolidation? Democratic Rule, Political Order, and Administrative Capacity'. *Governance*, 28(1): 5–24.

Carment, D., and Y. Samy (2019a). *Exiting the Fragility Trap: Rethinking Our Approach to the World's Most Fragile States*. Athens, OH: Ohio University Press.

Carment, D., and Y. Samy (2019b). 'Aid Targeting to Fragile and Conflict-Affected States and Implications for Aid Effectiveness'. *WIDER Working Papers* 8/2019. doi: 10.35188/UNU-WIDER/2019/642-5.

Cingolani, L., K. Thomsson, and D. de Crombrugghe (2015). 'Minding Weber More Than Ever? The Impacts of State Capacity and Bureaucratic Autonomy on Development Goals'. *World Development*, 72: 191–207.

Cronert, A. (2022). 'Precaution and Proportionality in Pandemic Politics: Democracy, State Capacity, and COVID-19-Related School Closures around the World'. *Journal of Public Policy*, 42(4): 705–729.

D'Arcy, M., and M. Nistotskaya (2017). 'State First, Then Democracy: Using Cadastral Records to Explain Governmental Performance in Public Goods Provision'. *Governance*, 30(2): 193–209.

Dhabaan, G.N., W.A. Al-Soneidar, and N.N. Al-Hebshi (2020). 'Challenges to Testing COVID-19 in Conflict Zones: Yemen as an Example'. *Journal of Global Health*, 10(1): 1–3.

ECDC (2020). 'Data on the Geographic Distribution of COVID-19 Cases Worldwide'. Available at: www.ecdc.europa.eu/en/publications-data/download-todays-data-geographic-distribution-covid-19-cases-worldwide.

Evans, D., and E. Werker (2020). 'What a Population's Age Structure Means for COVID-19's Impact in Low-Income Countries'. Available at: www.cgdev.org/blog/what-populations-age-structure-means-covid-19s-impact-low-income-countries.

Fukuyama, F. (2020). 'The Pandemic and Political Order'. *Foreign Affairs*, 99(4): 26–32, June–July.

Fuller, J.A., A. Hakim, K.R. Victory, K. Date, M. Lynch, and B. Dahl (2021). 'Mitigation Policies and COVID-19-Associated Mortality: 37 European Countries, January 23–June 30, 2020'. *Morbidity and Mortality Weekly Report*, 70(2): 1–5.

Gisselquist, R.M., and A. Vaccaro (2022). 'COVID-19 and the State: Exploring a Puzzling Relationship in the Early Stages of the Pandemic'. *Journal of International Development*, 35(5): 800–819. doi: 10.1002/jid.3702.

González-Bustamante, B. (2021). 'Evolution and Early Government Responses to COVID-19 in South America'. *World Development*, 137: 105180. doi: 10.1016/j.worlddev.2020.105180.

Grävingholt, J., S. Ziaja, and M. Kreibaum (2015). 'Disaggregating State Fragility: A Method to Establish a Multidimensional Empirical Typology'. *Third World Quarterly*, 36(7): 1281–1298.

Hale, T., N. Angrist, R. Goldszmidt, B. Kira, A. Petherick, T. Phillips, S. Webster, E. Cameron-Blake, L. Hallas, S. Majumdar, and H. Tatlow (2021a). 'A Global Panel Database of Pandemic Policies (Oxford COVID-19 Government Response Tracker)'. *Nature Human Behaviour*, 5(4): 529–538.

Hale, T., N. Angrist, A.J. Hale, B. Kira, S. Majumdar, A. Petherick, T. Phillips, D. Sridhar, R.N. Thompson, S. Webster, and Y. Zhang (2021b). 'Government Responses and COVID-19 Deaths: Global Evidence across Multiple Pandemic Waves'. *PLoS ONE*, 16(7): e0253116. doi: 10.1371/journal.pone.0253116.

Hertog, S. (2021). 'Taking Causal Heterogeneity Seriously: Implications for Case Choice and Case Study-Based Generalizations'. *Sociological Methods and Research*, 52: 1456–1492. doi: 10.1177/0049124120986206.

Holmberg, S., and B. Rothstein (2011). 'Dying of Corruption'. *Health Economics, Policy, and Law*, 6(4): 529–547.

Impouma, B., G.S. Williams, F. Moussana, F. Mboussou, B. Farham, C.M. Wolfe ... and I.S. Fall (2021). 'The First 8 Months of COVID-19 Pandemic in Three West African Countries: Leveraging Lessons Learned from Responses to the 2014–2016 Ebola Virus Disease Outbreak'. *Epidemiology and Infection*, 149: e258.

Kahn, M.E. (2005). 'The Death Toll from Natural Disasters: The Role of Income, Geography, and Institutions'. *The Review of Economics and Statistics*, 87(2): 271–284.

Karlinsky, A., and D. Kobak (2021). 'Tracking Excess Mortality across Countries during the Covid-19 Pandemic with the World Mortality Dataset'. *ELife*, 10: 1–21. doi: 10.7554/eLife.69336.

Keefer, P., E. Neumayer, and T. Plümper (2011). 'Earthquake Propensity and the Politics of Mortality Prevention'. *World Development*, 39(9): 1530–1541.

Knutsen, C.H., and P. Kolvani (2022). 'Fighting the Disease or Manipulating the Data? Democracy, State Capacity, and the COVID-19 Pandemic'. *V-Dem Working Paper Series* 2022: 127.

Koyama, M. (2021). 'Epidemic Disease and the State: Is There a Tradeoff between Public Health and Liberty?' *Public Choice*, 195(1–2): 145–167.

Liang, L.L., C.H. Tseng, H.J. Ho, and C.Y. Wu (2020). 'Covid-19 Mortality Is Negatively Associated with Test Number and Government Effectiveness'. *Scientific Reports*, 10: 12567. doi: 10.1038/s41598-020-68862-x.

Lieberman, E.S. (2005). 'Nested Analysis as a Mixed-Method Strategy for Comparative Research'. *American Political Science Review*, 99(3): 435–452.

Maeda, J.M., and J.N. Nkengasong (2021). 'The Puzzle of the COVID-19 Pandemic in Africa'. *Science*, 371(6524): 27–28.

Mobula, L.M., H. Samaha, M. Yao, A.S. Gueye, B. Diallo, C. Umutoni, and S. Ahuka-Mundeke (2020). 'Recommendations for the COVID-19 Response at the National Level Based on Lessons Learned from the Ebola Virus Disease Outbreak in the Democratic

Republic of the Congo'. *American Journal of Tropical Medicine and Hygiene*, 103(1): 12–17.

Møller, J., and S.E. Skaaning (2017). 'Explanatory Typologies as a Nested Strategy of Inquiry: Combining Cross-Case and Within-Case Analyses'. *Sociological Methods and Research*, 46(4): 1018–1048.

Mormina, M., and I.M. Nsofor (2020). 'What Developing Countries Can Teach Rich Countries about How to Respond to a Pandemic'. *The Conversation*, 15 October. Available at: https://theconversation.com/what-developing-countries-can-teach-rich-countries-about-how-to-respond-to-a-pandemic-146784.

Nguimkeu, P., and S. Tadadjeu (2021). 'Why Is the Number of COVID-19 Cases Lower Than Expected in Sub-Saharan Africa? A Cross-Sectional Analysis of the Role of Demographic and Geographic Factors'. *World Development*, 138: 105251.

Nordling, L. (2020). 'Africa's Pandemic Puzzle: Why So Few Cases and Deaths?'. *Science*, 369(6505): 756–757.

OWID (2020). COVID-19 dataset. https://github.com/owid/covid-19-data/tree/master/public/data.

Redlin, M. (2022). 'Differences in NPI Strategies against COVID-19'. *Journal of Regulatory Economics*, 62(1–3): 1–23.

Seawright, J. (2016). 'The Case for Selecting Cases That Are Deviant or Extreme on the Independent Variable'. *Sociological Methods and Research*, 45(3): 493–525.

Seawright, J., and J. Gerring (2008). 'Case Selection Techniques in Case Study Research: A Menu of Qualitative and Quantitative Options'. *Political Research Quarterly*, 61(2): 294–308.

Serikbayeva, B., K. Abdulla, and Y. Oskenbayev (2021). 'State Capacity in Responding to COVID-19'. *International Journal of Public Administration*, 44(11–12): 920–930.

Sjöstedt, M., and M. Povitkina (2017). 'Vulnerability of Small Island Developing States to Natural Disasters: How Much Difference Can Effective Governments Make?'. *Journal of Environment and Development*, 26(1): 82–105.

Stasavage, D. (2020). 'Democracy, Autocracy, and Emergency Threats: Lessons for COVID-19 from the Last Thousand Years'. *International Organization*, 74(S1): E1–E17.

Tikuisis, P., D. Carment, Y. Samy, and J. Landry (2015). 'Typology of State Types: Persistence and Transition'. *International Interactions*, 41(3): 565–582.

Toshkov, D., B. Carroll, and K. Yesilkagit (2022). 'Government Capacity, Societal Trust or Party Preferences: What Accounts for the Variety of National Policy Responses to the COVID-19 Pandemic in Europe?'. *Journal of European Public Policy*, 29(7): 1009–1028.

Vaccaro, A. (2023). 'Measures of State Capacity: So Similar, Yet So Different'. *Quality and Quantity* 57(3): 2281–2302.

Weber, M. (1946). 'Politics as a Vocation'. In H.H. Gerth and C.W. Mills (eds), *From Max Weber: Essays in Sociology*. New York: Oxford University Press, 77–128.

Wu, S.L., A.N. Mertens, Y.S. Crider, A. Nguyen, N.N. Pokpongkiat, S. Djajadi, and J. Benjamin-Chung (2020). 'Substantial Underestimation of SARS-CoV-2 Infection in the United States'. *Nature Communications*, 11: 4507.

Yanez, N.D., N.S. Weiss, J.A. Romand, and M.M. Treggiari (2020). 'COVID-19 Mortality Risk for Older Men and Women'. *BMC Public Health*, 20(1): 1–7.

Ziaja, S., J. Grävingholt, and M. Kreibaum (2019). 'Constellations of Fragility: An Empirical Typology of States'. *Studies in Comparative International Development*, 54(2): 299–321.

PART II
SUB-SAHARAN AFRICA

2

Harnessing Residual Capacity

Ghana's Struggle against Health System Constraints in the COVID-19 Response

Kofi Takyi Asante

2.1 Introduction: the political lives of pandemics

One of the great puzzles of the novel coronavirus (SARS-CoV-2, or COVID-19) pandemic has been its relatively mild overall impact on poorer countries.[1] While no definitive answer has yet emerged to explain this outcome, it is clear that any adequate explanation of the cross-national variations in health outcomes will need to address the political economy of public health emergency preparedness and response. This is important because public health emergencies, much like any other crisis, have a political life (Chigudu 2020). To contribute to this scholarly endeavour, this chapter examines the institutional and political contexts of Ghana's preparedness for and response to COVID-19.

The chapter specifically seeks to contribute to an emerging body of work that looks beyond aggregate outcomes to investigate the correlation between state effectiveness and pandemic outcomes. Insights from this emerging scholarship point to the centrality of state effectiveness (defined in terms of capacity and authority) in explaining the trajectory of the pandemic in different countries. For instance, a study published in *The Lancet* found that the mortality rate among COVID-19 patients in Africa who needed intensive care was much higher than for similar patients in other parts of the world, including Asia and South America, due to factors including the lack of critical care facilities (Biccard et al. 2021). At the analytical level, Gisselquist and Vaccaro (2023: 801–802) show that after controlling for relevant factors like per-capita income and population age structure, we can actually observe the '(expected) inverse relationship between state effectiveness and pandemic health outcomes', suggesting that effective states 'were indeed better prepared to cope with a pandemic than "weak" states'.

[1] I am grateful to Rachel Gisselquist, Andrea Vaccaro, Nana Amma Asante-Poku, Mark Kwaku Mensah Obeng, Esther Naa Dodua Darku, Adobea Yaa Owusu, and discussants at the 'COVID-19 and the State' workshop hosted by UNU-WIDER for useful feedback on early drafts of this chapter. Research assistance was provided by Huzeima Mahamadu and Nana Kwesi Asare.

Kofi Takyi Asante, *Harnessing Residual Capacity*. In: *How States Respond to Crisis*. Edited by: Rachel M. Gisselquist and Andrea Vaccaro, Oxford University Press. © UNU-WIDER (2025). DOI: 10.1093/9780198907237.003.0002

Three dimensions of the state are crucial in terms of its ability to effectively function in normal times and during periods of crises. These are authority (or the ability to maintain order), capacity (or the ability to deliver goods and services), and legitimacy (or the ability to win the allegiance and consent of citizens). Gisselquist and Vaccaro (2023) find that state capacity and authority had a more direct impact on health outcomes in the first year of the pandemic than legitimacy. Building on their insights, this chapter explores the state–pandemic nexus through an in-depth case study of Ghana's COVID-19 response during the first year of the outbreak. While analytically distinct, the dimensions of capacity and authority are closely related and often used interchangeably under the umbrella term of state effectiveness.

The chapter contributes to this emerging scholarship by showing that while Ghana lacked core state capacity, the country was able to leverage the proactive (sub)regional efforts and the residual capacity built from previous public health interventions to overcome the limitations of its weak and under-resourced public health systems. Building on this foundation, the government's strong early response allowed it to gain control of the situation in the crucial first few months of the outbreak. However, the longer the pandemic lasted, the more difficult it was for residual capacity to maintain its effectiveness and prevent the spread of infection. This demonstrates that while residual capacity could lay the much-needed foundation for crisis response, it is not enough to support effective response to protracted emergency situations.

The rest of the chapter proceeds as follows. The next section critically reviews the literature on the politics of state effectiveness in Ghana. The third section presents an overview of the capacity of Ghana's public health system, while the fourth describes the coordinated efforts at the African and West African levels to build preparedness against the pandemic. The fifth section analyses the government's response to the COVID-19 outbreak in Ghana. The chapter concludes with a brief discussion of the politics of pandemic response and the concept of residual capacity. The analysis draws on a variety of secondary data sources, including statistics on COVID-19 infections and deaths, reports on health system capabilities, official policy statements, and media accounts of the outbreak and government responses.

2.2 The politics of state capacity in Ghana

Despite its reputation as an oasis in an otherwise turbulent region (Aryeetey and Baah-Boateng 2015; Ateku 2017), there is broad consensus among scholars of the Ghanaian state that its overall capacity is substandard (Ansu 2013; Resnick 2019), a weakness often attributed to its having a 'public administration system that does not work and which severely reduces the ability of the government to implement reforms and programs' (Whitfield 2010: 735). The state capacity dataset compiled

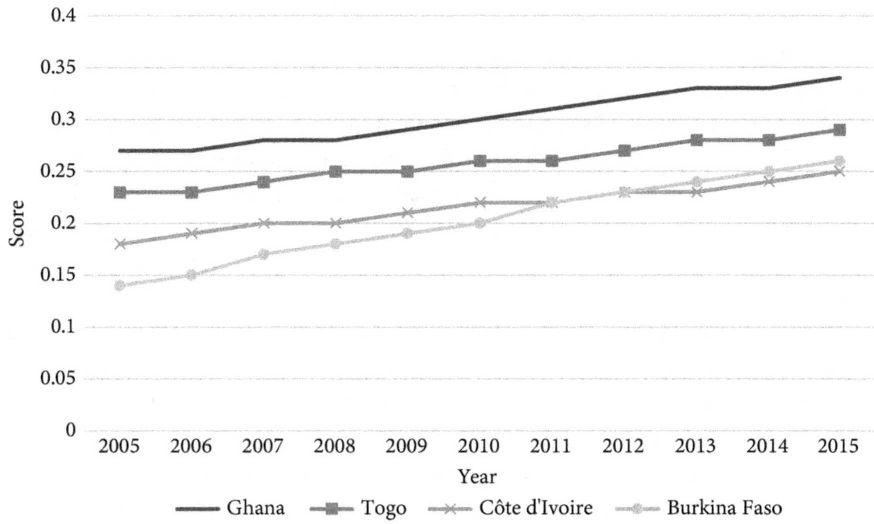

Figure 2.1 Historical trends in capacity levels: Ghana, Togo, Burkina Faso, Côte d'Ivoire.
Source: Author's illustration based on data from Grävingholt et al. (2018).

by the German Development Institute (DIE) rates Ghana's capacity as low, with a score of 0.34 out of a possible maximum score of 1. Ghana's capacity rose over the 10-year period covered by the DIE dataset, but the rate of improvement was unimpressive, increasing only by 0.07 between 2005 and 2015. The country's low rating is reflective of the generally poor performance across the West African subregion (see Figure 2.1).

Historical factors have affected the effectiveness of the country's institutions. Since the 1980s, when sweeping economic reforms were introduced as part of the Bretton Woods-led structural adjustment policies (SAPs), Ghana has abandoned interventionist policies for a market-driven strategy 'in which the government focuse[s] primarily on creating an enabling environment' rather than actively promoting or nurturing particular sectors (Diao et al. 2019: 6). Ghana has since achieved strong economic growth, but this has not been driven by and has not led to structural transformation of the national economy (Diao et al. 2019; Whitfield 2011). Activist governments are necessary to foster structural transformation (Resnick 2019), but given the abandonment of interventionist policies, 'some areas of the economy that are fraught with market failure problems have remained underdeveloped, and this has contributed to the limited growth of higher productivity sectors, and hence the low gains in productivity growth from structural change' (Diao et al. 2019: 8).

The introduction of multi-party politics since the promulgation of the Fourth Republican constitution of 1992 has further undermined the ability of the state to pursue long-term development. Consistent with theoretical expectations

(Khan 2005), the pressures of competitive politics have yielded broad human development dividends. Electoral pressures have forced the Ghanaian state to respond to the needs of citizens, but political liberalization has also led to the proliferation of interest groups making demands on the state (Boafo-Arthur 1999). Confronted with a weak economy where the industrial base is minuscule in comparison with the informal sector, political elites feel compelled to resort to short-term policy options, including the distribution of highly visible public goods (Appiah and Abdulai 2017; Asante 2021; Asante and Mullard 2021).

This results in a competitive clientelist political system where the alternation of political power in free and fair elections occurs alongside entrenched patronage politics (Asante and Khisa 2019; Oduro et al. 2014). Under competitive clientelism, democracy could be said to have 'become hostage to interest group pressures' where governments are motivated to sideline potentially beneficial policies if these would involve prioritizing the interests of an electorally marginal group over those of a larger or more powerful constituency (Resnick 2019: 54). This dynamic is at the root of policy failures across different sectors in the country (Asante 2023; Dye 2022).

Competitive clientelism undermines attempts to foster effective public agencies in Ghana (Appiah and Abdulai 2017). Political elites resort to ultimately self-sabotaging tactics involving 'short-term political survival strategies ... that undermine the capacity of the state bureaucracy, including politically-motivated changes in senior bureaucrats during election turnovers' (Abdulai 2021: 7). This frequent turnover of technocrats in the civil service 'undermines professionalism, continuity, long-term planning orientation, learning and innovation in the public service' (Ansu 2013: 512). This overall structural context shapes the performance of Ghana's public health system.

2.3 The capacity for healthcare delivery in Ghana

Ghana has a struggling public health system with statistics that paint a grim picture. Multiple factors militate against the ability of public hospitals and clinics to deliver timely care to patients. For example, by December 2017, the National Ambulance Service (NAS), established in 2004, had 133 stations across the country. However, only 45 of these stations were functional, and vehicle availability at the functional stations stood at 50 per cent owing to frequent breakdowns and inadequate funds for continual maintenance of the fleet (MoH 2018: 12). In 2018, there were only 55 functioning ambulances for the entire country (ISSER 2019). In 2019, the government made a timely procurement of 307 ambulances to replenish the existing stock, which were subsequently distributed to district, regional, and teaching hospitals in January 2020, two months before the country recorded its first cases of COVID-19 (ISSER 2020).

Poor infrastructure is another obstacle to timely care, especially in remote parts of the country where roads in a state of disrepair 'pose threats to stable patient management, timely scene response, and the longevity of the ambulances' that are already in shortly supply (Owusu and Asante 2020: 2). Another problem is shortage of beds, which leads to health facilities turning away patients needing urgent medical attention. However, a publication by the Institute of Statistical, Social, and Economic Research at the University of Ghana suggests that it was a 'lack of proper direction in Ghana's healthcare system, rather than the absence of beds for emergency admission', that lay at the root of the problem (ISSER 2019: 60). In fact, the report points out that between 2013 and 2016, about 40 per cent of all beds nationally were unoccupied.

To address some of these impediments to healthcare delivery, recent interventions have sought to leverage technological innovations to improve access to healthcare across the country. The most noteworthy of these was a collaboration between the Ghana Health Service (GHS) and Zipline in 2019 to use drones to deliver medical supplies to remote parts of the country. The director-general of the GHS at the time, Dr Anthony Nsiah-Asare, was optimistic that the innovation would help the country 'save money and save lives' (GhanaWeb 2019).

This turned out to be a timely investment, as the drone delivery system was quickly incorporated into the country's national COVID-19 response strategy.[2] However, the infrastructural deficit and inequitable distribution of health facilities which necessitated the use of drone delivery in the first place remain and require long-term planning and investment, which is undermined by the country's competitive clientelist political settlement.

Other factors affect the quality of and equitable access to the care provided by public health facilities. The ratio of population to health professionals is low but has seen slow improvements in recent years. The ratio of population to doctors has dropped steadily from 11,649 people to a doctor in 2009 to 8,098 people to a doctor in 2017. The ratio similarly improved for nurses, dropping from 1,494 in 2009 to 799 in 2017 (see Figure 2.2). However, this still puts Ghana behind its African peers. In a recent World Bank survey, Ghana placed 14th in sub-Saharan Africa in its doctor-to-patient ratio and 4th in West Africa (Pulse Ghana 2020).

To address disparities in access to health infrastructure, Community-based Health Planning and Services (CHPS) policy was introduced in 2000 as a service 'where Community Health Officers (CHOs) are engaged to live in compounds provided by the community or the District Assembly. The primary function of

[2] In April 2020, drone delivery of COVID-19 test samples began in Accra and Kumasi; and in March 2021, Ghana became the first country in the world to use drones to deliver COVID-19 vaccines (León 2020; Nwannekanma 2021; Vincent 2021).

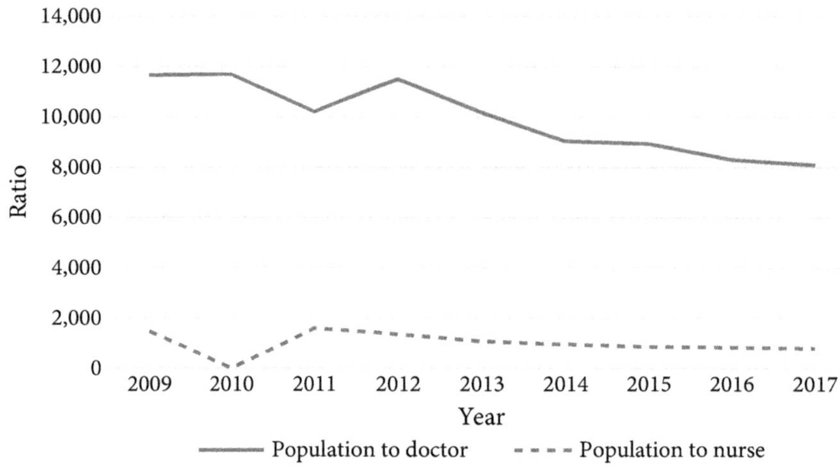

Figure 2.2 Ratio of population to health professionals, 2009–2017.

Source: Author's illustration based on data from Abdulai (2018) and MoH (2018).

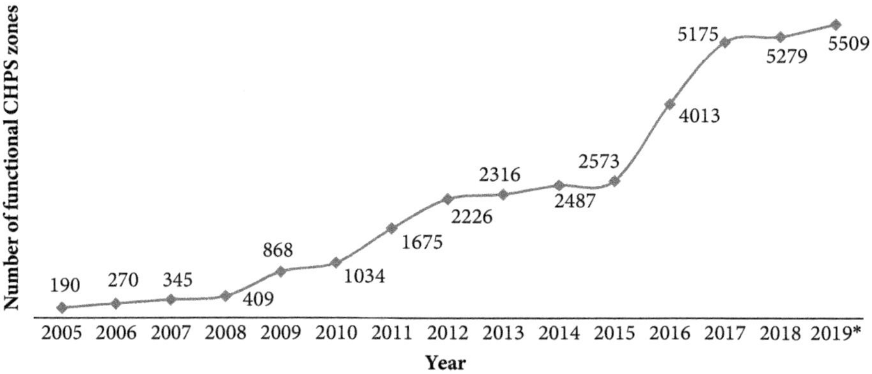

Figure 2.3 Number of functional CHPS zones, 2005–2019.

Note: *Provisional estimate.

Source: Author's illustration based on ISSER (2020).

CHOs is to deliver basic healthcare to the doorsteps of individuals within the selected communities, in addition to making prompt referrals, when necessary' (ISSER 2020: 194). In the implementation of the CHPS concept, 'a partnership is developed with the community leaders and members in a bid to come to a general consensus on the needs of the community thereby forging a feeling of ownership of the initiative within the community' (Nwameme et al. 2018: 2). Since its introduction, the number of functional CHPS zones has grown exponentially from 190 in 2005 to 5,509 in 2019 (see Figure 2.3).

In spite of these improvements, the health sector is still plagued by serious problems. Even though the ratio of health personnel to population is improving, there is a longstanding problem of health worker shortage, especially in rural areas (Okyere 2018). Additionally, resources to improve 'healthcare access are unequally distributed, with the poorer regions in the north having the poorest health status' (Asante and Zwi 2009: 372). Just like in other sectors of the economy (Banful 2011a, b), the disbursement of funds to health facilities does not follow the proposed formula. Instead, allocations are made based on factors like the capacity of local health facilities and the extent of involvement of donors at any point in time. Delays in the release of public sector health funds to districts also affect service delivery across the country. In some cases, the first of what is supposed to be quarterly disbursements is only received in the last quarter of the year (Asante et al. 2006; Asante and Zwi 2009).

With regard to the facilities necessary for treating COVID-19 patients, the situation is even more dire. A recent study found that in February 2020, there were only 16 operational intensive care unit (ICU) beds across 9 institutions in the country. Additionally, there was a severe deficit in the country's critical care bed capacity, with 0.5 ICU beds per 100,000 people (Siaw-Frimpong et al. 2021).

The longstanding problems affecting healthcare delivery in the country as well as the improvements that have been recorded over the past few decades can be traced to the unique configuration of forces that structure the prevailing competitive clientelist political system. This is manifested in the tendency to prioritize the building of large hospitals in urban areas rather than clinics or CHPS compounds in small towns and villages (Asante and Zwi 2009). Ironically, the implementation of the CHPS programme itself has focused more on building projects than on equipping the compounds with the necessary supplies and equipment and ensuring the stationing of medical staff. Between 2002 and 2014, the number of CHPS compounds increased from 39 to 2,948, but a 2010 review found that over half of them were not staffed with the requisite health personnel (Abdulai 2018: 16).

Given the many gaps in Ghana's public health system, how are we to understand the relatively mild impact of the COVID-19 pandemic on the country and neighbouring countries? The following sections address this question by looking at the actions taken by policy-makers in response to the outbreak of the virus.

2.4 Readiness and response to COVID-19 at the (sub)regional level

On the eve of the outbreak of COVID-19, the Global Health Security Index (GHSI), a global pandemic preparedness report, revealed huge gaps in the readiness for a major public health emergency across the world. The report uses six criteria (namely, prevention, detection and reporting, rapid response, health system, compliance with international norms, and risk environment) to comprehensively assess and benchmark the capability of health systems (Cameron et al. 2019). The index is scored on a 100-point scale, with a score below 33.4 considered low while a score above 66.6 is considered high. A country scoring between 33.3 and 66.7 has a medium level of preparedness. The report ranked Ghana 105th out of 195 countries but also revealed a worrying lack of preparedness worldwide, with a global average index score of about 40 (see Figure 2.4).

On all but six indicators, the global average score was below 50. West Africa performed worse than the global average on all indicators except 'compliance with IHR [International Health Regulations]', where the subregion marginally outperformed the global average by 0.6 points. Ghana performed better than its West African peers on four out of six of the indicators, and on the overall score (35.5 against 32.6), although Sierra Leone, Senegal, and Nigeria performed better than Ghana on the overall score (see Figure 2.5).

In fact, health systems across Africa have long suffered neglect, with the personnel and facilities needed to fight the pandemic sorely lacking. For instance, there were only 2,000 ventilators across 41 African countries and 5,000 intensive care beds across 43 countries. At the same time, the doctor-to-patient ratio in sub-Saharan Africa was 0.2 per 1,000 compared with 2.6 in North America, 3.7 in the European Union (EU), and a global average of 1.6. The Africa Centres for Disease Control (Africa CDC) describes this shortage as 'catastrophic' (Wadvalla 2020: 1).

In light of these gaps, coordination at the regional and subregional levels helped countries to prepare for and mitigate the impact of the domestic outbreaks. The Africa CDC 'activated its Emergency Operations Center for COVID-19 on 27 January 2020 after at least four Asian countries had announced cases' and began holding virtual weekly coordination meetings with its Regional Collaborating Centres and with national health institutions, and a system was developed across all five African Union (AU) regions to verify national alerts and reports (Loembé et al. 2020: 1000). By quickly leveraging this pre-existing operational capacity, the Africa CDC was able to assist member countries with weak health systems to strengthen their preparedness for the outbreak.

The Africa CDC also developed a Joint Continental Strategy for COVID-19 before the outbreak of the virus on the continent (Loembé et al. 2020: 1000). A collaborative taskforce was constituted to lead the implementation of this joint strategy. The early stages of its work involved enhancing national capacity for detecting and containing the virus. Technical know-how and earlier investments in emergency preparedness and response mechanisms during previous epidemic outbreaks like those of Ebola, Lassa fever, polio, and HIV were activated. This infrastructure includes a continent-wide exchange platform that was 'repurposed for training and information on COVID-19 diagnostics' as well as a dense network of 'community health agents that support the response to polio and other diseases ... leveraged for sensitization and to raise the alarm about suspected COVID-19 at the subnational level' (Loembé et al. 2020: 1001). Furthermore, in collaboration with AU partner countries, the number of testing labs was increased from 2 to 43 between February and mid-March 2020, and

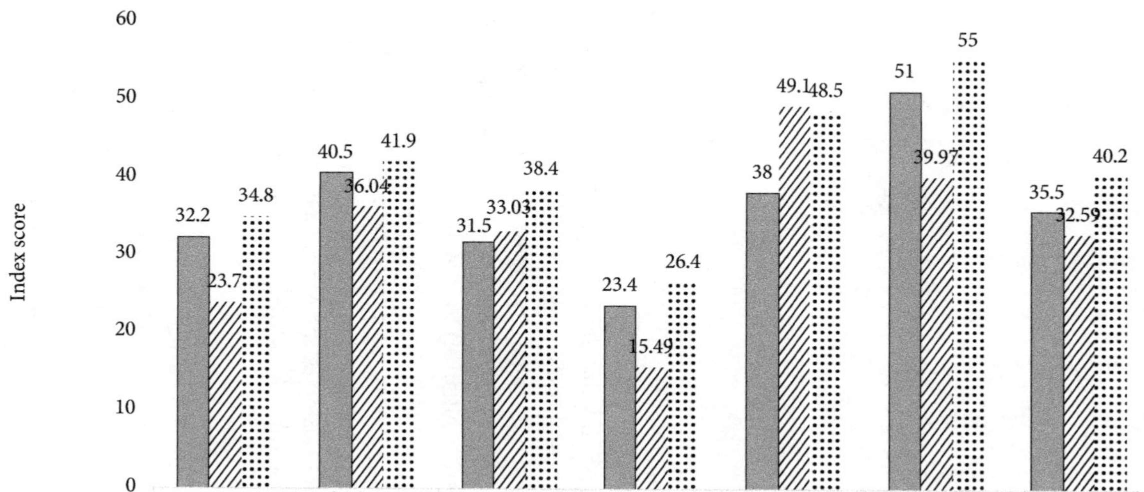

	Prevention	Early detection and reporting	Rapid response	Health system	Compliance with IHR	Risk environment	Overall
Ghana	32.2	40.5	31.5	23.4	38	51	35.5
West Africa	23.7	36.04	33.03	15.49	49.1	39.97	32.59
Global Average	34.8	41.9	38.4	26.4	48.5	55	40.2

Assessment criteria

Ghana West Africa Global Average

Figure 2.4 Ghana's average GHSI score in comparison with West Africa and global average.

Source: Author's illustration based on GHSI data (Cameron et al. 2019).

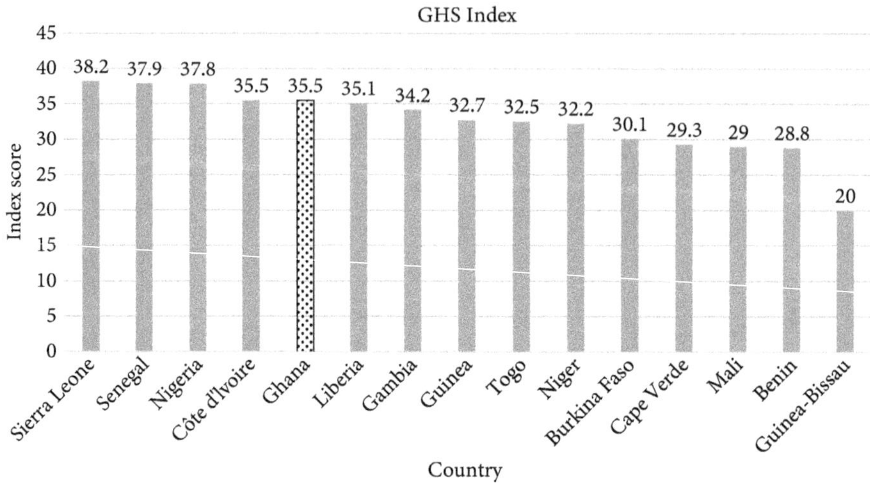

Figure 2.5 Overall GHSI score for West Africa.

Source: Author's illustration based on GHSI data (Cameron et al. 2019).

training workshops were held to increase surveillance capacity at entry points and to prevent and contain infections.

The AU COVID-19 Response Fund was set up on 26 March 2020 with the aim of 'strengthen[ing] the continental response to COVID-19 ... and mitigating the pandemic's socioeconomic and humanitarian impact on African populations' (AU n.d.). This fund enabled the Africa CDC to set up the Partnership to Accelerate COVID-19 Testing (the PACT initiative) to mobilize existing public health infrastructure for aggressive testing, tracing, and treatment (AU and Africa CDC 2020). In June 2020, following global shortages of medical supplies and the attendant increases in prices, the African Medical Supplies Platform was created as on online marketplace under the supervision of the Africa CDC, the United Nations (UN) Economic Commission for Africa, and the Africa Export–Import Bank, where member countries

> can shop for diagnostics and commodities at fixed, fair prices. For instance, at the start of the pandemic, global demand drove up the price of an N95 mask to \$30 (£24; €26) but this will cost \$2 on the platform. The Africa Export-Import Bank will handle payments and provide loans to member states to purchase equipment, while logistics partners including African national carriers and global freight companies will run delivery. (Wadvalla 2020: 2)

At the subregional level, health ministers from Economic Community of West African States (ECOWAS) held a meeting to develop a coordinated response to the outbreak two weeks after the World Health Organization (WHO) declared the outbreak a public health emergency of international concern. The ministers resolved to take early action, including setting up quarantine facilities and 'implementing robust measures to ensure availability of critical medical supplies' (Ahanhanzo et al. 2021: 2). These interventions were aided by the existence of institutions like the ECOWAS Regional Centre for Surveillance and Disease Control, which was established as an agency under the West African Health Organization (WAHO) in response to regional epidemics like those of Ebola and Lassa fever. These previous efforts had led to the building of reference laboratories and an increase in the number of epidemiologists in member countries through a field training programme. Surveillance, monitoring, and field investigations were carried out by a regional coordination platform involving National Public Health Institutes (NPHIs) across member states (Ahanhanzo et al. 2021).

These strong early actions and the efficient regional collaboration in Africa contrasted with the inaction and feet-dragging that characterized the initial response in wealthier countries. In the EU, for example, a study showed that delayed response and failure to deploy existing core capacity worsened the impact of the pandemic:

> Our results showed that one of the problems in northern Italy, for example, was that even though there were enough intensive care unit (ICU) beds across the country—and even in the region if they were able to cross a border (into another country)—that capacity was not used. (Gray 2020)

As observed above, Africa's strong early response was a tacit recognition of the stark reality that the continent could not afford the scale of infection witnessed by Italy, Spain, and the United States in the first two quarters of 2020. Given the fragility of national health systems, it was important to concentrate efforts on delaying national outbreaks for as long as possible, and to aggressively contain outbreaks once they occurred. However, once cases were recorded in individual countries, the national responses and attendant health outcomes were shaped by an attempt to balance public health and political considerations. In Ghana, where the sitting president, Nana Addo Danquah Akufo-Addo, was coming up for re-election in December, the political stakes were even higher, as will be seen in the next section.

2.5 Policy responses to the COVID-19 outbreak in Ghana

2.5.1 The trajectory of the COVID-19 outbreak in Ghana

The first two cases of COVID-19 in Ghana were reported on 12 March 2020. The following months witnessed a surge in infections, reaching 13,203 confirmed cases and 70 deaths in June. Before the end of December 2020, the country had recorded more than 54,000 confirmed cases and more than 330 deaths (see Figures 2.6–2.8).

By September 2021, Ghana had experienced three separate waves of the outbreak (see Figure 2.6). The first wave occurred in the middle of July 2020 after some

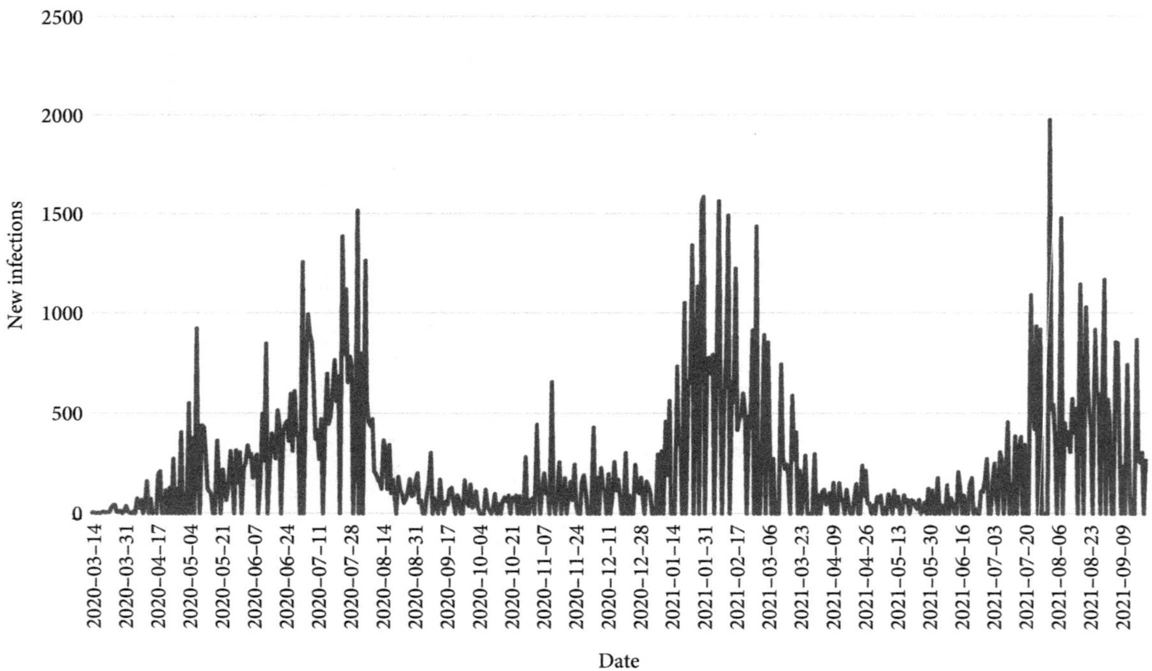

Figure 2.6 Daily recorded COVID-19 cases in Ghana.

Note: Based on data available at the time of writing; database updated weekly.
Source: Author's illustration based on Ritchie et al. (2020), with data from the COVID-19 Data Repository by the Center for Systems Science and Engineering (CSSE) at Johns Hopkins University (Dong et al. 2020).

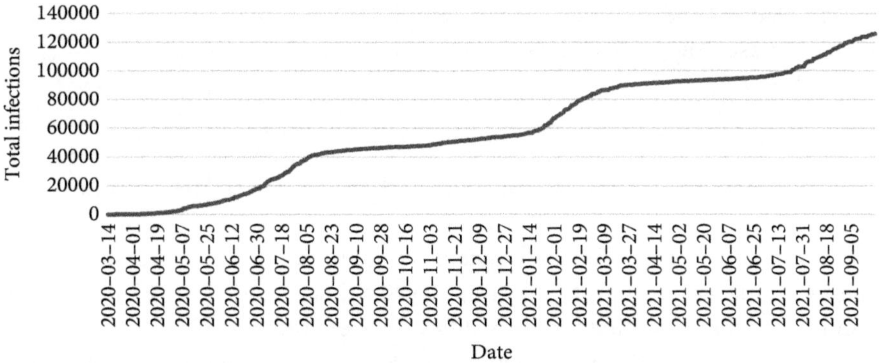

Figure 2.7 Trend in total COVID-19 cases in Ghana.

Note: Based on data available at the time of writing; database updated weekly.
Source: Author's illustration based on Ritchie et al. (2020), with data from the COVID-19 Data Repository (Dong et al. 2020).

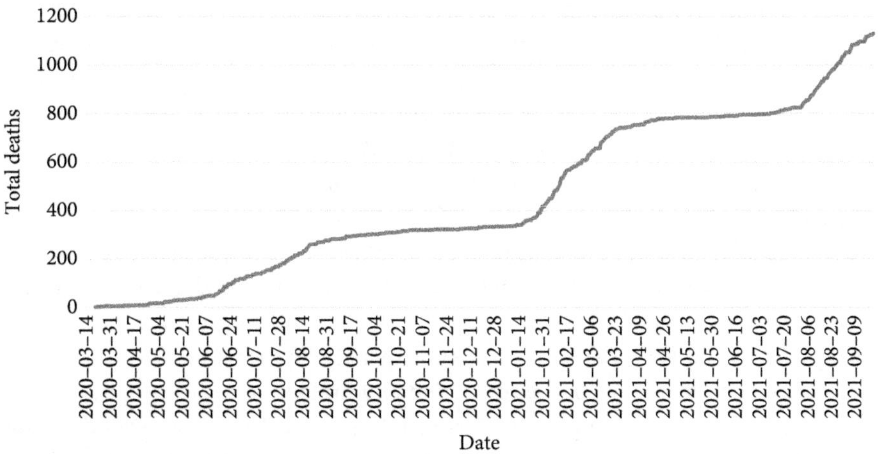

Figure 2.8 Trend in total COVID-19 deaths in Ghana.

Note: Based on data available at the time of writing; database updated weekly.
Source: Author's illustration based on Ritchie et al. (2020), with data from the COVID-19 Data Repository (Dong et al. 2020).

of the restrictions on social gatherings were lifted. In the following months, major government programmes requiring large gatherings—including registrations for the new national identification card, the compiling of a new voters' register, and presidential and parliamentary elections in December—were undertaken to much criticism from civil society organizations (CSOs) and professional associations. However, the second wave did not occur until the middle of January 2021, possibly linked to the Christmas and New Year festivities. The third wave was recorded in August 2021. The total number of deaths followed the same trajectory as the total number of cases, with rising fatalities as the number of recorded cases increased. By 27 September, the total number of deaths had risen to 1,150 (see Figure 2.8).

2.5.2 Residual capacity: Ghana's early response to the pandemic

As shown above, Ghana's health system was in a weak state at the outbreak of the pandemic. Policy-makers were thus worried that a sudden surge in infections would overwhelm existing health facilities. To avoid this situation, existing emergency public health structures were activated in the early months of 2020 even before the first cases were recorded. The Emergency Operation Centres (EOCs), Public Health Emergency Management Committees (PHEMCs), and National Disease Surveillance Department (NDSD) of the GHS conducted a readiness assessment and developed a response strategy. Additionally, a crash course on contact training was organized for alumni and residents of the Ghana Field Epidemiology and Laboratory Training Programme (Ghana FELTP) and staff of the GHS (Kenu et al. 2020). These measures, together with those put in place at the sub(regional) level, shored up the country's ability to control the spread of the virus in the crucial first few months of the outbreak. The rapid mobilization of pre-existing as well as ad hoc structures in response to the crisis is described in this chapter as 'residual capacity'.

Shortly after the first two cases were confirmed, the government imposed a number of restrictions including a partial lockdown in the Greater Accra, Kasoa, and Greater Kumasi areas (MoH 2020), and commenced 'enhanced surveillance ... to early detect, isolate and treat all confirmed cases' (Kenu et al. 2020: 72). For a summary of the restriction and mitigation measures put in place by the government, see appendix C in Asante (2022). To generate goodwill for the stringent measures put in place, the president held consultations with eminent clergymen and local leaders given the enormous influence that such leaders wield in the country (Asante 2020; Prempeh 2021).

Specific health-related interventions included the procurement of medical supplies needed to fight the pandemic, including coveralls, masks, goggles, non-contact thermometers, and test kits. Further, 2,000 community health workers and volunteers were employed to strengthen the pool of health personnel. This early response strategy prioritized aggressive disease surveillance, contact tracing, and testing (Quakyi et al. 2021). The government also ensured speedy availability of the resources necessary to fight the pandemic. Roughly 100 pick-up trucks and 2,500 tablets were mobilized for the exercise (Presidency of Ghana 2020a).

Before the pandemic, the country had only two testing centres. To boost testing and contact tracing, 14 more testing centres and facilities were added, including private providers (Presidency of Ghana 2020b). Given resource constraints, scientists at the University of Ghana's Noguchi Memorial Institute for Medical Research (NMIMR) developed an innovative batch-testing system (Owusu and Crentsil 2021). This cost-effective strategy allowed Ghana to significantly scale up testing, and by the end of May the country ranked above most other sub-Saharan African countries, second only to South Africa, the hardest-hit country on the continent (see figure 2.10 in Asante 2022).

To remedy the severe disparities in access to quality healthcare writ large by the pandemic, the president announced a long-term programme to provide each district and region with at least one hospital, a programme dubbed 'Agenda 111' (Presidency of Ghana 2020b). However, three years after this announcement, only 88 out of the target of 111 hospitals were under construction and none had yet been completed (ModernGhana 2023).

The ability to quickly mobilize pre-existing capacity like previous epidemic control measures, networks of volunteers, and fortuitously timed logistical acquisitions—such as ambulances and medical drones—was crucial in Ghana's early pandemic response strategy. However, residual capacity can only provide a short-term reprieve and cannot underscore sustainable public service delivery. In Ghana's competitive clientelist context, interventions requiring long-term planning and execution are more difficult to implement than short-term or emergency measures (Asante 2023), as evidenced by the government's inability to meet its target spelt out in Agenda 111. As the pandemic stretched out over the course of several months, the challenges became too daunting for residual capacity to effectively prevent the spread of infection, as will be shown in the next section.

2.5.3 'Fellow Ghanaians!': the politics of pandemic response

While residual capacity put Ghana in a strong position to implement an impactful early pandemic response, the country's ability to sustain this performance was constrained by the broader political context. The containment measures raised unforeseen obstacles in the months leading up to the general elections in December 2020, including initial confusion that elections may not be possible under pandemic conditions (Asiseh 2020; Bomfeh 2020; GhanaWeb 2020). However, given the constitutional complications that would ensue, there eventually emerged a tacit consensus among various stakeholders that the elections should go ahead (Agbele and Saibu 2021). The politics of pandemic response expressed itself in multiple ways.

First, the Electoral Commission (EC), the country's election management body, faced the unprecedented challenge of organizing general elections under pandemic conditions. The main obstacle it faced was how to proceed with its resolve to compile a fresh voters' register. This decision was a controversial one which the largest opposition party, the National Democratic Congress (NDC), had unsuccessfully contested at the Supreme Court. But apart from the political objections, questions were raised about the legality of a mass registration exercise when a ban on social gatherings was in place. The EC was also accused of recklessly endangering public health. In response, the EC assured the public that it had implemented safety protocols at registration centres, including social distancing, the use of face masks, the provision of handwashing stations, the use of temperature guns, and the introduction of a digital queuing system. However, a report by the Coalition of Domestic Election Observers (CODEO) indicated that some registration centres did not follow these protocols (Agbele and Saibu 2021).

Second, in a period when social gatherings had been restricted, the incumbent president, Nana Addo Danquah Akufo-Addo of the New Patriotic Party (NPP), enjoyed the advantage of incumbency. Appearing regularly on national television, he infused each appearance with an air of showmanship, especially when he was announcing mitigation packages such as subsidies on utilities. His speeches were intoned with a performative flair and his sartorial choice of wax print textiles, famous for their encoded messaging (Darku and Lubisi 2020), were meticulously curated for their symbolic impact. With a deadly disease raging and social life brought to a standstill, these broadcasts came to capture the public's attention with their well-rehearsed performance and spectacle. The president soon earned the nickname 'Fellow Ghanaians!', the signature greeting with which he opened each address. Later in the year, the Ghana Textiles Printing Company (GTP) outdoored a new design called 'Fellow Ghanaians' as one of the commemorative designs for the year (Aikins 2020). From March to December 2020, the president delivered 20 speeches, 19 of them before the general elections on 7 December 2020.

The incentive to exploit crisis for political advantage has been widely acknowledged in crisis scholarship (Boin and Hart 2003; Klein 2007). The nature of the pandemic and its containment measures provided an opportunity for the president to demonstrate competence and compassion while hobbling the opposition party's ability to mobilize for votes ahead of the election. The reality of the situation in Ghana and elsewhere was not lost on analysts, some of whom characterized the social support packages 'as a strategy by government to curry favour with electorates or score political points; while containment measures were seen as strategies to demobilise opposition parties from campaign activities during elections' (Tsikata and Torvikey 2021: 3–4).

However, as the elections drew closer, the government started to ease the containment measures. In May 2020, hotels, bars, and restaurants were allowed to open under enhanced social-distancing procedures (Graphic Online 2020a). In June, restrictions were further relaxed. Religious services with congregations not exceeding 100 were allowed, as were other social gatherings like private burials and weddings, provided they also did not exceed 100 attendees

(Graphic Online 2020c). With progressive relaxation of restrictions, compliance with the overall safety protocols, such as mask wearing, grew increasingly lax.

Along with the easing of restrictions, the seriousness of the pandemic receded in the public consciousness (Nikoi 2021). As attention was diverted to other matters, the public began 'throwing caution to the wind' (Agbele and Saibu 2021: 9). To compound the situation, with dwindling medical supplies and a growing backlog of samples, the director-general of GHS, Dr Patrick Kuma-Aboagye, announced on 21 July 2020 that the service was thenceforth going to prioritize the testing of only symptomatic cases (Graphic Online 2020b). This announcement effectively marked the end of the country's robust initial efforts: 'Contact tracing consequently scaled down to a near dormancy in parts of Ghana' (Quakyi et al. 2021: 1). This demonstrates that while residual capacity could lay the much-needed foundation for crisis response, it is not enough to support effective response to protracted emergency situations.

2.6 Conclusion: residual capacity and the politics of pandemic response

Institutional and political factors mediated the trajectory of the COVID-19 outbreak in Ghana in the first year of the outbreak. Institutionally, the country benefited from decisive early action at the continental and subregional levels, which laid a foundation for the national response. Ghana, like other West African countries, already had a public health emergency response infrastructure in place from earlier interventions, which was quickly reactivated and repurposed for the COVID-19 response. This included an extensive network of community health agents who were deployed for contact tracing and community sensitization. While Ghana's overall capacity remains weak, this public health response infrastructure and continental coordination helped the country to gain control of the public health emergency in the first few months of the outbreak. However, with an impending election later that year and fearing political backlash from the socioeconomic impact of its pandemic response measures, the government began easing restrictions even while the case count was still rising.

Ghana's case shows the need to rethink the way we conceptualize state capacity. It is necessary to distinguish between 'residual' capacity that may emerge only episodically and 'core' capacity that characterizes state performance in relatively settled times. Regional organizations like the AU and ECOWAS helped member countries to tap into a common pool of expertise and resources, allowing capacities embedded in individual countries to be 'abstracted' and 'distributed' across the region. Given the policy confusion, feet-dragging, and deeply statist responses that marked the early stages of the pandemic in wealthier countries with much higher levels of state capacity, this successful coordination by the

AU and ECOWAS is noteworthy. Additionally, sheer luck, such as Ghana's fortuitous procurement of ambulances and the deployment of drone delivery of medical supplies, allowed the country to leapfrog over entrenched infrastructural bottlenecks.

However, sustainable public service delivery over the long term cannot rely on residual capacity, which, because it is episodic and fleeting, cannot be the foundation of a long-term strategy. Moreover, the circumstances under which residual capacity can be activated remain uncertain. Residual capacity is, by definition, episodic and its successful deployment may not be guaranteed under all circumstances. The fundamental social and political disruptions caused by the pandemic opened the door for measures which would otherwise have been impossible. Future research could explore the possibility of deploying residual capacity in relatively more settled times and whether residual capacity could be leveraged to stimulate reforms that could trigger long-term public sector effectiveness.

References

Abdulai, A.-G. (2018). 'The Political Economy of Maternal Healthcare in Ghana.' Working Paper 107. Manchester: Effective States and Inclusive Development Research Centre (ESID), The University of Manchester. Available at: www.effective-states.org/working-paper-107 (accessed 20 July 2021). https://doi.org/10.2139/ssrn.3272848.

Abdulai, A.-G. (2021). 'Political Settlement Dynamics and the Emergence and Decline of Bureaucratic Pockets of Effectiveness in Ghana.' Working Paper 173. Manchester: ESID, The University of Manchester. Available at: www.effective-states.org/wp-content/uploads/esid_wp_173_abdulai.pdf (accessed 20 July 2021). https://doi.org/10.2139/ssrn.3894493.

Agbele, F., and G. Saibu (2021). 'Managing Elections under Covid-19 Pandemic Conditions: The Case of Ghana.' Case Study, 27 April. Strömsborg: International Institute for Democracy and Electoral Assistance (IDEA). Available at: www.idea.int/sites/default/files/managing-elections-under-covid-19-pandemic-conditions-the-case-of-ghana.pdf (accessed 1 October 2021).

Ahanhanzo, C., E.A.K. Johnson, E.A. Eboreime, S. Issiaka, B.I. Traoré, C.C. Adohinzin, T. Adesina, E.N. Diallo, N. Obgureke, and S. Okolo (2021). 'COVID-19 in West Africa: Regional Resource Mobilisation and Allocation in the First Year of the Pandemic.' BMJ Global Health, 6(5): e004762. https://doi.org/10.1136/bmjgh-2020-004762.

Aikins, A. de-Graft (2020). '"Colonial Virus"? Creative Arts and Public Understanding of COVID-19 in Ghana.' *Journal of the British Academy*, 8: 401–413. https://doi.org/10.5871/jba/008.401.

Appiah, D., and A.-G. Abdulai (2017). 'Competitive Clientelism and the Politics of Core Public Sector Reform in Ghana.' Working Paper 82. Manchester: ESID, The University of Manchester. Available at: www.effective-states.org/working-paper-82 (accessed 20 July 2021). https://doi.org/10.2139/ssrn.2954598.

Aryeetey, E., and W. Baah-Boateng (2015). "Understanding Ghana's Growth Success Story and Job Creation Challenges". WIDER Working Paper 2015/140. Helsinki: UNU-WIDER. https://doi.org/10.35188/UNU-WIDER/2015/029-4.

Asante, A.D., and A.B. Zwi (2009). 'Factors Influencing Resource Allocation Decisions and Equity in the Health System of Ghana.' *Public Health*, 123(5): 371–377. https://doi.org/10.1016/j.puhe.2009.02.006.

Asante, A.D., A.B. Zwi, and M.T. Ho (2006). 'Getting by on Credit: How District Health Managers in Ghana Cope with the Untimely Release of Funds.' *BMC Health Services Research*, 6(1): 1–9. https://doi.org/10.1186/1472-6963-6-105.

Asante, K.T. (2020). '"Citizens Not Spectators"? Civic Engagement and Informality of Citizenship in Ghana.' *Contemporary Journal of African Studies*, 7(2): 1–17. https://doi.org/10.4314/contjas.v7i2.1.

Asante, K.T. (2021). 'Political Economy of the Oil Palm Value Chain in Ghana.' Working Paper 54. Brighton: Future Agricultures Consortium. https://doi.org/10.19088/APRA.2021.008.

Asante, K.T. (2022). 'Residual Capacity and the Political Economy of Pandemic Response in Ghana.' WIDER Working Paper 2022/44. Helsinki: UNU-WIDER.

Asante, K.T. (2023). 'The Politics of Policy Failure in Ghana: The Case of Oil Palm.' *World Development Perspectives*, 31: 100509. https://doi.org/10.1016/j.wdp.2023.100509.

Asante, K.T., and M. Khisa (2019). 'Political Corruption and the Limits of Anti-Corruption Activism in Ghana.' In I. Amundsen (ed.), *Political Corruption in Africa*. Cheltenham: Edward Elgar Publishing, pp. 29–51.

Asante, K.T., and S. Mullard (2021). 'Social Accountability and Anti-Corruption in Ghana's Fertiliser Subsidy Programme.' U4, 2021(6). Bergen: Chr. Michelsen Institute.

Asiseh, T. (2020). 'The 2020 Elections Should Be Postponed.' GhanaWeb, 6 August. Available at: www.ghanaweb.com/GhanaHomePage/features/The-2020-elections-should-be-postponed-1027201 (accessed 2 September 2021).

Ateku, A.-J. (2017). 'Ghana Is 60: An African Success Story with Tough Challenges Ahead.' *The Conversation*, 7 March. Available at: https://theconversation.com/ghana-is-60-an-african-success-story-with-tough-challenges-ahead-74049 (accessed 20 November 2021).

AU (n.d.). 'About the Fund: AU COVID-19 Response Fund.' Available at: https://au.int/en/aucovid19responsefund (accessed 24 September 2021).

AU and Africa CDC (2020). 'Partnership to Accelerate COVID-19 Testing (PACT) in Africa: Resources.' Factsheet, 4 June. Addis Ababa: Africa CDC. Available at: https://africacdc.org/download/partnership-to-accelerate-covid-19-testing-pact-in-africa (accessed 1 October 2021).

Banful, A.B. (2011a). 'Do Formula-Based Intergovernmental Transfer Mechanisms Eliminate Politically Motivated Targeting? Evidence from Ghana.' *Journal of Development Economics*, 96(2): 380–390. https://doi.org/10.1016/j.jdeveco.2010.08.012.

Banful, A.B. (2011b). 'Old Problems in the New Solutions? Politically Motivated Allocation of Program Benefits and the "New" Fertilizer Subsidies.' *World Development*, 39(7): 1166–1176. https://doi.org/10.1016/j.worlddev.2010.11.004.

Biccard, B.M., P.D. Gopalan, M. Miller, W.L. Michell, D. Thomson, A. Ademuyiwa, E. Aniteye, G. Calligaro, M.S. Chaibou, and H.T. Dhufera (2021). 'Patient Care and Clinical Outcomes for Patients with COVID-19 Infection Admitted to African High-Care or Intensive Care Units (ACCCOS): A Multicentre, Prospective, Observational Cohort Study.' *The Lancet*, 397(10288): 1885–1894. https://doi.org/10.1016/S0140-6736(21)00441-4.

Boafo-Arthur, K. (1999). 'Ghana: Structural Adjustment, Democratization, and the Politics of Continuity.' *African Studies Review*, 42(2): 41–72. https://doi.org/10.2307/525364.

Boin, A., and P. Hart (2003). 'Public Leadership in Times of Crisis: Mission Impossible?' *Public Administration Review*, 63(5): 544–553. https://doi.org/10.1111/1540-6210.00318.

Bomfeh, J.K. (2020). 'Success of Registration Exercise Is Not the Vindication or Damnation of Any Position—Kabila'. YouTube, 14 August. Available at: www.youtube.com/watch?v=mTIBfGv8W50 (accessed 10 September 2021).

Cameron, E.E., J.B. Nuzzo, and J.A. Bell (2019). *Global Health Security Index: Building Collective Action and Accountability.* Washington, DC: Nuclear Threat Initiative, Baltimore, MD: Johns Hopkins Center for Health Security, and London: Economist Intelligence Unit. Available at: www.ghsindex.org/wp-content/uploads/2019/10/2019-Global-Health-Security-Index.pdf (accessed 2 September 2021).

Chigudu, S. (2020). *The Political Life of an Epidemic: Cholera, Crisis and Citizenship in Zimbabwe.* Cambridge: Cambridge University Press. https://doi.org/10.1017/9781108773928.

Darku, E. N., and Lubisi, N. (2020). '"We Have Rights to Designs": Interrogating Design Pirating on the Ghanaian Textiles Market'. *The Journal of Legal Pluralism and Unofficial Law*, 52(1): 28–45.

Diao, X., P. Hazell, S. Kolavalli, and D. Resnick (2019). 'Introduction'. In X. Diao, P. Hazell, S. Kolavalli, and D. Resnick (eds), *Ghana's Economic and Agricultural Transformation: Past Performance and Future Prospects.* Oxford: Oxford University Press, pp. 1–18. https://doi.org/10.2499/9780198845348_01.

Dong, E., H. Du, and L. Gardner (2020). 'An Interactive Web-Based Dashboard to Track COVID-19 in Real Time'. *The Lancet Infectious Diseases*, 20(5): 533–534. https://doi.org/10.1016/S1473-3099(20)30120-1.

Dye, B.J. (2022). 'When the Means Become the Ends: Ghana's "Good Governance" Electricity Reform Overwhelmed by the Politics of Power Crises'. *New Political Economy*, 28(1): 91–111. https://doi.org/10.1080/13563467.2022.2084517.

European Centre for Disease Prevention and Control (multiple dates). 'COVID-19 Situation Update Worldwide'. Available at: www.ecdc.europa.eu/en/geographical-distribution-2019-ncov-cases (accessed 15 October 2021).

GhanaWeb (2019). 'Zipline Begins Test Flights in Ghana'. GhanaWeb, 1 March. Available at: www.ghanaweb.com/GhanaHomePage/NewsArchive/Zipline-begins-test-flights-in-Ghana-727211 (accessed 20 September 2021).

GhanaWeb (2020). 'NPP Does Not Want 2020 General Elections Postponed—John Boadu'. GhanaWeb, 16 April. Available at: www.ghanaweb.com/GhanaHomePage/NewsArchive/NPP-does-not-want-2020-general-elections-postponed-John-Boadu-925465 (accessed 20 September 2021).

Gisselquist, R. M., and A. Vaccaro (2023). 'COVID-19 and the State: Exploring a Puzzling Relationship in the Early Stages of the Pandemic'. *Journal of International Development*, 35(5): 800–819. https://doi.org/10.1002/jid.3702.

Graphic Online (2020a). 'Drinking Bars, Restaurants, Hotels to Resume Operations'. *Graphic Online*, 13 May. Available at: www.graphic.com.gh/news/general-news/drinking-bars-restaurants-hotels-to-resume-operations.html (accessed 20 September 2021).

Graphic Online (2020b). 'COVID-19: Symptomatic Persons to Be Prioritised for Testing as GHS Clears Backlog of 23,000 Samples'. *Graphic Online*, 21 July. Available at: www.graphic.com.gh/news/general-news/covid-19-symptomatic-persons-to-be-prioritised-for-testing-as-ghs-clears-backlog-of-23-000-samples.html (accessed 20 September 2021).

Graphic Online (2020c). 'Why President Akufo-Addo Relaxed Covid-19 Restrictions [FULL ADDRESS]'. *Graphic Online*, 31 May. Available at: www.graphic.com.gh/news/politics/why-president-akufo-addo-relaxed-covid-19-restrictions-full-address.html (accessed 20 September 2021).

Grävingholt, J., S. Ziaja, C. Ruhe, P. Fink, M. Kreibaum, and C. Wingens (2018). *Constellations of State Fragility v1.0*. Bonn: German Development Institute/Deutsches Institut für Entwicklungspolitik (DIE). https://doi.org/10.23661/CSF1.0.0.

Gray, R. (2020). 'Lack of Solidarity Hampered Europe's Coronavirus Response, Research Finds'. Horizon: The EU Research and Innovation Magazine, 12 November. Available at: https://ec.europa.eu/research-and-innovation/en/horizon-magazine/lack-solidarity-hampered-europes-coronavirus-response-research-finds (accessed 20 December 2020).

ISSER (2019). *Ghana Social Development Outlook 2018*. Accra: Institute of Statistical, Social and Economic Research.

ISSER (2020). *The State of the Ghana Economy in 2019*. Accra: Institute of Statistical, Social and Economic Research.

Kenu, E., J. Frimpong, and K. Koram (2020). 'Responding to the COVID-19 Pandemic in Ghana'. *Ghana Medical Journal*, 54(2): 72–73. https://doi.org/10.4314/gmj.v54i2.1.

Khan, M.H. (2005). 'Markets, States and Democracy: Patron–Client Networks and the Case for Democracy in Developing Countries'. *Democratisation*, 12(5): 704–724. https://doi.org/10.1080/13510340500322157.

Klein, N. (2007). *The Shock Doctrine: The Rise of Disaster Capitalism*. New York: Macmillan.

León, R. de (2020). 'Zipline Begins Drone Delivery of Covid-19 Test Samples in Ghana'. CNBC, 20 April. Available at: www.cnbc.com/2020/04/20/zipline-begins-drone-delivery-of-covid-19-test-samples-in-ghana.html (accessed 10 September 2021).

Loembé, M.M., A. Tshangela, S.J. Salyer, J.K. Varma, A.E.O. Ouma, and J.N. Nkengasong (2020). 'COVID-19 in Africa: The Spread and Response'. *Nature Medicine*, 26(7): 999–1003. https://doi.org/10.1038/s41591-020-0961-x.

ModernGhana (2023). '88 Out of "Agenda 111" Hospitals under Construction—Kojo Oppong Nkrumah'. ModernGhana, 29 June. Available at www.modernghana.com/news/1241363/88-out-of-agenda-111-hospitals-under-constructio.html (accessed 14 July 2023).

MoH (2018). *Holistic Assessment of the Health Sector Programme of Work 2017*. Accra: Ministry of Health.

MoH (2020). *National Strategic Covid-19 Response Plan. Period: July 2020–December 2024*. Accra: Ministry of Health.

Nikoi, N.K. (2021, 3 March). 'Propagandizing a Pandemic: The Narrative of "Progress" in Ghana's COVID19 Response'. Africa ProActive, 3 March. Available at: www.africaproactive.com/blog/propagandizing-a-pandemic-the-narrative-of-progress-in-ghanas-covid19-response (accessed 3 September 2021).

Nwameme, A.U., P.T.-N. Tabong, and P.B. Adongo (2018). 'Implementing Community-Based Health Planning and Services in Impoverished Urban Communities: Health Workers' Perspective'. *BMC Health Services Research*, 18(1): 1–11. https://doi.org/10.1186/s12913-018-3005-1.

Nwannekanma, B. (2021,3 March). 'Zipline Begins World's First Ever Drone Delivery of COVID-19 Vaccine in Ghana'. *The Guardian Nigeria News*, 3 March. Available at: https://guardian.ng/news/zipline-begins-worlds-first-ever-drone-delivery-of-covid-19-vaccine-in-ghana (accessed 20 October 2021).

Oduro, F., A. Mohammed, and M. Ashon (2014). 'A Dynamic Mapping of the Political Settlement in Ghana'. Working Paper 28. Manchester: ESID, The University of Manchester. https://doi.org/10.2139/ssrn.2386788.

Okyere, E. (2018). '*Assessing Policies and Strategies to Reduce the Impact of Health Worker Shortages in Primary Health Care Facilities in Ghana*'. PhD thesis. Adelaide: College of Medicine and Public Health, Flinders University.

Owusu, A.Y., and K.T. Asante (2020). 'Emergency Medical Care in Ghana: A Focus on the National Ambulance Service, Support Systems and Beds in Healthcare Institutions'. Policy Brief 4 (September). Accra: ISSER.

Owusu A.Y., and A.O. Crentsil (2021). 'COVID-19, Employment, Social Protection, and Basic Services'. In ISSER (ed.), *The Impact of the COVID-19 Pandemic in Ghana*. Accra: ISSER.

Prempeh, C. (2021). 'Religion and the State in an Episodic Moment of COVID-19 in Ghana'. *Social Sciences & Humanities Open*, 4(1): 100141. https://doi.org/10.1016/j.ssaho.2021.100141.

Presidency of Ghana (2020a). 'Address to the Nation by President Akufo-Addo on Updates to Ghana's Enhanced Response to the Coronavirus Pandemic'. Accra: Presidency of Ghana. Available at: www.presidency.gov.gh/index.php/briefing-room/speeches/1545-address-to-the-nation-by-president-of-the-republic-nana-addo-dankwa-akufo-addo-on-updates-to-ghana-s-enhanced-response-to-the-coronavirus-pandemic-on-friday-27th-march-2020 (accessed 10 September 2021).

Presidency of Ghana (2020b). 'President Akufo-Addo Provides Update on Ghana's Enhanced Response to COVID-19'. Available at: www.presidency.gov.gh/index.php/briefing-room/speeches/1582-president-akufo-addo-provides-update-on-ghana-s-enhanced-response-to-covid-20 (accessed 10 September 2021).

Pulse Ghana (2020). 'World Bank Report: Ghana Ranks 14th in Doctor-to-Patient Ratio in Sub-Saharan Africa'. *Pulse Ghana*, 21 April. Available at: www.pulse.com.gh/news/local/world-bank-report-ghana-ranks-14th-in-doctor-to-patient-ratio-in-sub-saharan-africa/dfk42ve (accessed 10 September 2021).

Quakyi, N.K., N.A.A. Asante, Y.A. Nartey, Y. Bediako, and N.A. Sam-Agudu (2021). 'Ghana's COVID-19 Response: The Black Star Can Do Even Better'. *BMJ Global Health*, 6(3): e005569. https://doi.org/10.1136/bmjgh-2021-005569.

Quartey, P., and K.T. Asante (2021). 'Overview Chapter: The Socio-Economic Impacts of Pandemics'. In ISSER (ed.), *The Impact of the COVID-19 Pandemic in Ghana*. Accra: ISSER.

Resnick, D. (2019). 'Strong Democracy, Weak State: The Political Economy of Ghana's Stalled Structural Transformation'. In X. Diao, P. Hazell, S. Kolavalli, and D. Resnick (eds), *Ghana's Economic and Agricultural Transformation: Past Performance and Future Prospects*. Oxford: Oxford University Press, pp. 49–94. https://doi.org/10.1093/oso/9780198845348.003.0003.

Ritchie, H., E. Mathieu, L. Rodés-Guirao, C. Appel, C. Giattino, E. Ortiz-Ospina, J. Hasell, B. Macdonald, S. Dattani, and M. Roser (2020). 'Ghana: Coronavirus Pandemic Country Profile'. Our World in Data. Available at: https://ourworldindata.org/coronavirus/country/ghana (accessed 20 October 2021).

Siaw-Frimpong, M., S. Touray, and N. Sefa (2021). 'Capacity of Intensive Care Units in Ghana'. *Journal of Critical Care*, 61: 76–81. https://doi.org/10.1016/j.jcrc.2020.10.009.

Tsikata, D., and D. Torvikey (2021). *Africa's COVID-19 Responses: Proactivity, Hits and Misses and Deepening Inequalities*. Leiden: INCLUDE, African Studies Centre Leiden. Available at: https://includeplatform.net/wp-content/uploads/2021/06/Synthesis-Report-COVID19-in-Africa.pdf (accessed 15 October 2021).

Vincent, J. (2021). 'Self-Flying Drones Are Helping Speed Deliveries of COVID-19 Vaccines in Ghana'. *The Verge*, 9 March. Available at: www.theverge.com/2021/3/9/22320965/drone-delivery-vaccine-ghana-zipline-cold-chain-storage (10 October 2021).

Wadvalla, B.-A. (2020). 'How Africa Has Tackled Covid-19'. *British Medical Journal*, 370: m2830. https://doi.org/10.1136/bmj.m2830.

Whitfield, L. (2010). 'The State Elites, PSRPs, and Policy Implementation in Aid-Dependent Ghana.' *Third World Quarterly*, 31(5): 721–737. https://doi.org/10.1080/01436597.2010.502692.

Whitfield, L. (2011). 'Growth without Economic Transformation: Economic Impacts of Ghana's Political Settlement.' Working Paper 2011:28. Copenhagen: Danish Institute for International Studies (DIIS).

3

The Effects of Limited Capacity, Ideational Legitimacy, and Weak Authority on the Tanzanian State Response to COVID-19

Amy S. Patterson

3.1 Introduction

As a lower-middle-income country with 58 million residents and a gross national income per capita of US$1,080 in 2020 (Piatti-Fünfkirchen and Ally 2020), the United Republic of Tanzania (hereafter Tanzania) received significant global attention for its response to COVID-19 during 2020–2021.[1] This was not because the country's attempts were hampered by its huge geographic area, inadequate road infrastructure, or largely rural population (65 per cent of its residents) (Trading Economics 2021), though such factors mattered. Rather, Tanzania garnered attention because of its unorthodox approach. High-level state officials, and particularly the late president John Magufuli, publicly supported herbal cures, declared the country 'COVID-free', shunned mask wearing, argued that prayer kept the virus at bay, questioned the value of testing, and refused the COVID-19 vaccine. At the same time, district and regional health officials educated the public about the virus, engaged in contact tracing, and cared for the sick (Yamanis et al. 2021). After the president's death on 17 March 2021 (due to what opposition party leaders claimed was COVID-19), his successor, Samia Suluhu Hassan, began to align the country's response with global health practices (Mirondo 2021). What explains Tanzania's pandemic response from March 2020 until March 2021? Although it is tempting to merely focus on the 'big man' explanation, there is more to the story (Becker 2021). This chapter interrogates state capacity, legitimacy, and authority—some of which are closely tied to but not synonymous with the late president—to argue that the state's formation, its ideational underpinning,

[1] The author is grateful to Laura Botros for research assistance, as well as Rachel Gisselquist, Julio Teehankee, and Andrea Vaccaro for helpful comments.

Amy S. Patterson, *The Effects of Limited Capacity, Ideational Legitimacy, and Weak Authority on the Tanzanian State Response to COVID-19*. In: *How States Respond to Crisis*. Edited by: Rachel M. Gisselquist and Andrea Vaccaro, Oxford University Press. DOI: 10.1093/9780198907237.003.0003

and its shaky authority as evidenced through its reliance on electoral authoritarianism undergird a response that minimized the pandemic threat, shunned global cooperation, and promoted nationalist solutions.

This chapter incorporates a systematic analysis of 140 news articles from 2020 and 2021 in the *Citizen* (an independent English-language newspaper with a corresponding Kiswahili version, *Mwananchi*) and global media sources such as allAfrica.com and *Al Jazeera*. It also uses data from Afrobarometer, a pan-African, non-partisan survey network working in 34 countries, and the World Bank Governance Index to demonstrate state capacity, legitimacy, and authority (World Bank 2020).[2] Author observations, informal conversations, and key informant interviews in Dodoma and Dar es Salaam with non-governmental organization (NGO) officials, scholars, and government health officials between November 2019 and March 2020 provide additional insights.[3]

This chapter proceeds as follows. First, it argues that although state capacity, authority, and legitimacy matter for effective pandemic responses (see Gisselquist and Vaccaro 2021), those state components are rooted in particular historical processes of state formation, discourses on legitimatization, and strategies of control, the combination of which shapes pandemic responses. Section 3.3 describes Tanzania's response to COVID-19 during the pandemic's first year. Sections 3.4 and 3.5 incorporate the approaches of historical and discursive institutionalism to dissect how patterns established under the first postcolonial president, Julius Nyerere (president from 1961 to 1985), shaped state capacity and legitimacy. Historical institutionalism recognizes how 'institutions emerge from and are embedded in current temporal processes' (Thelen 1999: 371). Broadly defining institutions and recognizing how political actors affect institutions, this approach shies away from a deterministic path dependency to see institutions as a reflection of social processes (Thelen 1999). Discursive institutionalism adds that ideas and discourses shape these processes. Defined as 'programmatic beliefs' (Berman 1998), values or norms (Finnemore and Sikkink 1998), national traditions (Katzenstein 1996), policy problem definitions (Shiffman 2017), and 'deep core' worldviews (Sabatier and Jenkins-Smith 1993), discourses and ideas bring meaning to institutions (Schmidt 2008). Section 3.6 examines the state's struggle for authority through its use of electoral authoritarianism and actions to curtail debates on its COVID-19 response (Paget 2020b). The chapter concludes that African states may exhibit agency in contexts of significant uncertainty.

[2] The World Bank Governance Index includes six indicators: political stability, government effectiveness, control of corruption, rule of law, regulatory quality, and voice and accountability. Countries receive cumulative and indicator-specific scores from −2.5 to +2.5. The cumulative average in 2020 was −0.68 for sub-Saharan Africa and −0.60 for Tanzania.

[3] All respondents were assured of anonymity in publications. The broader research project, which examined mental health policy, was approved by the Tanzanian Commission for Science and Technology (2019-627-NA-2019-375) and the University of the South.

3.2 African state capacity, legitimacy, and authority: beyond 'big man' politics

The African state 'include[s] the territory, laws, bureaucratic and military apparatus, and some ideological justification for the state's existence' (Englebert 2009: 4). The state is a dynamic, flexible institution (Becker 2020), 'amalgamated thorough the exercise of power' (Lund 2006). It claims control over people and territories, has the capacity to 'command, regulate and extract' (Linz and Stepan 1996: 7), and has some level of autonomy from civil society (Skocpol et al. 1985). A focus on the state does not deny that leaders operate within this institutional context, but it does move beyond the 'big man' trope that portrays individual rulers as erratic decision-makers who rely on patronage, ethnic and family networks, and personal loyalty to retain power and control institutions (Sigman and Lindberg 2020; van de Walle 2001). The narrative of the 'mad dictator' with unfettered power is 'generally misleading' because it 'pass[es] off as a personal failure' broader structural conditions of the state (Becker 2021: 189).

The combination of capacity, legitimacy, and authority shape a state's effectiveness in promoting economic growth, providing public goods, fostering development, and fostering positive health outcomes (Gisselquist and Vaccaro 2021). These dimensions take on unique characteristics depending on the state, thereby leading to outcomes that can be specific to a particular time, place, or external threat. Capacity is the 'ability of a state to provide its citizens with basic life chances' (Grävingholt et al. 2015: 1290), including protection from pathogenic threats. Although many African states have some developmental capacity to solve problems and provide security, far fewer have the administrative and responsive capacity to make services accessible, efficient, and equitable (Bratton and Chang 2006: 1068). Legitimacy is the population's consent that the state has the right to rule. Most Africans consider that their state is 'authentically constituted', despite most states' colonial histories and ethnic and religious pluralism, but they question legitimacy based on accountability and upholding the rule of law (Bratton and Chang 2006). State legitimacy also may rest on ideas and discourses, such as nationalism and family (Bhandari and Mueller 2019).

Authority is the state's ability to control violence across its territory and establish public order. Authority is not divorced from precolonial, indigenous governance that focused on personal loyalty (Herbst 2000); colonial exploitation (Young 2012); nationalist struggles (Cheeseman 2015); and neoliberal attempts to minimize the state (Bratton and van de Walle 1997). In its struggle for public authority, the state must contend with civil society organizations, donors, NGOs, and traditional and religious authorities (Brass 2016; Lund 2006; Migdal 1988). Neopatrimonial rule through personal networks and patronage challenges the African state's autonomy from civil society (Chabal and Daloz 1999: 5–7). Tensions between the 'primordial public' (the realm of ethnic, lineage, and religious affiliations to which individuals give freely) and the 'civic public' (the realm of state institutions which citizens obey only grudgingly) shape state authority. To solidify its authority, the state may use repression (Bates 2008), extraction (Englebert 2009), and/or electoral manipulation, with the latter allowing the state to tacitly meet global norms of democratic competition (Schedler 2006). This chapter shows how these three state components shaped Tanzania's COVID-19 response.

3.3 The Tanzanian state responds to COVID-19

Tanzania's first case of COVID-19 appeared on 16 March 2020, when a Tanzanian woman returning from Belgium became ill. State officials quickly shut schools and universities and mandated social distancing on public transportation (author observations, Dar es Salaam, 19 March 2020). International travellers were required to undergo and pay for 14 days of quarantine in designated hotels, and on 11 April 2020 state officials suspended all international flights. District and regional health authorities were provided personal protective equipment (PPE) and received guidelines on screening and isolating patients, setting up treatment units, quarantining confirmed cases, and urging social distancing and handwashing (Mfinanga et al. 2021). Early fear of the virus contributed to stigma and avoidance of those who had travelled (Yamanis et al. 2021: 565). On 22 March 2020, the president declared the virus to be 'the devil', which could not survive in the 'body of Christ', and state officials urged the population to pray and to engage in handwashing. They did not publicly support mask wearing (Bariyo and Parkinson 2020; *Citizen* 23 April 2020a).

Within two months, the state began to minimize the pandemic threat. After 8 May 2020, when Tanzania reported 509 cases and 21 deaths, the state released no more health statistics until June 2021 (Kombe 2021). On 22 May 2020, Magufuli declared Tanzania to be 'COVID-19 free' and ordered students to return to school and universities to reopen (*Citizen* 17 May 2020d; Dahir 2020). International flights resumed by mid-May, and by late June isolation centres were closed. In response, the US Embassy publicly warned tourists against visiting the country. In an August 2020 crowded church service, the late president credited God with saving the country and demonized those who challenged the official narrative: 'Our enemies will say a lot, but here in Tanzania, we are safe' (Dahir 2020). Further illustrating exceptionalism, Tanzania was one of only four African states (of 50 examined) that did not close workplaces, issue stay-at-home orders, or place restrictions on in-country movement (Hale et al. 2020). Unlike two-thirds of other African countries, it did not implement any social policies such as income support (Yamanis et al. 2021: 571).

As the pandemic continued, state officials publicly challenged public health recommendations on testing and vaccines, claiming these were inaccurate, unreliable, untested, and potentially unsafe. To illustrate problems at the National Community Health Laboratory, Magufuli secretly asked scientists to use the tests on a goat, quail, and papaya, all of which allegedly tested positive for the virus (Dahir 2020). Tanzania accepted donations of the COVID-Organics mixture from Madagascar to 'cure' the disease, despite the fact that no data on the product's efficacy had been shared with the World Health Organization (WHO) or the Africa Centres for Disease Control (Africa CDC) (*Al Jazeera* 8 May 2020b). In February 2021, as COVAX—the international collaboration to ensure equitable access to vaccines in low-income countries—compiled its distribution list, Tanzania announced that it would not accept vaccines because they were sourced abroad and had not been proven safe. Magufuli publicly challenged health officials to shun the vaccine: 'You should stand firm. Vaccinations are dangerous. If the White man was able to come up with vaccinations he would have found a vaccination for AIDS by now .... He would have found a vaccination for malaria by now; he would have found a vaccination for cancer by now' (Makoni 2021). In late February 2021, the health ministry de facto admitted that Tanzania had cases, but put a positive spin on the country's experience with the virus: 'As said by the president, we won last year and the economy continued to grow ... and Corona still existed. We did not set lockdowns, and even now, we will not impose lockdowns because God is on our side' (*Citizen* 22 February 2021). A few weeks later, Magufuli died.

3.4 Historical institutionalism: *ujamaa*, state capacity, and the pandemic response

Ziaja et al. (2019) classify Tanzania as a 'low-capacity' country, an assessment echoed in the World Bank 'government effectiveness' measure that assesses the quality, competence, effectiveness, and independence of the civil service. The country scored −0.77, the average sub-Saharan Africa score. To understand how low capacity informs Tanzanian governance, this chapter examines the actions of Nyerere, who had a 'towering influence on Tanzania's political and economic affairs for almost forty years' (Lofchie 2014: 3). After Tanzanian independence from Britain in 1961 and unification with Zanzibar in 1964, Nyerere established the *ujamaa* (familyhood) socialist policies in the 1967 Arusha Declaration (Shivji 2012). *Ujamaa* included nationalization of privately owned properties and the resettlement and expropriation of African-held land. Villagers were relocated to 8,000 new communities, many composed of people from different ethnic groups and lineages. Half of the country's rural population moved between 1967 and 1976 (Boone and Nyeme 2015; Green 2010). This 'state-initiated social engineering' resulted from state officials' overconfidence about scientific and technical progress, an authoritarian state structure, and a prostrate civil society unable to resist (Scott 1988: 4). Nyerere hoped to generate economies of scale for health and educational services, to create opportunities for large-scale and mechanized farming (Schneider 2014), and to weaken the landowning class and generate tax revenue for industrialization. *Ujamaa* villages were envisioned to be efficient, productive models of cooperative socialist development (Lofchie 2014).

Although Tanzania resembled East Asian developmental states in its authoritarianism, unlike those states, it was ruling party elites, not professionalized civil servants, who set Tanzania's development agenda. Similar to the more recently established developmental states of Rwanda and Ethiopia, Nyerere's Tanzania linked economic policies to the political objective of controlling society and preventing conflict (Matfess 2015; Singh and Ovadia 2018). Thus, despite his initial support for a bottom-up, participatory policy, Nyerere bowed to pressure from elites in the ruling Tanganyika African National Union (TANU) to centralize policy implementation (Shivji 2012; Schneider 2014: 49, 58–59). By 1973, some state officials used their discretionary power to coerce villagers to collectivize. For example, state officials informed people in Dodoma (a drought-prone region in central Tanzania) that only residents of collective villages would receive food aid during the hungry season (Scott 1998: 233).

Ujamaa had two long-term effects on state capacity. First, it amplified a hierarchical, bureaucratic governance preoccupied with 'adherence to forms and practices rather than ... a concern with content' (Green 2010: 18). When famine hits, for example, local officials tend to focus on how many sacks of grain are delivered or whether bureaucratic forms are correctly completed, not human suffering (Phillips 2018). In this governance, 'titles, office holding, meetings, and [written] plans' symbolize power even in the absence of activity (Green 2010: 25), as the state strives to make the population 'legible', or easy to document, locate, and ultimately control (see Englebert 2009).

Hierarchical relations and accountability to the next level condition the public health system. Although it was officially decentralized in the 1990s to make district health centres the first line of care (above the village), the system relies on regional health officers under the President's Office-Regional Authority and Local Government (PO-RALG) (Sirili and Simba 2021). Health services (through PO-RALG offices in the 31 regions) receive funding from the finance ministry, not the health ministry (interview, Dodoma, 30 January 2020), leading the central government, not local authorities, to spend over half of public health funding (Piatti- Fünfkirchen and Ally 2020: 9). At times, there can be confusion about jurisdictional issues related to budgets and health policies (interview, Dodoma, 6 February 2020). The regional health officer ensures that the budgetary plans of district health management teams comply with national health ministry priorities (e.g. childhood survival targets). Although district health teams ask for public input on budgets, they have limited discretion since there are expenditure limits (interview, Dodoma, 18 February 2020).

A second effect of *ujamaa* was that it made the state the main protector of citizens' interests and the dominant provider of citizen services. In 1962, the postcolonial government abolished the position of chief, a local leader who in traditional society would adjudicate local conflicts or represent people to the state. As a result, the state now orders, arranges, judges, and represents (Boone and Nyeme 2015). Additionally, through a series of actions in 1964, 1970, and 1971, the government nationalized church-run schools and the largest church-run hospitals. Neoliberal policies of the 1990s led the state to return some of these institutions, though state officials continue to oversee faith-based district hospitals (Mhina 2010). As a result, people turn to state institutions, not civil society, for many services. Indeed, 76 per cent of those surveyed said they had had contact with a public clinic or hospital in the last 12 months.[4] In addition, trust for central state authorities, such as the president, is higher than for subnational authorities—62 per cent compared to 49 per cent for local authorities and 20 per cent for traditional leaders (Afrobarometer 2016/2018).

Although a hierarchical bureaucracy is one component of a well-functioning state, Rauch and Evans (2000) point to other necessary elements such as competitive salaries, merit-based hiring and promotion, and clarity in personnel procedures, factors less apparent in Tanzania. An insufficient number of personnel, outdated equipment, inadequate resources, limited training, and poor incentives undermine state operations (Phillips 2018; interviews, Dodoma, 3 December 2019 and 17 January 2020). In 2017, health spending was 2.5 per cent of GDP (the target was 5 per cent), and health received just 6 per cent of the government's gross expenditures (vs. a target of 15 per cent). Since 2010, the health sector has suffered a 3.5 per cent decline in its share of the government budget (Piatti-Fünfkirchen and Ally 2020: 8). Low spending levels mean Tanzania has less than half the health workforce it needs to provide basic health services (Sirili and Simba 2021): 0.06 physicians and 0.58 nurses/midwives per 1,000 residents in 2017 (World Bank 2017a, b).

A 'contradiction' exists: despite centralized control, the state's overall low capacity creates gaps in policy implementation (Becker 2021) and confusion in interpretation across levels. Because the state has centralized service provision but lacks capacity, demand is high and often unmet; overworked staff sometimes show disdain for clients (interview, Dodoma, 24 February 2020). In health, 36 per cent of surveyed Tanzanians said it was 'difficult' or 'very difficult' to obtain the healthcare they needed, compared to the Africa regional average of 27 per cent (Afrobarometer 2016/2018). An overstretched state creates space for state officials to use discretion as they 'wield power [and] enforce dependencies'

[4] The average for Afrobarometer-surveyed countries was 60 per cent.

(Philips 2018: 12). With a transactional logic (Camargo 2017), citizens may play along, exhibiting a certain complicity, conviviality, illicit cohabitation, and collaboration to ensure access to needed resources and bureaucratic approval (Green 2010; Phillips 2018: 10, 138, 154). This pattern allowed corruption to significantly increase throughout the 2000s, as a weak state became the tool for a rising business class linked to the ruling party (Rahman et al. 2019).

The state's structural shortcomings made it both a target and a tool for Magufuli after his election in 2015. On one hand, he promised to increase state accountability and diminish discretion with his attack on corruption among 'lazy' mid-level officials, 'greedy' business leaders, and 'exploitative' foreigners (Paget 2020a: 1247; 2020b). His slogan *Hapa kazi tu* ('There is only work here') stressed productivity and honesty, and his anti-corruption actions garnered support among the *wanyonge* (downtrodden) and *wananchi* (citizens) (Paget 2020a). One informant exclaimed: 'It's much better! When you go to public offices now, people are actually working' (informal conversation, Dodoma, 2 February 2020). On the other hand, Magufuli used the state's hierarchical, centralized structure to adopt Nyerere-like policies, aiming to create a 'New Tanzania' through industrialization and state economic intervention. He bolstered the ruling party's access to economic resources through parastatals and military-owned enterprises (Becker 2021). He revitalized Air Tanzania; transferred government ministries to Dodoma (Nyerere's 1973 goal); invested in new trainlines, rural electrification, and highways; and pushed state shares in foreign mining projects (Collord 2019; Jones 2020; Paget 2020a; Thiong'o 2021). These policies had divergent effects on state capacity: Tanzania improved its World Bank 'control of corruption' score from –0.69 in 2015 to –0.39 in 2020, but its score for 'regulatory quality' (a measure of infrastructure and market-friendly policies) dropped from –0.37 in 2015 to –0.66 in 2020.[5]

State centralization (and its accompanying low capacity) had several implications for the response to COVID-19. First, the government may have adopted a less aggressive approach because it did not want to call attention to weaknesses in the country's health system (Becker 2021). Indeed, inadequate infrastructure hampered the pandemic response: hospitals lacked PPE and space to isolate patients, and low laboratory capacity delayed testing (Yamanis et al. 2021). Second, low capacity may have led the state, despite its focus on bureaucratic records, to not collect case counts after May 2020. Because legibility historically was used to control populations, not necessarily to respond to local problems (Scott 1998), high-level officials may not have prioritized COVID-19-related documentation. Third, high-level officials' pronouncements set policy guidance on testing, lockdowns, and vaccines, with some of this information coming to public health centres even before cases occurred (Yamanis et al. 2021). Yet this happened in a context where

[5] The average scores for sub-Saharan Africa in 2020 were –0.62 for 'control of corruption' and –0.73 for 'regulatory quality'.

some citizens embraced an official narrative that minimized the pandemic threat. One informant wrote, 'Here in Dodoma [COVID-19] is not an issue at all' (correspondence with author via WhatsApp, 15 January 2021). Local health officials found their job to be more complicated because not all individuals took the virus seriously (Yamanis et al. 2021: 569).

Finally, the gaps in state capacity and the consequent 'street-level discretion' enabled district officials to act in the context of confusing national-level statements or inaction (Carlitz et al. 2021). Health centre directors, for example, sometimes interpreted policies as they wished, but because these individuals lack many resources, operate within ill-defined parameters, and fear sharing ideas in a hierarchical bureaucratic culture, they could not publicly challenge the state's policies on masks, vaccines, or case counts. The result was mixed messages: individual doctors anonymously told the media about hospitals full of patients, while Mabula Mchembe, the permanent secretary in the health ministry, said people in the hospitals were suffering from hypertension, kidney failure, or asthma, not COVID-19. Many district health workers wore masks, but when Mchembe told people to wear masks, he back-tracked and said that this was 'not because of corona, like some people think, but it's to prevent respiratory diseases' (*BBC News* 6 February 2021a). The multiple messages were evident in a study of women's understanding of pandemic prevention in Mwanza (a western city): respondents framed prevention in terms of both health measures and traditional cures and prayer (Mchome et al. 2021).

3.5 Discursive institutionalism: nationalism, state legitimacy, and the pandemic response

Measures of Tanzanian state legitimacy are indirect and somewhat contradictory. On one hand, the World Bank's 'rule of law' indicator, which measures confidence in and willingness to abide by the rules of society and to enforce contracts and property rights, seems to indicate low (and declining) legitimacy. Tanzania's score moved from −0.37 in 2015 to −0.60 in 2020.[6] On the other hand, indicators of nationalism show a high level of state legitimacy. As a 'collective sentiment or identity ... binding together those who share a sense of large-scale political solidarity' (Marx 2005: 6), nationalism may support or undermine state power, divert attention from state malfeasance, and justify access to state resources (Englebert 2009: 198–206). In Tanzania, nationalism and its accompanying discourses of self-reliance and paternalism have contributed to state legitimacy. Forty-seven per cent of Tanzanians report that they identify solely as Tanzanians, and another

[6] The 2020 average for sub-Saharan Africa was −0.69.

10 per cent say they identify more as Tanzanian than as a member of a specific ethnic group (Afrobarometer 2016/2018).[7] Legitimacy is reflected in strong social networks, institutional trust, and civic participation, with the Legatum Institute (2021) placing 42 other sub-Saharan African countries below Tanzania on these 'social capital' elements. In addition, state legitimacy is apparent in citizens' perceptions of equitable treatment, with 94 per cent of Tanzanians saying that they 'never' thought that their ethnic group was treated unfairly (Afrobarometer 2016/2018).[8]

Tanzania's nationalist discourse promotes unity in a country with roughly 120 ethnic groups and several religious traditions. To achieve this aim, Nyerere declared that citizenship would be non-racial (Lofchie 2014) and mandated that Kiswahili be used for all official documents and instruction in primary schools and most secondary school subjects. A national Kiswahili culture of poetry, music, and literature reinforces this widespread language use (Lofchie 2014: 13), and this cultural spectacle of 'performing the nation' emphasizes shared experiences (Askew 2002). The nationalist discourse is credited with preventing conflict and violence (but see Green 2011), although it downplays specific ethnic, religious, and regional concerns and can marginalize dissent (Phillips 2018: 15).

At times, this discourse has helped to silence civil society. On one hand, 28 per cent of citizens report being an active member of a community or voluntary organization, more than the regional average of 19 per cent (Afrobarometer 2016/2018). Yet, much of this participation has focused on service delivery and communal labour, not advocacy. In addition, civil society groups have historically been linked to the ruling party and thus the state. For example, the labour unions, farmer cooperatives, and youth leagues that mobilized against colonial rule operated under TANU's direction (Kimambo et al. 2017). In the post-*ujamaa* era, much civil society mobilization has centred around entrepreneurship and development, with the number of NGOs dramatically increasing. Many of these organizations are decidedly 'apolitical', focusing on accessing donor funds for technical projects (Green 2012). The state controls such NGOs through registration processes and, at times, has organized such groups into federations (see Patterson 2018). A discourse of national unity and state centralization means that when challenges emerge, the state arbitrates or, if needed, paternalistically corrects wayward voices. For example, when university students in 1966 went on strike to protest mandatory national service and the remittance of 40 per cent of their salary to the state, Nyerere expelled them, saying they were 'a class of exploiters' (Shivji 2012: 107; Brennan 2006). This label juxtaposed the students with the ideal citizen who works in solidarity to develop the nation.

[7] The averages for the region were 33 per cent and 9 per cent, respectively.
[8] The regional average was 66 per cent.

Nationalism revolves around ideas of *kujenga taifa* (building the nation) and *kujitegemea* (self-reliance), which were embedded in state programmes such as youth national service in the 1960s (Burgess 1999) and the present-day obligation for *michango* (communal labour) to construct schools, roads, or sanitation projects in rural areas (Phillips 2018). Citizens are expected to give generously and unquestioningly to build the nation, and when they do not, others may act to 'enforce' their participation (Phillips 2018: 16, 138). For Nyerere, self-reliance also entailed challenging Western power, as Tanzania did through involvement in the Non-Aligned Movement, support for liberation groups in southern Africa, and refusal to adopt neoliberal economic policies in the early 1980s in return for desperately needed World Bank loans (Langwick 2011: 68; Shivji 2012). In health, self-reliance stressed traditional medicines as a path towards development and independence from Western pharmaceutical companies. In the 1970s, the state established the Institute of Traditional Medicine at Muhimbili Medical Centre in Dar es Salaam, and traditional healers and health ministry officials conducted joint research throughout the 1980s and 1990s. In 2002, a Traditional Healer Desk was established at the ministry of health (Langwick 2011: 62–71).

Nationalism has tended to stress notions of familyhood and paternalism. Nyerere is referred to as *Baba wa Taifa* (father of the nation) or *Mwalimu* (teacher), ruling party members are *Ndugu* (brother), and the ruling Chama Cha Mapinduzi (CCM; the Party of the Revolution, which succeeded TANU in 1977) is a 'political family' (Phillips 2018: 20). In this 'moral matrix', the president is a caring father who guides the childlike nation. The metaphor bestows political legitimacy, as the father figure presides over, administers, decides, and adjudicates; he (in the metaphor, the president is usually 'he') may also discipline, punish, forgive, and pardon the children who challenge him (Schatzberg 2001: 23–26). Survey results echo this discourse: 42 per cent of Tanzanians strongly agreed that 'government is like a parent', while 37 per cent strongly agreed that 'government is like an employee' (Afrobarometer 2016/2018).[9] Magufuli blended paternalism with populism to stress how the party elite must stand for the people, while he simultaneously underplayed the power and privilege of those very elites (Paget 2020a). This discourse legitimated state actions because the 'state knows best', but concern over lost legitimacy may lead state officials to underreport negative events such as epidemics or famines. This is because it is shameful to not meet the moral obligation to care for citizen-children (Philips 2018: 21, 113–117).

These broader state discourses of national unity, self-reliance, and paternalism shaped how Magufuli responded to the pandemic, as a letter from Tanzanian health experts to *The Lancet* indicated (Mfinanga et al. 2021). The writers claimed that the government had always taken the pandemic seriously, but it also wanted to prevent unwarranted suspicion, panic, or rumours. As a 'wise father', Magufuli

[9] There are no data for other countries for the same time period.

weighed the cost of pandemic prevention measures against citizens' economic survival, access to healthcare, and food security, particularly in light of predictions that over 2 million Tanzanians would need food aid in 2020 (World Food Programme 2020). In defending the decision to not close Tanzania's borders, Magufuli acted paternalistically towards those countries' populations too. Border closures would destroy those economies because 'they get maize, rice, meat ... and milk from us. If we close the borders, you also close economic opportunities to people but more importantly, you deny food to those who depend on you' (*Citizen* 17 May 2020a). Lockdowns could also prevent 'public access to health services, especially for patients with chronic conditions like tuberculosis and HIV infection' (Mfinanga et al. 2021: 1542). These concerns were not unwarranted: lockdowns, fear of contracting coronavirus at health facilities, and limited access to transportation undermined access to lifesaving medications for people with HIV, tuberculosis, and malaria in 24 African countries (Global Fund 2021).

The discourse of self-reliance led state officials to resent interference by external actors. In response to donors' criticism about limited lockdowns, the president invoked Nyerere: 'Our founding father was not someone to be directed to be told what to do' (*BBC News* 18 March 2021b). On 4 May 2020, the president said he suspected a 'dirty game' at the national laboratory (*Al Jazeera* 5 May 2020a), and he speculated that some workers 'may have been put on the payroll of imperialists' (*Citizen* 4 May 2020b). Alleged laboratory problems were not attributed to low state capacity but rather to potential problems with 'imported reagents and swaps [sic] used in the testing processes' (*Citizen*, 4 May 2020b). Magufuli cautioned about foreign donations, saying, 'I want to urge you Tanzanians to not accept donations of masks. Instead, tell the donors to go and use them with their wives and children' (*BBC News* 18 March 2021). In keeping with themes of self-reliance, the permanent secretary of the ministry of foreign affairs, Wilbert Ibuge, summoned the US acting ambassador, Inmi Patterson, to the ministry in response to 'inaccurate information' on the US Embassy Twitter page that reported that hospitals in Dar es Salaam were overrun with COVID-19 patients. Ibuge challenged the US official to provide 'certified information' from government sources before speaking out (*Citizen* 26 May 2020f). Similarly, in September 2019, the US Embassy and WHO said the country had not met its international obligation to report Ebola cases after media speculation about two such cases. In response, the health minister said that since the cases were not positive, Tanzania did not have to report them or have the WHO independently verify the results (*Africa News* 2019).

Finally, the discourse of self-reliance led the state to adopt traditional medicines for treatment, an approach that would foster self-sufficiency and 'reduce dependency' on Western imports (Richey et al. 2021). In May 2020, state officials announced research plans for COVID-19, including projects on how traditional medicines and Tanzanian lifestyles might be protective and/or curative

(*Citizen* 10 May 2020c). In early 2021, the health minister, Dorothy Gwajima, urged citizens to use steam baths and to drink mixtures with ginger, lemon, pepper, and onion to ward off illness (*BBC News* 6 February 2021). The aforementioned adoption of COVID-Organics stressed both self-reliance and the country's long history of supporting pan-Africanist solidarity. Just as Nyerere 'arrived at continental pan-Africanism through Tanganyikan nationalism' (Shivji 2012), Magufuli saw African solidarity intertwined with national interests. When Madagascar offered the medicine to African states, the minister of foreign affairs—not the health minister—travelled to retrieve the donation, an act symbolizing African solidarity. Yet, once the country had the medicine, it was not distributed widely. Instead, Tanzanian healers produced alternative products, an adaptive form of 'import substitution' that supported the state's nationalist and industrialization agenda (Richey et al. 2021) and built on the propensity of many Tanzanians to visit traditional healers (Langwick 2011; interview, Dodoma, 20 December 2019).

As the COVID-Organics example illustrated, self-reliance could directly challenge African solidarity (Patterson and Balogun 2021: 148). Such tensions were evident in at least three other examples. First, in August 2020, Kenya reported that it would continue to quarantine Tanzanian visitors for 14 days, while visitors from 100 other countries were released from the requirement. In response, Tanzania banned Kenyan airlines' flights over its airspace, including flights to Zanzibar and Kilimanjaro (*Citizen* 30 August 2020g). Second, Tanzania's decision to not report case counts after May 2020 led Africa CDC director John Nkengasong to say he was 'deeply worried' about health in the region (Dahir 2020). Third, in January 2021, Nkengasong situated Tanzania's stance on the vaccine in the context of regional health: 'Not cooperating will make it dangerous for everybody' (Makoni 2021). Tanzanian discourses of nationalism, familyhood, and self-reliance help foster state legitimacy, making state actions on COVID-19 permissible, even when they might undermine African solidarity.

3.6 State authority, electoral authoritarianism, and the pandemic response

As one measure of state authority, the World Bank assigns Tanzania –0.41 for 'political stability and limited violence', a better grade than the regional average of –0.66. However, this measure does not capture the struggle for state authority in Tanzania and the ways that electoral authoritarianism manifests these struggles. Jockeying for authority led the state as a 'twilight institution', or one whose authority waxes and wanes (Lund 2006), to respond to COVID-19 in particular ways.

In 1985, Nyerere voluntarily stepped down and Tanzania underwent a democratic 'transition from above' without protests or violence (Cheeseman 2015: 97).

For the next 20 years there were significant press and associational freedoms, and public debate was relatively open (Becker 2021; Whitehead 2012). However, the CCM continued to win sizeable electoral victories because of the opposition's inability to raise funds, the CCM's credentials as the 'party of Nyerere', and the CCM's grassroots party organization (Bakari and Whitehead 2013; Fouéré 2015). Tanzania is a 'party-state', with the CCM formally or informally fused into all aspects of governance (local government, public services, electoral management, parliament, security forces), civil society, the media, NGOs, and business (Whitehead 2012). Despite this control, political liberalization over time had given other parties some space. Between 2005 and 2015, the opposition Chama cha Demokrasia na Maendeleo (CHADEMA; the Party of Democracy and Development) deepened its organizational strategy and capitalized on increasing disappointment with the government's actions on poverty, rural development, and corruption (Paget 2021a). Younger voters disproportionately supported the opposition (McDonald 2018), and in some rural strongholds state officials' corruption turned voters from the CCM (Collord 2015; Phillips 2018). In the run-up to the 2015 election, the CCM was internally divided, and when Edward Lowassa (a former prime minister under outgoing president Jakaya Kikwete) did not get the party's nomination, he left the CCM to become CHADEMA's candidate. Magufuli—a party stalwart, minister of roads, and someone perceived to be outside the party's 'grand corruption'—became the 'happenstance' CCM nominee. In the election, CHADEMA won 40 per cent of the vote (compared to 6 per cent in 2005), and the CCM received its lowest share ever with 58 per cent.

The 2015 election outcome threatened the party-state, pushing it to become increasingly authoritarian in its efforts to maintain control over civil society, the economy, and the population (Paget 2021b). The state detained journalists and regulated foreign journalists, outlawed publication of 'false statistics', prosecuted opposition members for sedition, and passed laws to curtail NGO funding and membership (Congressional Research Service 2020; Freedom House 2021). The attempted assassination of CHADEMA's Tundu Lissu in 2017 stoked fear among opposition party members, pushing them into hiding. Between 2016 and 2020, a large number of CHADEMA members—including Lowassa—defected to the CCM (Paget 2021b). These actions significantly curtailed the political space and created an atmosphere of fear and silence (author observations, September 2019 to March 2020). Afrobarometer (2016/2018) found that 83 per cent of Tanzanians said they would never attend a protest or demonstration, compared to the Africa average of 60 per cent.

The state's search for authority was most apparent in the electoral authoritarianism that characterized the 2019 local and 2020 national elections (Paget 2021b). In electoral authoritarianism, 'electoral contests are subject to state manipulation so severe, widespread, and systematic that they do not qualify as democratic' (Schedler 2006: 3). Before the elections, the party-state restricted political rallies, banned internal opposition party meetings, detained CHADEMA members, disallowed online criticism of the regime, and disqualified most opposition candidates (particularly in the local elections). Fearful of retribution, most opposition leaders did not protest these actions, and some were violently attacked during the campaign (Congressional Research Service 2020; Freedom House 2021). In the 2020 election, opposition polling agents were barred from many voting stations, the internet was partially blocked, and journalists were silenced; the election commission refused to allow the EU, over 100 Tanzanian NGOs, and the Tanzanian Episcopal Conference (TEC), the body that represents Catholic bishops, to serve as election observers (Tanzania Election Watch 2020). Magufuli won re-election with 84 per cent of the vote, and the CCM gained 93 per cent of National Assembly seats and 99 per cent of local government positions (Paget 2021b).

Electoral authoritarianism built on the discourse of national unity to stress how alternative voices could destabilize the 'pure social order' (Paget 2020a). This view also led the state to suspend one journalist, close two media offices, and fine three media outlets for their COVID-19 stories (Human Rights Watch 2021). As a result, pandemic coverage declined from a monthly average of 34 pandemic-related articles in the *Citizen* between March and May 2020 to a monthly average of 4.2 articles between June 2020 and March 2021, and stories increasingly framed the pandemic as a global crisis, not a national one (Kiptinness and Okoye 2021). Second, the state criminalized the publication of 'information with regards to the outbreak of a deadly or contagious disease in the country or elsewhere without the approval of the respective authorities' (Reporters without Borders 2020). In early 2021, a presidential order allowed only the health minister, the president, and three other officials to speak publicly on the pandemic (*BBC News* 6 February 2021). As a result, lower-level state officials attributed deaths to pneumonia or employed euphemisms—*kushindwa kupumua* (failure to breathe)—to describe the sick (Becker 2021).

State efforts to deepen authority shaped civil society actions on the pandemic. Although local organizations educated people about COVID-19, urged hand-washing, and cared for the sick (Yamanis et al. 2021), they engaged in little advocacy for state policies. This muted response reflects not only the rise in authoritarianism after 2015 but also a discourse of national unity that limited challenges to the state. There were two notable exceptions: opposition parties and the Catholic Church. Lissu asserted that the state's response was an 'irresponsible disaster', Zitto Kabwe, the leader of the opposition ACT-Wazalendo, wrote that the government had 'abandoned its constitutional duty to protect Tanzanians', and opposition leaders in parliament demanded testing for lawmakers in August 2020 (Dahir 2020; Kabwe 2020). These actions occurred five months into the pandemic, and did little to shape state actions.

In contrast, the Catholic Church was slower to speak out, but arguably more effective. In January 2021, the TEC said that coronavirus was a serious national threat and urged people to take precautions. In March 2021 it revealed that 25 priests and 60 nuns had died from COVID-19 in a two-month period, a figure that the state disputed (*Crux* 6 March 2021). Catholic leaders' subtle challenges occurred in a context where the late president (himself a devout Catholic) often appealed to conservative Church leaders by stressing traditional values on issues such as drug use, homosexuality, and premarital sex (Paget 2020a). When the Church expressed concerns about COVID-19, it challenged its historical pattern of shunning politics in Tanzania's religiously pluralist society (Pew-Templeton 2020). Public trust (and global connections) empowered the Church: 74 per cent of Tanzanians report high levels of trust for religious leaders (Afrobarometer 2016/2018). The president himself repeatedly acknowledged the Church's legitimacy and sway when he made pandemic pronouncements in church services (see *Citizen* 17 May 2020c; Kalumbia 2020). These performances illustrated how churches can be sites of spiritual and political power (Ellis and ter Haar 1998). The Church's actions may have led the president to finally acknowledge cases at a church service on 21 February 2021 (Said 2021). Yet, for most of the pandemic's first year, authority over nonstate actors such as opposition leaders, the media, and religious organizations allowed the state's narrative on COVID-19 to dominate.

3.7 Conclusion

This chapter has illustrated how the capacity, legitimacy, and authority of the Tanzanian state shaped the COVID-19 response during the pandemic's first year. Despite the state's focus on bureaucratic hierarchy, the state's overall low capacity in terms of personnel and clear procedures undermined its ability to address the pandemic and created spaces of local-level discretion. Centralization, a relic of socialism, led to high-level pronouncements and lower-level bureaucrats' inability to fully counter them. The state's legitimacy through its discourse of unity, nationalism, and paternalism meant that civil society organizations only indirectly challenged state actions. The nationalist discourse of 'Tanzania first' and self-reliance made it less likely that Tanzania would cooperate with international actors or its neighbours. Paternalistic discourses led to assumptions that state officials—led by the president—were looking out for the population's interests. State legitimacy facilitated actions that countered global norms and expectations. As it continuously sought control in a public space crowded with donors, civil society groups, NGOs, opposition leaders, and religious actors, the state used strategies such as electoral authoritarianism to deepen its authority. The struggle for authority, and the closing of political space that accompanied it, made it more difficult for civil society organizations, opposition parties, and the media to hold the state accountable for its pandemic response.

The Tanzania case highlights some broader lessons about the 'state versus big man' debate. Since Magufuli's death, Tanzania has significantly changed its

COVID-19 strategy: by late 2021, it was administering COVAX-procured vaccines, publishing case counts, and urging citizens to wear masks and avoid crowds. As the pandemic's economic costs rose due to a below-expected GDP growth rate, drops in tourism revenue, and an increasing account deficit, it received almost US$600 million in loans from the International Monetary Fund (IMF) (2021). On first glance, this 'about-face' seems to indicate that the COVID-19 response was driven by one leader (first Magufuli and then Samia Suluhu Hassan). Although leaders matter, the change in Tanzania's COVID-19 response is in keeping with a broader understanding of how leaders operate within state structures and how conditions may change to provide states new incentives to act. The state components that drove the Magufuli-era response remain, but they have now created a new scenario. Low state capacity necessitates IMF loans and COVAX help; legitimating discourses of state paternalism and national unity mean both that the state knows best and that few will criticize its significant change in policies; the state's perennial need for authority means that embracing globally accepted COVID-19 policies muzzles criticism from civil society groups. At the same time, state exertions of authority continued with the arrest of CHADEMA leader Freeman Mbowe in August 2021 (Fabricius 2021).

Finally, Tanzania shows how African states can manifest agency despite their relatively weak position in global structures (Brown 2013; Patterson and Balogun 2021). Sovereignty, and the rise of Chinese and Russian involvement in Africa, may have enabled Tanzania to dismiss WHO, donor, and Africa CDC policy suggestions (Collord 2019). Donors, who provided almost 60 per cent of public health expenditures in 2017 (the last date for data), continued their health funding, with the US offering US$5.75 million in COVID-19 assistance in June 2020 (Piatti-Fünfkirchen and Ally 2020: 9; USAID 2020). Continued aid may have relieved some short-term pressures for the state to change course during the first year of COVID-19. The state's relative autonomy from donor demands meant that capacity, legitimacy, and authority mattered for Tanzania's unorthodox approach. Future research should more closely examine how state agency intersects with these attributes to influence state actions during moments of crisis and uncertainty.

References

Africa News (2019). 'Tanzania Defends Decision Not to Share Ebola Information with WHO', 3 October. Available at: www.africanews.com/2019/10/03/there-is-no-ebola-in-tanzania-minister (accessed 26 October 2021).

Afrobarometer (2016/2018). 'The Online Data Analysis Tool'. Available at: https://afrobarometer.org/online-data-analysis/analyse-online (accessed 15 October 2021).

Al Jazeera (2020a). 'Tanzania COVID-19 Lab Head Suspended as President Questions Data', 5 May. Available at: www.aljazeera.com/news/2020/5/5/tanzania-covid-19-lab-head-suspended-as-president-questions-data (accessed 21 October 2021).

Al Jazeera (2020b). 'Tanzania Gets Madagascar's Anti-Coronavirus Drink Disputed by the WHO', 8 May. Available at: www.aljazeera.com/news/2020/5/8/tanzania-gets-madagascars-anti-coronavirus-drink-disputed-by-who (accessed 1 October 2021).

Askew, K. (2002). *Performing the Nation: Swahili Music and Cultural Politics in Tanzania.* Chicago, IL: University of Chicago Press.

Bakari, M., and R. Whitehead (2013). 'Tanzania: Nurturing Legacies of the Past'. In R. Doorenspleet and L. Nijzink (eds), *One Party Dominance in African Democracies.* Boulder, CO: Lynne Rienner, pp. 93–116.

Bariyo, N., and J. Parkinson (2020). 'Tanzanian Leader Urges People to Worship in Throngs against Coronavirus', *Wall Street Journal.* 8 April. Available at: www.wsj.com/articles/tanzanias-leader-urges-people-to-worship-in-throngs-against-coronavirus-11586347200 (accessed 7 October 2021).

Bates, R. (2008). *When Things Fell Apart: State Failure in Late-Century Africa.* Cambridge: Cambridge University Press. https://doi.org/10.1017/CBO9780511790713.

BBC News (2021a). 'Coronavirus in Tanzania: The Country That's Rejecting the Vaccine', 6 February. Available at: www.bbc.com/news/world-africa-55900680 (accessed 23 October 2021).

BBC News (2021b). 'John Magufuli: Tanzania's Late President in His Own Words', 18 March. Available at: www.bbc.com/news/world-africa-56441421 (accessed 21 October 2021).

Becker, F. (2020). 'Locating the "Customary" in Post-Colonial Tanzania's Politics: The Shifting Modus Operandi of the Rural State'. *Journal of Eastern African Studies*, 14(1): 145–163. https://doi.org/10.1080/17531055.2019.1711311.

Becker, F. (2021). 'Tanzania's Authoritarian Turn: Less Sudden Than It Seems'. *Current History*, 120(826): 189–194. https://doi.org/10.1525/curh.2021.120.826.189.

Berman, S. (1998). *The Social Democratic Movement: Ideas and Politics in the Making of Interwar Europe.* Cambridge, MA: Harvard University Press. https://doi.org/10.4159/9780674020849.

Bhandari, A., and L. Mueller (2019). 'Nation-State or Nation-Family? Nationalism in Marginalized African Societies'. *Journal of Modern African Studies*, 57(2): 297–322. https://doi:10.1017/S0022278X1900003X.

Boone, C., and L. Nyeme (2015). 'Land Institutions and Political Ethnicity in Africa: Evidence from Tanzania'. *Comparative Politics*, 48(1): 67–86. http://doi.org/10.5129/001041515816075123.

Brass, J. (2016). *Allies or Adversaries: NGOs and the State in Africa.* Cambridge: Cambridge University Press. https://doi.org/10.1017/CBO9781316678527.

Bratton, M., and E. Chang (2006). 'State Building and Democratization in Sub-Saharan Africa'. *Comparative Political Studies*, 39(9): 1059–1083. https://doi.org/10/1177/0010414005280853.

Bratton, M., and N. van de Walle (1997). *Democratic Experiments in Africa.* Cambridge: Cambridge University Press. https://doi.org/10.1017/CBO9781139174657.

Brennan, J.R. (2006). 'Blood Enemies: Exploitation and Urban Citizenship in the Nationalist Political Thought of Tanzania, 1958–75'. *Journal of African History*, 47(3): 389–413. https://doi.org/10.1017/S0021853706001794.

Brown, W. (2013). 'Sovereignty Matters: Africa, Donors and the Aid Relationship'. *African Affairs*, 112(447): 262–282. https://doi.org/10.1093/afraf/adt001.

Burgess, T. (1999). 'Remembering Youth: Generation in Revolutionary Zanzibar'. *Africa Today*, 46(2): 29–50. https://doi.org/10.1353/at.1999.0003.

Camargo, C. (2017). 'Corruption, Social Norms and Behaviours: A Comparative Assessment of Rwanda, Tanzania and Uganda'. Report. London: DFID. Available at: https://baselgovernance.org/sites/default/files/2019-01/earf_comparative_report.pdf (accessed 23 October 2021).

Carlitz, R., T. Yamanis, and H. Mollel (2021). 'Coping with Denialism: How Street-Level Bureaucrats Adapted and Responded to COVID-19 in Tanzania'. *Journal of Health Politics, Policy and Law*, 46(6): 989–1017. https://doi.org/10.1215/03616878-9349128.

Chabal, P., and J.P. Daloz (1999). *Africa Works: Disorder as Political Instrument*. Bloomington, IN: Indiana University Press.

Cheeseman, N. (2015). *Democracy in Africa*. Cambridge: Cambridge University Press. https://doi.org/10.1017/CBO9781139030892.

Citizen (2020a). 'Tanzania Government Defends Its Handling of Outbreak', 23 April. Available at: www.thecitizen.co.tz/tanzania/news/tanzania-government-defends-its-handling-of-outbreak-2708092 (accessed 3 October 2021).

Citizen (2020b). 'Magufuli: Why I Don't Trust Covid-19 Results', 4 May. Available at: www.thecitizen.co.tz/tanzania/news/national/magufuli-why-i-don-t-trust-covid-19-test-results-2708680 (accessed 4 October 2021).

Citizen (2020c). 'Tanzania Lays Down Research Priorities for Covid-19', 10 May. Available at: www.thecitizen.co.tz/tanzania/news/-tanzania-lays-down-research-priorities-for-covid-19-2708982 (accessed 3 October 2021).

Citizen (2020d). 'Magufuli: Our Economy Comes First in Covid-19 Fight', 17 May. Available at: www.thecitizen.co.tz/tanzania/news/magufuli-our-economy-comes-first-in-covid-19-fight-2709358 (accessed 27 October 2021).

Citizen (2020e). 'Magufuli Says God Has Responded to Prayers with Massive Reduction in Covid-19 Cases', 17 May. Available at: www.thecitizen.co.tz/tanzania/news/magufuli-says-god-has-responded-to-tanzania-s-prayers-with-massive-reduction-in-covid-19-cases-2709346 (accessed 27 October 2021).

Citizen (2020f). 'US Ambassador to Tanzania Summoned over Covid-19 Statement', 26 May. Available at: www.thecitizen.co.tz/tanzania/news/us-ambassador-to-tanzania-summoned-over-covid-19-statement-2709842 (accessed 2 October 2021).

Citizen (2020g). 'No End in Sight in the Row between Kenya and Tanzania over Covid-19 Rules', 30 August. Available at: www.thecitizen.co.tz/tanzania/news/africa/no-end-in-sight-in-the-row-between-kenya-and-tanzania-over-covid-19-rules-2715376 (accessed 16 October 2021).

Citizen (2021). 'Tanzania's Ministry of Health Now Urges Precaution against Covid-19', 22 February. Available at: www.thecitizen.co.tz/tanzania/news/tanzania-s-ministry-of-health-now-urges-precaution-against-covid-19-3299084 (accessed 24 October 2021).

Collord, M. (2015). 'An Improbable "Liberation": How Tanzania's Ruling Party Lost a Rural Stronghold'. Available at: www.africaresearchinstitute.org/newsite/blog/an-improbable-liberation-how-tanzanias-ruling-party-lost-a-rural-stronghold (accessed 17 October 2021).

Collord, M. (2019). 'Drawing the Wrong Lessons from Magufuli's Rule in Tanzania', *Africa Is a Country*. 5 June. Available at: https://africasacountry.com/2019/05/drawing-the-wrong-lessons-from-the-magufuli-experience-in-tanzania (accessed 22 October 2021).

Congressional Research Service (2020). 'Tanzania: Recent Governance Trends and 2020 Elections in Brief'. Available at: https://sgp.fas.org/crs/row/R46579.pdf (accessed 11 October 2021).

Crux (2021). 'Church in Tanzania Urges COVID Precautions in Face of Govt Denial', 6 March. Available at: https://cruxnow.com/church-in-africa/2021/03/church-in-tanzania-urges-covid-precautions-in-face-of-govt-denial (accessed 27 October 2021).

Dahir, A.L. (2020). 'Tanzania President Says Country Is Virus Free. Others Warn of Disaster', *New York Times*. 4 August. Available at: www.nytimes.com/2020/08/04/world/africa/tanzanias-coronavirus-president.html (accessed 26 October 2021).

Ellis, S., and G. ter Haar (1998). 'Religion and Politics in Sub-Saharan Africa'. *Journal of Modern African Studies*, 36(2): 175–201. https://doi.org/10.1017/S0022278X9800278X.

Englebert, P. (2009). *Africa: Unity, Sovereignty and Sorrow*. Boulder, CO: Lynne Rienner.

Fabricius, P. (2021). 'Tanzania's President Samia Walking a Razor's Edge over Detention of Opposition Figures', *Daily Maverick*. 20 August. Available at: www.dailymaverick.co.za/article/2021-08-20-tanzanias-president-samia-walking-a-razors-edge-over-detention-of-opposition-figures (accessed 28 October 2021).

Finnemore, M., and K. Sikkink (1998). 'International Norm Dynamics and Political Change'. *International Organization*, 52: 887–917. https://doi.org/10.1162/002081898550789.

Fouéré, M.-A. (ed.) (2015). *Remembering Julius Nyerere in Tanzania: History, Memory, Legacy*. Dar es Salaam: Mkuki na Nyota Publishers. https://doi.org/10.2307/j.ctvh8qz4m.

Freedom House (2021). 'Tanzania'. Available at: https://freedomhouse.org/country/tanzania/freedom-world/2021 (accessed 20 October 2021).

Gisselquist, R.M., and A. Vaccaro (2021). 'COVID-19 and the State'. WIDER Working Paper 2021/80. Helsinki: UNU-WIDER. https://doi.org/10.35188/UNU-WIDER/2021/018-4.

Global Fund (2021). *The Impact of Covid-19 on HIV, TB and Malaria Services and Systems for Health: A Snapshot from 502 Health Facilities across Africa and Asia*. Geneva: Global Fund.

Grävingholt, J., S. Ziaja, and M. Kreibaum (2015). 'Disaggregating State Fragility: A Method to Establish a Multidimensional Empirical Typology'. *Third World Quarterly*, 36(7): 1281–1298. https://doi.org/10.1080/01436597.2015.1038340.

Green, E. (2011). 'The Political Economy of Nation Formation in Modern Tanzania: Explaining Stability in the Face of Diversity'. *Commonwealth & Comparative Politics*, 49(2): 223–244. http://doi.org/10.1080/14662043.2011.564474.

Green, M. (2010). 'Ujamaa? Cultures of Governance and the Representation of Power in Tanzania'. *Social Analysis: The International Journal of Anthropology*, 54(1): 15–34. http://doi.org/10.3167/sa.2010.540102.

Green, M. (2012). 'Anticipatory Development: Mobilizing Civil Society in Tanzania'. *Critique of Anthropology*, 32(3): 309–333. https://doi.org/10.1177/0308275X12449107.

Hale, T., S. Webster, A. Petherick, T. Phillips, and B. Kira (2020). *Oxford COVID-19 Government Response Tracker*. Available at: https://covidtracker.bsg.ox.ac.uk (accessed 1 October 2021).

Herbst, J. (2000). *States and Power in Africa*. Princeton, NJ: Princeton University Press.

Human Rights Watch (2021). 'Tanzania'. Available at: www.hrw.org/world-report/2021/country-chapters/tanzania-and-zanzibar (accessed 18 October 2021).

International Monetary Fund (2021). 'IMF Executive Board Approves US$567.25 Million in Emergency Support to Tanzania to Address the COVID-19 Pandemic', 7 September. Available at: www.imf.org/en/News/Articles/2021/09/07/pr21256-tanzania-imf-executive-board-approves-us-million-emergency-support-address-covid-19-pandemic (accessed 27 October 2021).

Jones, H. (2020). 'Magufuli 2.0: A More Nuanced Approach?', *New African*. 15 December. Available at: https://newafricanmagazine.com/24929 (accessed 21 October 2021).

Kabwe, Z. (2020). 'Tanzanian President's Handling of the Pandemic Is the Epitome of Incompetence', *Daily Maverick*. 27 May. Available at: www.dailymaverick.co.za/article/2020-05-27-tanzanian-presidents-handling-of-pandemic-is-the-epitome-of-incompetence (accessed 27 October 2021).

Kalumbia, L. (2020). 'Magufuli Calls on World Leaders to Put God First in Fight against Covid-19', *Citizen*. Available at: www.thecitizen.co.tz/tanzania/news/magufuli-calls-on-world-leaders-to-put-god-first-in-fight-against-covid-19-3239170 (accessed 19 October 2021).

Katzenstein, P. (1996). *The Culture of National Security: Norms and Identity in World Politics*. New York: Columbia University Press.

Kimambo, I., G. Maddox, and S. Nyuanto (2017). *A New History of Tanzania*. Dar es Salaam: Mkuki na Nyota Publishers. https://doi.org/10.2307/j.ctvh8r3f5.

Kiptinness, E.M., and J.B. Okoye (2021). 'Media Coverage of the Novel Coronavirus (Covid-19) in Kenya and Tanzania: Content Analysis of Newspaper Articles in East Africa'. *Cogent Medicine*, 8(1): 1956034. https://doi.org/10.1080/2331205X.2021.1956034.

Kombe, C. (2021). 'Tanzania Publishes First COVID-19 Data in Over a Year', *Voice of America*. 29 June. Available at: www.voanews.com/a/africa_tanzania-publishes-first-covid-19-data-over-year/6207608.html (accessed 1 October 2021).

Langwick, S. (2011). *Bodies, Politics and African Healing: The Matter of Maladies in Tanzania*. Bloomington, IN: Indiana University Press.

Legatum Institute (2021). 'Prosperity Index'. Available at: www.prosperity.com/rankings (accessed 3 February 2022).

Linz, J., and A. Stepan. (1996). *Problems of Democratic Transition and Consolidation: Southern Europe, South America, and Post-Communist Europe*. Baltimore, MD: Johns Hopkins University Press.

Lofchie, M. (2014). *The Political Economy of Tanzania: Decline and Recovery*. Philadelphia, PA: University of Pennsylvania Press. https://doi.org/10.9783/9780812209365.

Lund, C. (2006). 'Twilight Institutions: Public Authority and Local Politics in Africa'. *Development and Change*, 37(4): 685–705. https://doi.org/10.1111/j.1467-7660.2006.00497.x.

Makoni, M. (2021). 'Tanzania Refuses COVID-19 Vaccines'. *The Lancet*, 397: 566–567. https://doi.org/10.1016/S0140-6736(21)00362-7.

Marx, A. (2005). *Faith in Nation: Exclusionary Origins of Nationalism*. London: Oxford University Press.

Matfess, H. (2015). 'Rwanda and Ethiopia: Developmental Authoritarianism and the New Politics of African Strong Men'. *African Studies Review*, 58: 181–204. https://doi:10.1017/asr.2015.43.

McDonald, R. (2018). 'Age and Gender Voting Trends in the 2015 Tanzanian General Election'. *Journal of Eastern African Studies*, 12(1): 44–62. https://doi.org/10.1080/17531055.2017.1410759.

Mchome, Z., G. Mshana, E. Peter, D. Aloyce, S. Kapiga, and H. Stöckl (2021). 'Women's Narratives about COVID-19 Preventive Practices and Sources of Information in Northwestern Tanzania'. *International Journal of Environmental Research and Public Health*, 18(10): 5261. https://doi.org/10.3390/ijerph18105261.

Mfinanga, S., N. Mnyambwa, D. Minja, N.E. Ntinginya, E. Ngadaya, J. Makani, and A. Makubi (2021). 'Tanzania's Position on the COVID-19 Pandemic'. *Lancet*, 397: 1542–1543. http://doi.org/10.1016/S0140-6736(21)00678-4.

Mhina, A. (2010). 'Faith Based Organizations and Development in Tanzania.' *The African Review: A Journal of African Politics, Development and International Affairs*, 37(1/2): 64–86.

Migdal, J. (1988). *Strong Societies, Weak States*. Princeton, NJ: Princeton University Press.

Mirondo, R. (2021, 6 April). 'Tanzania to Re-evaluate Its Position on COVID-19, Says President Samia', *Citizen*. Available at: www.thecitizen.co.tz/tanzania/news/tanzania-to-re-evaluate-its-position-on-covid-19-says-president-samia-3351224 (accessed 1 October 2021).

Paget, D. (2020a). 'Again, Making Tanzania Great: Magufuli's Restorationist Developmental Nationalism.' *Democratization*, 27(7): 1240–1260. https://doi.org/10.1080/13510347.2020.1779223.

Paget, D. (2020b). 'Mistaken for Populism: Magufuli, Ambiguity and Elitist Plebeianism in Tanzania.' *Journal of Political Ideologies*, 26(2): 121–141. https://doi.org/10.1080/135692317.2020.179345.

Paget, D. (2021a). 'Lone Organizers: Opposition Party-Building in Hostile Places in Tanzania.' *Party Politics*, 28(2), 223–235. https://doi.org/10.1177/13540688211041034.

Paget, D. (2021b). 'Tanzania: The Authoritarian Landslide.' *Journal of Democracy*, 32(2): 61–76. https://doi.org/10.1353.jod.201.0019.

Patterson, A.S. (2018). *Africa and Global Health Governance*. Baltimore, MD: Johns Hopkins University Press.

Patterson, A.S., and E. Balogun (2021). 'African Responses to COVID-19: The Reckoning of Agency'. *African Studies Review*, 61(4): 144–167. https://doi.org/10.1017/asr.20.

Pew-Templeton (2020). 'Global Religious Futures Project: Tanzania.' Available at: www.globalreligiousfutures.org/countries/tanzania#/?affiliations_religion_id=0&affiliations_year=2010&region_name=All%20Countries&restrictions_year=2016 (accessed 29 October 2021).

Phillips, K. (2018). *An Ethnography of Hunger*. Bloomington, IN: Indiana University Press. https://doi.org/10.2307/j.ctv4rfqsv.

Piatti-Fünfkirchen, M., and M. Ally (2020). *Tanzania: Health Sector Public Expenditure Review 2020*. Washington, DC: World Bank. https://doi.org/10.1596/34620.

Rahman, K., R.M. Kukutschka, P. Banoba, and B. Cooksey (2019). 'Overview of Corruption and Anti-corruption in Tanzania.' Report. Berlin: Transparency International.

Rauch, J., and P. Evans (2000). 'Bureaucratic Structure and Bureaucratic Performance in Less Developed Countries'. *Journal of Public Economics*, 75(1): 49–71. https://doi.org/10.1016/S0047-2727(99)00044-4.

Reporters without Borders (2020). 'Tanzanian Media Unable to Cover Covid-19 Epidemic', 5 November. Available at: https://rsf.org/en/news/tanzanian-media-unable-cover-covid-19-epidemic (accessed 18 October 2021).

Richey, L.A., L.E. Gissel, O. Kweka, P. Baerendtsen, P. Kragelund, H.Q. Hambati, and A. Mwamfupe (2021). 'South–South Humanitarianism: The Case of COVID-Organics in Tanzania.' *World Development*, 141, 105375. https://doi.org/10.1016/j.worlddev.2020.105375.

Sabatier P., and H.D. Jenkins-Smith (1993). *Policy Change and Learning: An Advocacy Coalition Approach*. Boulder, CO: Westview Press.

Said, K. (2021, 12 March). 'In the Name of Jesus: How the Church Forced Tanzania to Change Its Stance on COVID-19', *Elephant*. Available at: www.theelephant.info/long-reads/2021/03/12/in-the-name-of-jesus-how-the-church-forced-tanzania-to-change-its-stance-on-covid-19 (accessed 19 October 2021).

Schatzberg, M. (2001). *Political Legitimacy in Middle Africa: Father, Family, Food*. Bloomington, IN: Indiana University Press.

Schedler, A. (2006). *Electoral Authoritarianism: The Dynamics of Unfree Competition.* Boulder, CO: Lynne Rienner.

Schmidt, V. (2008). 'Discursive Institutionalism: The Explanatory Power of Ideas and Discourse'. *Annual Review of Political Science*, 11: 303–326. https://doi.org/10.1146/annurev.polisci.11.060606.135342.

Schneider, L. (2014). *Government of Development: Peasants and Politicians in Postcolonial Tanzania.* Bloomington, IN: Indiana University Press.

Scott, J. (1998). *Seeing Like a State: How Certain Schemes to Improve the Human Condition Have Failed.* New Haven, CT: Yale University Press.

Shiffman, J. (2017). 'Four Challenges That Global Health Networks Face'. *International Journal of Health Policy and Management*, 6(4): 183–189. https://doi.org/10.15171/ijhpm.2017.14.

Shivji, I.G. (2012). 'Nationalism and Pan-Africanism: Decisive Moments in Nyerere's Intellectual and Political Thought'. *Review of African Political Economy*, 39(131): 103–116. https://doi.org/10.1080/03056244.2012.662387.

Sigman, R., and R. Lindberg (2020). 'Neopatrimonialism and Democracy'. In G. Lynch and P. Von Doepp (eds), *Routledge Handbook of Democratization in Africa.* London: Routledge, pp. 17–37. https://doi.org/10.4324/9781315112978-2.

Singh, J.N., and J.S. Ovadia (2018). 'The Theory and Practice of Building Developmental States in the Global South'. *Third World Quarterly*, 39(6): 1033–1055. https://doi.org/10.1080/01436597.2018.1455143.

Sirili, N., and D. Simba (2021). 'It Is beyond Remuneration: Bottom-Up Health Workers' Retention Strategies at the Primary Health Care System in Tanzania'. *PLoS One*, 16(4): e0246262. https://doi.org/10.1371/journal.pone.0246262.

Skocpol, T., D. Rueschmeyer, and P. Evans (eds) (1985). *Bringing the State Back In.* Cambridge, MA: Harvard University Press.

Tanzania Election Watch (2020). 'Final Observation Report on the General Elections Held in Tanzania on October 28, 2000'. Available at: https://tanzaniaelectionswatch.org (accessed 2 October 2021).

Thelen, K. (1999). 'Historical Institutionalism in Comparative Politics'. *Annual Review of Political Science*, 2: 369–404. https://doi.org/10.1146/annurev.polisci.2.1.369.

Thiong'o, J. (2021). 'President John Magufuli: A Man after Julius Nyerere's Own Heart', *Standard.* 19 July. Available at: www.standardmedia.co.ke/politics/article/2001406767/magufuli-in-the-footsteps-of-julius-nyerere-with-nationalist-agenda (accessed 21 October 2021).

Trading Economics (2021). 'Tanzania: Rural Population'. Available at: https://tradingeconomics.com/tanzania/rural-population-percent-of-total-population-wb-data.html (accessed 20 October 2021).

USAID. (2020). 'The US Agency for International Development's COVID-19 Response in Tanzania'. Available at: www.usaid.gov/sites/default/files/documents/1860/Tanzania-Fact-Sheet-on-COVID-19-Assistance.pdf (accessed 29 October 2021).

van de Walle, N. (2001). *African Economies and the Politics of Permanent Crisis, 1979–1999.* Cambridge: Cambridge University Press.

Whitehead, R. (2012). 'Historical Legacies, Clientelism and the Capacity to Fight: Exploring Pathways to Regime Tenure in Tanzania'. *Democratization*, 19(6): 1086–1116. https://doi.rg/10.1080/13510347.2011.626913.

World Bank (2017a). 'Nurses and Midwives (per 1,000 People): Tanzania'. Available at: https://data.worldbank.org/indicator/SH.MED.NUMW.P3?locations=TZ (accessed 21 October 2021).

World Bank (2017b). 'Physicians (per 1,000 People): Tanzania.' Available at: https://data.worldbank.org/indicator/SH.MED.PHYS.ZS?locations=TZ (accessed 21 October 2021).

World Bank (2020). 'Worldwide Governance Indicators.' Available at: https://info.worldbank.org/governance/wgi (accessed 2 February 2022).

World Food Programme (2020). 'Food Security Overview Tanzania.' Available at: www.wfp.org/publications/wfp-tanzania-food-security-overview-context-covid-19-may-2020 (accessed 20 October 2021).

Yamanis, T., R. Carlitz, and H. Mollel (2021). 'Adapting COVID-19 Containment in Africa: Lessons from Tanzania.' In S. Greer, E. King, E. Massard da Fonseca, and A. Peralta-Santos (eds), *Coronavirus Politics: The Comparative Politics and Policy of COVID-19*. Ann Arbor, MI: University of Michigan Press, pp. 560–579.

Young, C. (2012). *The Postcolonial State in Africa: Fifty Years of Independence, 1960–2010*. Madison, WI: University of Wisconsin Press.

Ziaja, S., J. Grävingholt, and M. Kreibaum (2019). 'Constellations of Fragility: An Empirical Typology of States.' *Studies in Comparative International Development*, 54: 299–321. https://doi.org/10.1007/s12116-019-09284-3.

PART III
ASIA

4
Pandemic Populism amid Weak State Capacity in the Philippines

Julio C. Teehankee

4.1 Introduction

Among the 10 members of the Association of Southeast Asian Nations (ASEAN), the Philippines is one of three countries that has struggled to contain the spread of the COVID-19 pandemic, its dismal performance coming despite the country implementing one of the strictest and longest lockdowns in the world.[1] While populist president Rodrigo Duterte appeared victorious in his assault on human rights and media freedom, his government's record in fighting the virus has been spotty at best. Duterte's inadequate performance in handling the pandemic has been highlighted as the Philippines has consistently appeared last in Nikkei Asia's COVID-19 Recovery Index and Bloomberg's COVID Resilience Ranking (Li 2021; Bloomberg News 2021).

Yet Duterte's populism has proven to be resilient, with a record approval rating of 92 per cent at the height of the pandemic. For some observers, the continuing COVID-19 pandemic presents an ideal chance for 'strongmen' and autocrats to further solidify their authority and control in the face of a massive worldwide humanitarian calamity (Lührmann et al. 2020). Indeed, there has appeared to be a trade-off between limiting individual liberties and the necessity for the government to impose these limits by a command to stop the spread of the fatal virus. Hence, it is puzzling that the Philippines has struggled with the pandemic despite Duterte's strongman leadership, high state legitimacy, and popular trust. What has the role been of state capacity (or the lack thereof) in the poor pandemic response? This chapter will unpack Duterte's deployment of 'brute-force governance' (which he earlier employed in his bloody 'war on drugs') in addressing the COVID-19 crisis in the Philippines. It seeks to delineate how factors such as political deployment and state capacity have shaped the government's pandemic response

[1] I would like to thank Rosa Babel Calilung-Teehankee for her invaluable research assistance and Rachel M. Gisselquist and Amy S. Patterson for insightful comments that helped to crystallize the arguments of this chapter.

Julio C. Teehankee, *Pandemic Populism amid Weak State Capacity in the Philippines*. In: *How States Respond to Crisis*. Edited by: Rachel M. Gisselquist and Andrea Vaccaro, Oxford University Press. © UNU-WIDER (2025).
DOI: 10.1093/9780198907237.003.0004

and account for Duterte's enduring popularity despite his mismanagement of the coronavirus crisis.

4.2 State capacity and the politics of deployment

The onslaught of the COVID-19 pandemic has underlined the integral role of state capacity in containing the spread of the virus. The literature initially focused on regime types (Alon et al. 2020; Berengaut 2020; Kleinfeld 2020). The swift and disciplined approach at first helped some authoritarian regimes to flatten the COVID-19 curve. Indeed, authoritarian regimes were quick to impose strict public health measures compared with democracies (Diamond 2020). But advocates of democratic governance argue that democracy offers a more effective way of addressing the pandemic by mobilizing social capital and public trust between citizens and government. However, countries with strong democratic institutions were slower in implementing measures to address the pandemic (Bunyavejchewin and Sirichuanjun 2021; Dobbs 2022).

Drawing on political science and health politics research, Greer et al. (2020, 2021) identify four broad hypotheses for research on COVID-19 political responses:

1. Social policy matters to crisis management as well as recovery—the preexisting social policies of the country plus the importance of communication and trust in generating compliance.
2. Regimes matter—the regime type of a country, such as whether it is democratic or autocratic. Authoritarian regimes are bad at maintaining the internal and external flow of good information, while only some are good at forceful action (e.g. China and Russia). Democratic regimes might have more difficulty taking forceful or appropriate action but benefit from better information flow and public trust (e.g. Germany under Angela Merkel and New Zealand under Jacinda Ardern).
3. Formal political institutions matter—this refers to the vertical and horizontal institutions of governance: unitary or federal, presidential or parliamentary.
4. State capacity matters—whether state capacity is strong or weak significantly impacts the shaping of policy options and the implementation of a more effective response to the pandemic.

However, the performance outcomes of regimes and political institutions have varied in response to the pandemic. Some democratic federal countries have succeeded, while others have failed. Some authoritarian unitary governments have been able to flatten the curve, but not all. Rather than the regime type dictating a country's ability to respond effectively, characteristics such as legitimacy, capacity, and trust have been more likely to determine a country's success rate in combating this worldwide pandemic (Dobbs 2022; Hartley and Jarvis 2020). For Fukuyama (2020: 26), 'It is not a matter of regime type. Some democracies have performed well, but others have not, and the same is true for autocracies.' Hanson (2015) was among the first to ask whether it is more important to have democracy or a capable state in achieving development outcomes. Recently, the literature has shifted its focus onto the critical role of state capacity in government pandemic response. The absence of state capacity is frequently cited as a barrier to development. Initially referring to the ability to produce income, state capacity encompasses various skills relevant to the development process, including protecting private property rights, enforcing contracts, supporting and augmenting markets through regulation, and providing public goods (Serikbayeva et al. 2020).

Gisselquist and Vaccaro (2021) identify three core dimensions of the state: authority, capacity, and legitimacy. Authority refers to the ability of the state to provide order and security within its territorial boundaries. Ideally, state authority should be associated with improved pandemic outcomes since states with greater power should be more successful at implementing COVID-19-related limitations such as quarantine and stay-at-home regulations than states with less jurisdiction. Capacity is the state's ability to provide basic public services. To a lesser extent, capacity and authority are inextricably linked to what is occasionally referred to as state effectiveness. Effective states provide a range of beneficial socioeconomic outcomes, including economic development, improved supply of public goods, and improved public health outcomes.

Additionally, a well-functioning state apparatus is believed to be critical in minimizing the harmful consequences of external shocks such as natural disasters. It is assumed that states with 'high capacity' will be more prepared to respond to crises than states with 'low capacity', such as through having proper pandemic response plans and preventative infrastructure in place. Legitimacy is the ability to acquire consent to govern from the population of a country. State legitimacy appears to affect pandemic outcomes mainly through the state's ability to enforce rules and deliver services (i.e. via state authority and capacity). States with a high degree of legitimacy may rely more on the population's voluntary compliance with the regulations. Individuals living in legitimate states are also more likely to have a higher level of social trust, allowing voluntary compliance with rules and support for government actions.

Mao (2021) underscores the importance of state capacity for crisis management. State capacity is critical for developing an effective crisis management system because it helps the government to manage crises by coordinating many entities, analysing data, and providing public services. Mao conceptualizes state capacity for crisis management in four dimensions: information capacity, decision-making and implementation capacity, coercive capacity, and mobilization and cooperation capacity. He also acknowledges that political institutions shape the state's capacity. As a result, both consolidated democracies and authoritarian regimes can have strong state capability. Stable democracies can increase state capacity through institutionalized administration and bottom-up control of civil society. Through strong top-down control, consolidated authoritarian states can bolster state capacity.

Nevertheless, countries with varying political institutions have different degrees of state capacity. State capacity has a critical role in shaping the strength of the lines of accountability that connect rulers to service providers. When state capacity is high, rulers can more effectively supply increased levels of public services. When states lack capacity, funds may not reach service providers and policy-makers may lack the tools to hold service providers accountable for their performance (Hanson 2015).

Comparing authoritarian China with democratic South Korea, for example, offers two effective pandemic responses within various political institutions and state capacities. China has followed a policy of mandatory lockdown that is highly reliant on authoritarian governance. However, in the early stages of the pandemic, a lack of state information capability hampered the rapid response. In comparison, as a democratic country, South Korea has maintained a robust information capability that enables timely crisis responses. Considering the government's limited coercive capacity, this capability has supported society's openness and opposes COVID-19 through state–society synergy. Voluntary social cooperation, such as public compliance with anti-crisis measures, affects effectiveness (Mao 2021).

Underpinning the functionality of state capacity, particularly during a crisis, is public trust and political legitimacy. As countries worldwide have fought to limit the COVID-19 pandemic, analysts have frequently observed that those with greater regime legitimacy, state capacity, and political trust have been more likely to contain the virus's spread. Fukuyama (2020) highlights the factors responsible for successful pandemic responses: state capacity, social trust, and leadership. A competent state apparatus is defined by a government that citizens trust and listen to and successful leaders who have performed admirably, mitigating the harm they have sustained. Countries with dysfunctional state apparatus, polarized communities, or ineffective leadership, on the other hand, have performed poorly in pandemic response, leaving their populations and economies exposed and vulnerable. However, Dobbs (2022) discovered that countries with higher legitimacy and trust have also had a rise in COVID-19 cases, though the correlation is only moderate.

Some puzzles have emerged in the role of legitimacy and trust in facilitating the state's capacity for crisis response. Hong Kong may have been expected to falter in reacting to the COVID-19 pandemic as sociopolitical tensions erupted into significant street protests against the government's perceived facilitation of Chinese Communist Party control over the city in the year preceding the outbreak. And yet, it initially succeeded in containing the first wave of the virus. For Hartley and Jarvis (2020), the Hong Kong experience called into question the applicability of academic theories of response capacity that are primarily concerned with the state.

This society riven by legitimation crisis and low trust in government still managed to successfully respond to the crisis through 'community capacity'.

State capacity can also be defined by politics, or the mechanisms by which leaders with authority over bureaucracies are selected and sanctioned, beginning at the village level. Politics influences the incentives of state workers and their beliefs and expectations, and thus the performance of government agencies (Khemani 2019). According to Centeno et al. (2017), two significant inputs are required to deploy state capacity into a range of outcomes: political coalitions (including leadership, classes, and parties) and a balance of social forces. The 'politics of deployment' depends on the quality of decision-making of the state leadership and the political coalitions forged to support such decision-making. Decisions, in turn, depend on the balance of social forces—the resistance or support of various sectors in society. A state's performance cannot be divorced from the expectations imposed on it, the opposition it may face in achieving its objectives, and the degree of support or cooperation it enjoys. We must account for societal resistance posed by either a sizeable segment of the population (e.g. a refusal to observe the law) or a sizeable and influential minority (objecting to some health measure). State capacity will depend on the means available to mobilize support, quell resistance, or fulfil requests in certain instances. While states' coercive capacity to enforce decisions is frequently emphasized, equal weight should be given to the political instruments available to garner and demonstrate support (Centeno et al. 2017).

This chapter will utilize process-tracing to account for Duterte's political deployment during the coronavirus outbreak. Process-tracing is 'an analytic tool for drawing descriptive and causal inferences from diagnostic pieces of evidence—often understood as part of a temporal sequence of events or phenomena' (Collier 2011: 824). It will systematically examine trajectories of change and causation, considering Duterte's populist resilience despite his poor pandemic response. Specifically, the chapter will probe into a sequence of three critical elements in the Philippine response to the coronavirus pandemic (see Figure 4.1). These elements

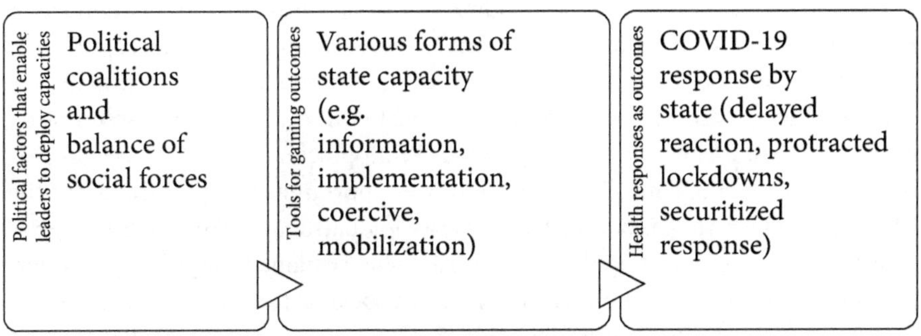

Figure 4.1 Political deployment and state capacity amid the COVID-19 pandemic.
Source: Author's illustration based on Mao (2021) and Centeno et al. (2017).

are: political factors that enable leaders to deploy state capacity; state capacity as a tool for gaining outcomes; and health responses as outcomes.

4.3 Populist mobilization amid a pandemic

There is a tendency to focus on structural explanations for the success or failure of state response to the COVID-19 pandemic. Even when capable states exist, we must consider whether political agents aim to deploy the organizational capacity of the state. A well-functioning state bureaucracy is essentially a tool. It can only fulfil its potential if deployed in the proper direction and partially insulated from interference, and if it has mechanisms to deal with competing pressures. It is critical to distinguish between public failures caused by state capacity (organizational or institutional structures) and those driven primarily by leadership quality, preferences, or tactics. It is critical to evaluate the leaders who spearhead a project and the political coalitions formed to support those efforts when analysing political agency (Centeno et al. 2017).

4.3.1 Duterte's political coalition

The liberal political order's inability to enact critical social and political reforms and increase state capacity (most notably in criminal justice systems and disaster management) fostered a 'politics of anger' that Duterte exploited during the 2016 election (Teehankee and Thompson 2016). This outpouring of anger was sparked by widespread voter discontent and rising demand for a strong leader capable of restoring law and order. The outpouring of rage manifested itself as a movement centred on an anti-establishment and unorthodox mayor from the South who promised the arrival of genuine change ('tunay na pagbabago') (Teehankee 2017).

Despite the lack of reliable party support and political machinery, the former mayor of Davao City in Mindanao rode a wave of angry votes to capture the single-term presidency in 2016. Starting as an almost party-less candidate, his allies swelled to hundreds of national and local politicians upon his assumption of the presidency. However, unlike previous Philippine presidents, he did not personally endeavour to consolidate his political support under his political party, the PDP-Laban. Duterte has succeeded in bypassing patronage-based political party formation in favour of populist mobilization—a 'sustained, large-scale political project that mobilizes ordinarily marginalized social sectors into publicly visible and contentious political action, while articulating anti-elite, nationalist rhetoric that valorizes ordinary people' (Jansen 2011: 82).

Duterte's populist mobilization triggered the rise of illiberal democracy that promoted intense polarization and spawned brute-force governance in the country. Illiberal democracy 'upholds participation rights while violating personal liberties' (Thompson 2019: 41). The country restored its democracy in 1986 after 14 years of authoritarian rule under Ferdinand Marcos. Its steep decline into illiberal democracy was first manifested in Duterte's bloody 'war on drugs' and later replicated in his militarized COVID-19 response. When institutions are unable to generate favourable governance outcomes, particularly when issues have been 'securitized', resulting in expectations of quick solutions, and when a lack of accountability allows for widespread human rights violations, brute-force governance results (Thompson 2020).

4.3.2 The populist public

As with other populist politicians abroad, Duterte originally minimized the threat posed by the novel coronavirus. Duterte and his populist peers globally have discovered an unfamiliar 'enemy' in the COVID-19 pandemic problem. It is tough to maintain a narrative of the people versus the elite in the face of a viral and existential threat. A virus cannot just be disciplined. And the population is fearful, hungry, and dying (Teehankee 2021). However, for his die-hard supporters, Duterte embodies their 'tatay' or daddy—a severe father figure who has the Filipino people's best interests at heart (Aquino 2019). They are a segment of the 'populist public' who are disgruntled, angry, and distrustful of liberal reformism's 'hypocrisy', as represented by the previous presidential administration, which was believed to be governed by 'elites' and 'oligarchs'. As one enthusiastic Duterte admirer puts it, '[we] support Duterte because [we] are Duterte' (Arguelles 2019: 431).

Nonetheless, the pandemic has created a perfect opportunity for populist leaders worldwide to consolidate power (Balfour 2020; Katsambekis and Stavrakakis 2020; Meyer 2020; Serhan 2020; Urbinati 2020). Populist mobilizations begin, develop, and flourish during times of crisis. Crises foster widespread worry and uncertainty in society, which is especially favourable to populist support. Popular support is generated by capitalizing on public fears, securitizing the epidemic, and alienating the people. In the Philippines, the effective implementation of these initiatives has created an environment favourable to the public renewing its support for Dutertismo (Arguelles 2021).

While various populisms have emerged in different parts of the world in recent years, Lasco (2020) points to 'medical populism' as a significant variant that spreads with contagion. He defines medical populism as 'a political style based on performances of public health crises that pit "the people" against "the establishment"', and proposes that this type of populism is characterized by 'simplifying the pandemic by downplaying its impacts or touting easy solutions or treatments, spectacularizing ... responses to crisis, forging divisions between the "people" and dangerous "others", and making medical knowledge claims to support the above' (Lasco 2020: 1417).

In the Philippines, most pundits and analysts shared the conventional wisdom that the government's dismal performance in addressing the pandemic would somehow impact the president's popularity. Hence, it was a tremendous surprise for most observers of Philippine politics that in a national survey by Pulse Asia in September 2020, Duterte's government gained a 92 per cent approval rating for its response to the COVID-19 pandemic. Moreover, 84 per cent of respondents said that they approved of Duterte's performance in controlling the spread of the virus. Another 84 per cent approved of his government providing assistance and livelihood to those affected by the pandemic.

Duterte's high approval mark was evident across geographical locations and classes. His highest level of support came from his bailiwick, Mindanao, and from the lower-middle to lower classes. But he also rated highly in the other geographical constituencies and even the upper to middle classes. The following subsection will delineate how Duterte leveraged his popularity to mount a highly militarized, albeit mismanaged, pandemic response anchored on a weak state.

Several possible factors have been posited as having contributed to Duterte's continuing popularity amid the mismanagement of the pandemic crisis. Some analysts point out that the possible 'fear factor' of the Duterte administration may have prompted survey respondents to positively rate the president's COVID-19 response. Citizens became even more reliant on government assistance and services during the stringent lockdowns, thus the intense desire to be on the good side of government authorities. Pollsters do not rule out the idea that fear influences the polling process, even though it is hard to estimate (Arguelles 2021). According to Social Weather Stations (SWS) fellow Geoffrey Ducanes, the 'fear factor' relates to how much of the survey response is motivated by the fear of expressing dissatisfaction, such that what is observed is not genuine satisfaction. Another factor can be 'social desirability bias', making survey respondents fudge their responses. A list experiment conducted by Yuko Kasuya (Keio University), Hirofumi Miwa (Gakushuin University), and Ronald Holmes (De La Salle University) found that Filipinos who believed that their neighbours supported Duterte were more susceptible to this social desirability bias. For Jose Ramon Albert, a senior research fellow at the Philippine Institute for Development Studies, the Social Amelioration Program (the government's pandemic financial support) contributed to the high satisfaction ratings since it covered 75 per cent of households across the country (Albert 2021).

Another potential factor is the 'rally-around-the-flag' effect. Presidents benefit from this during times of war and other such crises: they enjoy brief increases in popular approval due to the imagined necessity for national unity and citizen support for government leadership. The effective use of crisis rhetoric, which is frequently characterized by discourses of national unity in the face of hardship, is critical to this phenomenon. However, Duterte's addresses during the pandemic have mainly been unclear and polarizing. Populist leaders thrive amid crises. Crises foster a climate of widespread uncertainty and insecurity that enables populist support. These leaders garner support by exploiting fears, securitizing crises, and polarizing societies. According to Arguelles (2021), Duterte's populist brand is crisis.

For Pernia (2022), the unexpected spike in popular trust and confidence in political institutions under Duterte can be attributed to citizens' latent authoritarian values being activated. The 'populist' politics of Duterte have appealed to the public's need for strong leadership and a government that shows (or signals) legitimacy by decision responsiveness. It is possible that Duterte merely mirrors an innate political orientation among citizens that values order and hierarchy. According to political psychology research, a 'beneficial strategy' deals with life's complexity and disorder. This would explain Filipinos' continued admiration of and support for Duterte. Healthy authoritarians comprise a sizeable segment of the Filipino population who remained loyal to the government because it offered a semblance of decisive action (e.g. cash aids, rehabilitation programmes, and lockdowns) that could alleviate their anxieties and powerlessness during disasters and other related crises. Despite the country's substandard healthcare system—which is often indicative of poor institutional performance—the government could generate trust among the populace.

4.4 The Philippines' weak state capacity

The state is a formidable structure that towers above other formal and informal social formations because it seeks primacy via rules that govern citizens' conduct. State capabilities are the state's 'capacities to penetrate society, regulate social relationships, extract resources, and appropriate and use resources in determined ways' (Migdal 1988: 4–5). The Philippines is frequently said to be a weak state. The capacity of the Philippine state is insufficient to withstand challenges to its autonomy, particularly in the face of various elite interests. The country is Southeast Asia's oldest democracy, yet democratic institutions consistently fail to demonstrate coherence in what is usually viewed as a resilient oligarchical state that maintains power over the state, economy, and society by continually adapting and shifting in response to changing political dynamics (Teehankee and Calimbahin 2020).

Moreover, state capacity is a multidimensional concept that relates to the ability of the state to achieve administrative, extractive, and coercive goals.

Administrative capacity relates to the ability to formulate and implement policies. Coercive capacity demonstrates how the state exerts control over society and suppresses dissent using coercive force. The ability of a state to extract income from its citizens to cement its authority is referred to as its extractive capacity (Hanson 2018). State capacity is critical to developing an efficient crisis management system because it helps the government deal with crises by coordinating many organizations, analysing information, and providing public services (Christensen et al. 2016). Mao (2021) adapts these dimensions into a state-capacity-driven crisis management framework that includes information capacity, decision-making and implementation capacity, coercive capacity, and mobilization and cooperation capacity. The following subsections will assess these capacities in the Philippines' response to the pandemic.

4.4.1 Information capacity

Information collection, processing, and sharing are integral to crisis response and management. Coordination and collaboration at the intergovernmental level facilitate effective information collecting and sharing, prompt decision-making, and the execution of crisis response measures. Inadequate information capacity may result in the government responding slowly to crises (Mao 2021). For example, one of the contributing elements to the initial success of Vietnam in containing the virus was its strong and effective information capacity. Timely notification by government and the media of any pandemic developments, together with the Vietnamese scientific community's latest understanding of the new virus, combined to provide reliable sources of information. The government also ran an effective social media information campaign (Hartley et al. 2021).

COVID-19 data in the Philippines are critically deficient. Currently, the country's Department of Health (DOH) collects COVID-19-related data through disease reporting units, local government units, and health facilities. However, when an information system fails, the data-collecting process is halted. The DOH does not collect official statistics on COVID-19 excess fatalities. The Philippines has limited capability for surveying public health threats and low capacity for community reporting. COVID-19 statistics that are incomplete or delayed undermine the government's response to the public health situation (Del Castillo 2021).

On top of the state's information infrastructure is the chief executive, who acts as the government's chief communicator. World leaders' communication styles are being compared, from New Zealand prime minister Jacinda Ardern's Facebook press conferences to Singaporean prime minister Lee Hsien Loong's crisp statements, to US president Donald Trump's ranting (Ranada 2020). Duterte's unorthodox and unfiltered communication style was designed for reality television and social media. When he was mayor of Davao City in Mindanao, he hosted a local television show called 'Gikan sa Masa, Para sa Masa' ('From the Masses to the Masses') for years, where he called out and cursed incompetent local and national bureaucrats, suspected criminals, and other erring government officials. Thus, Duterte, like Donald Trump in the US, exemplifies 'performative populism'—a kind of populism in the era of television and digital media that draws on a 'repertoire of performance' and establishes a link between the leader as a performer and the follower as the audience (Moffitt 2016).

Even in the face of a crisis that needs clarity, analytical rigour, and consistency, Duterte has continued to deliver lengthy, rambling speeches filled with digressions, rants against opponents, and personal thoughts that drowned out clear commands and crucial messaging. Throughout the coronavirus pandemic, brutal messaging has trumped science-based communication. Duterte has used swear words more often than he has used the terms 'testing', 'test kits', or 'tracing' (Ranada 2020). He has reacted angrily to public criticism, devoting his late-night briefings, which were intended to provide updates on the government's response to the virus's spread, to maligning and threatening his critics (Arguelles 2021). As the nation waited every week for updates regarding the state of the COVID-19 response, they expected the same discipline that was exacted from them with the demanding requirements of community quarantine. Unfortunately, these periodic televised reports by the president and his task force members have only highlighted how unorganized and uncoordinated COVID-19 response efforts have been.

4.4.2 Decision-making and implementation capacity

The capacity of a government to make decisions and implement policies is critical to enhancing disaster preparation and institutional quality in responding to crises. Strong decision-making and implementation capacity require effective intergovernmental coordination to overcome institutional frictions between different levels of government (Mao 2021). Who decides and how decisions are made impact the implementation of crisis response.

Duterte constituted an Inter-Agency Task Force for the Management of Emerging Infectious Diseases (IATF-EID) comprising health professionals, technocrats, and business leaders, led by controversial health secretary Francisco Duque III, who has been publicly chastised for incompetence and alleged irregular transactions. Duque has been blamed for the slow and ineffective government response to the spread of the pandemic, as well as billion-peso anomalies in the corruption-laden Philippine Health Insurance Corporation (PhilHealth), where he sits as chair.

Despite running on an electoral platform of shifting the Philippine form of government to federalism, Duterte has eschewed decentralization in his pandemic response and adopted a highly centralized 'whole-of-government' strategy with a top-down approach to policy-making decisions. This set-up has left local government units as mere implementers, following the orders of the national government (Navarro et al. 2020; Espia et al. 2021). For Hutchcroft and Gera (2022), the Philippine state amid the pandemic has not provided the type of 'central steering' required of the national government to address COVID-19. Drawing on the work of Kjellberg (1995), this strategy attempts to guarantee that although the basic goals of public action remain the purview of the national government, the means to achieve them are defined more explicitly by local governments. Instead, populist president Rodrigo Duterte's action has relied on 'strong-arming' local politicians. This has concealed the government's weak steering and provided the illusion that a 'strongman' is in control of the situation. Nonetheless, this approach has been ineffective in terms of the central steering required for pandemic response. At the outset, the pandemic necessitated strong and effective coordination by the national government, mainly through the IATF-EID. However, the critical central agencies led by the DOH have consistently failed to deliver. Thus, a number of local governments have picked up the slack to compensate for the slow and faulty response of the national government. However, not all local governments have the capacity and resources to address the onslaught of the pandemic.

4.4.3 Coercive capacity

State–society relations shape coercive, mobilization, and cooperation capacities. Combating crises requires not only government action but also public compliance, social mobilization, and cooperation. For example, when a state exerts strong control over its society through coercive force, the government's capacity to coerce public compliance with anti-crisis measures is enhanced (Mao 2021).

The Philippines, however, implemented one of the world's most draconian lockdowns. Its flight capacity, which indicates how far air transport has recovered, is 74 per cent lower than in 2019, and its borders remain closed to travellers. Yet the Philippines has also underperformed in COVID-19 containment. While cases per capita are less than a fifth of what vaccine leader Israel has seen, the Philippines has the second-worst positive test rate in Bloomberg's ranking, at 27 per cent (Bloomberg News 2021).

Consistent with his leadership approach, President Duterte viewed the pandemic problem as a war against the virus—shutting down its transmission barriers by stopping the movement of people and mobilizing the police and military to keep citizens indoors. He has also relied heavily on another body, composed of former military generals, the National Task Force COVID-19 (NTF), which he tasked with implementing the National Action Plan to manage the spread of virulent disease in the country. On the prodding of his military advisors, Duterte implemented a lockdown patterned after the military's decades-long tactics for border control in its fight against armed insurgent groups (Dizon 2020; Olanday and Rigby 2020).

Duterte's government has focused its efforts on slowing down the spread of the virus by curbing the movement of people through martial-law-like mechanisms. This approach, however, has not been combined with mass testing and aggressive contact tracing. While governments of countries with the first confirmed cases of COVID-19 ramped up their testing strategies and capacities, the Philippine government continued to ignore the advice of health experts to include mass testing in its prevention and control measures. According to health experts, Vietnam effectively prevented and limited the spread of the virus because it made urgent decisions to restrict entry into the nation, enforce quarantine protocols, and strengthen its testing and contract tracing capacities. By 19 March 2020, Vietnam had conducted 14,950 tests (Vu et al. 2020) compared with the 1,200 tests conducted by the Philippines (DOH 2020).

4.4.4 Mobilizational and cooperative capacity

When a state and its society are connected, the government is more likely to have high capacity for social mobilization and cooperation, enabling the private sector and citizens to participate more effectively in crisis response (Mao 2021). The Philippines has a rich history of community capacity through its vibrant civil society, non-governmental, and not-for-profit organizations (Teehankee and Calimbahin 2020). However, the populist Duterte has exploited the enormous anxiety caused by the viral pandemic. He has securitized the pandemic by militarizing crisis response, empowering security agencies to administer it, and using war rhetoric. For Duterte, the pandemic response is a 'war against COVID-19' or 'war against an invisible enemy'. After the COVID-19 crisis was securitized, the people saw Duterte as the ideal crisis manager. He has portrayed himself as a ruthless, tough, and uncompromising commander-in-chief, always ready for war. And lastly, while the coronavirus crisis could have served as an opportunity for Duterte to champion national unity and rally the country to a common cause, he instead doubled down on the use of polarizing rhetoric (Arguelles 2021).

Hence, Duterte's pandemic response has been akin to a war cabinet. He has deployed an ad hoc coalition of bureaucrats, the military, the police, allied parties, petty village and suburb heads, and online die-hard supporters. More importantly, he has relied on populist mobilization or the rallying of mass supporters towards contentious political action with minimum institutional intermediation (Teehankee and Kasuya 2020). Populists thrive on direct communication with their supporters, relying mainly on the media and public demonstrations (Kenny 2017). Arguelles (2019) argues that the populist publics are not irrational, dumb, or gullible voters but are part of a growing constituency who are frustrated, angered, and sceptical of the 'hypocrisy' of liberal reformism. Cas Mudde (2015) points out that 'populism is an illiberal democratic response to undemocratic liberalism'.

In 2016, Duterte won the presidency on a narrative of 'the people versus the corrupt elite'. Drawing on the politics of anger and resentment amplified through social media, he managed to sustain his popularity despite his consistent bad behaviour, bloody war on drugs, and assault on media freedom. Since Duterte's government implemented a long and strict lockdown and seems to enjoy high levels of legitimacy (as high approval ratings suggest), it could seem puzzling that the Philippines has been struggling to control the pandemic (Teehankee 2021). The irony of Duterte's populist resilience amid his poor pandemic response serves to highlight his mastery of political deployment within a weak state.

4.5 The pitfalls of Duterte's pandemic response

The COVID-19 pandemic caught the global community off guard. While health experts and risk assessors have always considered a pandemic scenario, world leaders did not expect it to happen so soon on their watch. In an instant, national leaders faced an ambiguous and uncertain situation that could impact their population's health and survival and economic and political stability. The Philippines was unprepared for the magnitude and severity of the impact of the COVID-19 virus.

While Duterte exploited the crisis to his advantage, his government committed a series of severe missteps in the early phase of the outbreak that exacerbated the impact of the virus. These significant policy errors in the first year of the pandemic included:

(1) The government's delayed acknowledgement of the severity of the coronavirus pandemic, causing the country to be reactive in its action.
(2) Once it was too late to avert widespread virus transmission, Duterte's government piled in, imposing a series of protracted total lockdowns without providing appropriate support for vulnerable localities.
(3) Duterte's securitized response to a public health emergency, which aggravated an already lethal virus. Unsurprisingly, Duterte has viewed the virus epidemic as a law-and-order issue, cracking down on allegedly 'pasaway' or 'undisciplined' residents who are said to be responsible for COVID-19's quick spread (Arguelles 2021).

4.5.1 Delayed reaction

With other leaders announcing travel restrictions and closely monitoring their airports as an urgent response to the virus's global spread, the Duterte administration adopted a 'wait and see' approach and even downplayed the virus. Since his assumption of the presidency, Duterte has closely pivoted the country's foreign policy towards China. He has frequently mentioned his close friendship with President Xi Jinping in his public speeches. He has anchored the nation's COVID-19 recovery on the development of the Chinese vaccine, urging China to prioritize supplies to the Philippines at a time when the world was demanding accountability for China's involvement in the COVID-19 outbreak.

As early as 9 January 2020, the World Health Organization (WHO) had already announced the outbreak of coronavirus-related pneumonia in Wuhan, China. Even with the unprecedented move of China to put Wuhan under strict lockdown on 23 January, it was only on 28 January that President Duterte ordered a temporary ban on the entry of Chinese nationals from China's Hubei province. Two days after his announcement of the travel ban, the first case of COVID-19 was confirmed by the DOH. The first documented case arrived in the Philippines on 21 January 2020, from Wuhan, China, via Hong Kong.

With the virus already in the country and its local transmission inevitable, the Duterte administration needed to work quickly (De Jesus and Dayrit 2021). Early intervention is critical in dealing with an infectious virus like COVID-19, to remain ahead of the disease. However, President Duterte continued to downplay the disease even after the country had reported its first COVID-19 fatality on 2 February 2020, involving a 44-year-old Chinese man who was the first victim's companion. His death on 1 February was the first to be reported outside of China (Romero and Baculinao 2020). In a press briefing the following day, the president said, 'let's start with narratives by saying that everything is well in the country, that there is nothing really to be extra scared of the coronavirus thing' (Baclig 2021).

The Philippines has experienced four COVID-19 surges. The initial wave was moderate, peaking at 316 on a 7-day rolling average in early April 2020. Cases began to progressively climb in early June 2020, building up to the second wave, which peaked at roughly 4,300 daily cases in late August. The third wave peaked at 11,000 daily instances on average in mid-April 2021. The fourth wave, fuelled by the Delta variation, was the most devastating since the epidemic began. By 8 August 2021, the daily average had risen to nearly 19,000 instances (Cristino 2021). By September, the Philippines had breached 2 million cases, with a total death toll of 33,533 (Magsambol 2021).

4.5.2 Protracted lockdowns

With the total number of cases in the Philippines rising to 24 and a confirmed case of local transmission, President Duterte signed Proclamation 922 on 8 March 2020, declaring a state of public health emergency in the country. This declaration was soon followed by the imposition of a 'community quarantine' in Metro

Manila on 12 March. Domestic land, air, and sea travel to and from Manila were suspended from 15 March to 14 April 2020.

To make up for the time lost through the late imposition of travel restrictions from China and other countries with notable cases of COVID-19, the Duterte administration announced, on 15 March 2020, the lockdown of Metro Manila, giving its citizens minimal time to prepare provisions for what was at the time projected to be a month-long quarantine. After two days, the lockdown was extended to Luzon, and soon after, the rest of the country was put under community quarantine and subjected to interzonal travel restrictions. The country has been recognized globally as having had the longest general lockdown (general community quarantine) and strictest lockdown, with at least four hard lockdown cycles (enhanced community quarantine). President Duterte mobilized the police and the military to enforce a curfew and keep citizens indoors.

For weeks, police officers, petty bureaucrats, and village authorities cracked down on violators of the heightened community quarantine enforced by the 'Bayanihan to Heal as One Act'—the law that granted Duterte special powers to handle the COVID-19 outbreak. Around 130,000 quarantine violators were apprehended (ABS-CBN News 2020b). According to some human rights groups, quarantine violators were also subjected to verbal abuse and physical punishments (Castaneda 2020). In a developing nation like the Philippines, where a significant proportion of the urban population lives in confined slum neighbourhoods and survives on daily wage labour, social distancing and work-from-home arrangements are luxuries reserved for the country's middle and upper classes. Slow and sometimes missed delivery of crucial government food support and subsidies to the poor and vulnerable sectors led to hunger and desperation that have further threatened social order in the metropolis (Gutierrez 2020). Nonetheless, the well-heeled have not been entirely spared, as the police barging into exclusive villages and condominiums in search of quarantine violators has also been reported (ABS-CBN News 2020a; De Leon 2020).

The Bayanihan Law, which took effect on 26 March, punishes those 'creating, perpetuating, or spreading false information regarding the [COVID-19] crisis on social media and other platforms, such information having no valid or beneficial effect on the population, and [being] geared to promote chaos, panic, anarchy, fear, or confusion', according to Section 6(6) (Buan 2020). The definition of fake news, on the other hand, is hazy, and decisions are left to the whims of law enforcement (Ramos 2020).

On-and-off lockdowns have also harmed the economy. Lockdown can help a country enhance its healthcare and test-trace-treat systems—the basic elements of better disease control. However, failing to enhance these mechanisms wastes the time that lockdown gives. Despite having had the world's longest lockdowns, the country failed to flatten its COVID-19 curve (Mendoza 2021). Moreover, the 'low downs' of the protracted lockdowns, such as displacement, inefficiencies, and uneven distribution of resources from the presidential palace, continued to hamper the country's recovery efforts (Hall 2023).

4.5.3 Securitized response

Strong-arming became the default mode of Duterte's highly securitized pandemic response, drawing heavily from his bloody 'war on drugs' (Hutchcroft and Gera 2022). This securitized approach blamed the so-called undisciplined others or 'pasaway' for justifying the imposition of a 'disciplinary quarantine' to protect the virtuous from those elements set to derail the war against COVID-19 (Kusaka 2020; Hapal 2021). The reliance of Duterte on 'strong-arming' is akin to what Michael Mann (1984: 188–190) termed 'despotic power' or 'power by the state over civil society'. This highlights the lack of 'infrastructural power', which Mann (1984: 189–190) characterized as the capacity of the state to 'centrally coordinate the activities of civil society through its own infrastructure'.

Duterte's use of the military to help police to enforce national mandates in the cities blurred the line between these two state security agents, and local governments did not object because they thought of the police and military as resources that could be used to implement their own policies. The use of uniformed personnel to address a public health emergency and the administration's aggressive enforcement strategy were viewed as having little effect on the rising tide of positive cases and inviting repressive action against the opposition under the guise of pandemic countermeasures. It widened the military's functional mandate and perceived institutional reach, even as President Duterte appointed ex-generals to various cabinet positions to coordinate government initiatives in testing, contact tracing, and vaccination. Military personnel were present on the ground and in decision-making positions at the highest levels (Hall 2022).

While a significant amount of political communication during the early stages of the COVID-19 epidemic did securitize the pandemic and attacked the opposition, the degree to which securitizing players did so varied, thereby creating layers of legitimizing actors for securitization and repression. This also enabled Duterte to be depicted as a strong leader throughout the epidemic, thus explaining some of his continuing popularity.

Duterte exploited the pandemic to attack his enemies and declare war on many fronts. His administration and his allies in Congress spent a great deal of time and effort enacting severe anti-terrorism legislation and terminating the franchise of the country's leading television network, ABS-CBN. Maria Ressa, the CEO of the Rappler news website, was also convicted of cyber libel during this period (Teehankee 2020b).

In the early days of the pandemic, Duterte threatened to declare martial law on the Philippines' largest island, Luzon, to punish those who disobeyed the quarantine law. In a televised address, he told the military and police to 'shoot them dead'. 'Dead. Instead of causing chaos, I'll just bury you' (Gregorio 2020). 'I am warning everybody and putting notice [to the] armed forces and the police, I might declare martial law', he later reiterated (CNN Philippines 2020).

However, the immediate implementation of lockdown measures was not supported by social and economic safety nets, leaving those who did not have the financial capacity to stockpile to leave their homes and look for food. These so-called 'pasaway' or undisciplined residents became the target of the president, singling them out as the cause of the rapid transmission of the virus. Thousands of people have been arrested for violating curfew and other health protocols (such as not wearing masks). Duterte even publicly threatened to order a tougher crackdown, ordering the military and police to 'shoot to kill' the 'pasaway' (violators) (Agojo 2021; Hapal 2021).

4.6 Conclusion

The Philippines was among the last countries in the ASEAN region to roll out its vaccination programme. It only started its vaccination programme on 1 March 2021, with the arrival of the 600,000 doses of Sinovac. With the limited arrival of vaccines and limited capacity of laboratories and healthcare facilities, the primary strategy of the Duterte administration in addressing the pandemic continued to be community quarantine. The surge in COVID-19 cases in April and September 2021 further overwhelmed the already-strained healthcare system.

Rodrigo Duterte rose to power by riding the wave of popular anger and frustration towards the ruling elite's failure to institute socioeconomic and political reforms. The COVID-19 pandemic has threatened his populist legacy as a strongman president. His government has consistently fumbled in its handling of the pandemic despite implementing one of the most heavy-handed lockdowns in the world. Just like his fellow populists around the world, Duterte has found it challenging to sustain an 'us versus them' narrative against an existential threat like the virus. His unorthodox and disruptive populist leadership has amplified the country's weak state capacity in crisis management, particularly information gathering and dissemination and decision-making and implementation. He has relied wholly on the state's coercive capacity to mount an 'all-out war' against the COVID-19 pandemic to the point of transgressing institutional checks and balances and violating fundamental human rights (Teehankee 2022).

As a political institution, the Philippine presidency has accrued enough constitutional power to have a formal semblance of a 'strong presidency'. As a result, strong Philippine presidents appear to reign over a state with weak capacity, malleable to presidential whims and vulnerable to social pressure. The Philippine presidency is a classic case of what Latin American political scientist Guillermo

O'Donnell (1994) called a 'delegative democracy', with little accountability, limited capacity and professionalism within the administrative and security apparatuses, and a lack of autonomy in the face of powerful domestic and foreign political actors. Nonetheless, even an apparently 'strong' presidency can become susceptible to societal challenges (Teehankee 2020a).

Despite his missteps in addressing the pandemic, Duterte remains popular, especially with his die-hard supporters—the populist public. He could have used this vast social capital to mobilize a unified nation with healing leadership to address the crisis. Rather than presenting a clear strategy to fight the virus's rise and spread, the president used the moment to attack his political adversaries and renew his declaration of war on several fronts. In the end, he turned out to be a weak president against the COVID-19 virus.

References

ABS-CBN News (2020a). 'Cops Allegedly Trespass into Taguig Condo, Accost Residents over COVID-19 Lockdown Violations', ABS-CBN News. 20 April. Available at: https://news.abs-cbn.com/news/04/20/20/cops-trespass-pacific-plaza-towers-shout-accost-residents-lockdowncoronavirus (accessed 10 November 2020).

ABS-CBN News (2020b). 'No More Warnings: PNP to Make Arrests in "Martial Law-Type" Lockdown—Chief', ABS-CBN News. 20 April. Available at: https://news.abs-cbn.com/video/news/04/20/20/no-more-warnings-pnp-to-make-arrests-in-martial-law-type-lockdown-chief (accessed 27 October 2020).

Agojo, K.N.M. (2021). 'Policing a Pandemic: Understanding the State and Political Instrumentalization of the Coercive Apparatus in Duterte's Philippines'. *Journal of Developing Societies*, 37(3): 363–386. https://doi.org/10.1177/0169796X21996832.

Albert, J.R. (2021). '[Analysis] Part 1: Survey Says or Not', Rappler. 27 October. Available at: www.rappler.com/voices/thought-leaders/analysis-what-surveys-says-or-not-lecture-series-public-service-business-government-part-1 (accessed 22 November 2021).

Alon, I., M.F., and S. Li (2020). 'Regime Type and COVID-19 Response'. *FIIB Business Review*, 9(3): 152–160. https://doi.org/10.1177/2319714520928884.

Aquino, N.P. (2019). '"Tatay Digong" Thrives on Pathos to Keep Rock-Star Status', BusinessWorld. 22 July. Available at: www.bworldonline.com/tatay-digong-thrives-on-pathos-to-keep-rock-star-status (accessed 20 November 2020).

Arguelles, C.V. (2019). '"We Are Rodrigo Duterte": Dimensions of the Philippine Populist Publics' Vote'. *Asian Politics and Policy*, 11(3): 417–437. https://doi.org/10.1111/aspp.12472.

Arguelles, C.V. (2021). 'The Populist Brand Is Crisis: Durable Dutertismo amidst Mismanaged COVID-19 Response'. In D. Singh and M. Cook (eds), *Southeast Asian Affairs 2021*. Singapore: ISEAS-Yusof Ishak Institute, pp. 257–274. https://doi.org/10.1355/9789814951753-016.

Baclig, C.E. (2021). 'Timeline: One Year of Covid-19 in the Philippines', Inquirer.net. 12 March. Available at: https://newsinfo.inquirer.net/1406004/timeline-one-year-of-covid-19-in-the-philippines?utm_source=pocket_mylist (accessed 12 November 2021).

Balfour, R. (2020). 'Why Populism Can Survive the Pandemic', Carnegie Europe. 15 June. Available at: https://carnegieeurope.eu/2020/07/15/why-populism-can-survive-pandemic-pub-82293 (accessed 8 September 2020).
Berengaut, A.A. (2020). 'Democracies Are Better at Fighting Outbreaks', *The Atlantic*. 24 February. Available at: www.theatlantic.com/ideas/archive/2020/02/why-democracies-are-better-fighting-outbreaks/606976 (accessed 12 September 2020).
Bloomberg News (2021). 'Why the Philippines Became the Worst Place to Be in Covid', *Bloomberg*. 29 September. Available at: www.bloomberg.com/news/articles/2021-09-29/why-the-philippines-just-became-the-worst-place-to-be-in-covid (accessed 8 November 2021).
Buan, L. (2020). 'NBI Summons "More Than a Dozen" for Coronavirus Posts', *Rappler*. 2 April. Available at: www.rappler.com/nation/256746-nbi-summons-more-than-dozen-people-social-media-coronavirus-posts (accessed 2 May 2020).
Buan, L. (2021). '"Who Instructed You?" Pharmally's Advance Delivery Surprises PS-DBM Staff', Rappler. 17 September. Available at: www.rappler.com/nation/pharmally-advance-delivery-surprises-procurement-service-dbm-staff (accessed 20 September 2021).
Bunyavejchewin, P., and K. Sirichuanjun (2021). 'How Regime Type and Governance Quality Affect Policy Responses to COVID-19: A Preliminary Analysis'. *Heliyon*, 7(2): 1–5. https://doi.org/10.1016/j.heliyon.2021.e06349.
Castaneda, J. (2020). 'Say a Prayer for Lockdown Victims in the Philippines', *Asia Times*. 15 April. Available at: https://asiatimes.com/2020/04/say-a-prayer-for-lockdown-victims-in-the-philippines (accessed 10 November 2020).
Centeno, M.A., A. Kohli, D.J. Yashar, and D. Mistree (2017). *States in the Developing World*. Cambridge: Cambridge University Press. https://doi.org/10.1017/CBO9781316665657.
Christensen, T., P. Lægreid, and L.H. Rykkja (2016). 'Organizing for Crisis Management: Building Governance Capacity and Legitimacy'. *Public Administration Review*, 76(6): 887–897. https://doi.org/10.1111/puar.12558.
CNN Philippines (2020). 'Duterte Threatens to Declare Martial Law if "Lawlessness" of NPA Continues', CNN Philippines. 24 April. Available at: https://cnnphilippines.com/news/2020/4/24/duterte-lawlessness-martial-law.html (accessed 9 October 2020).
Collier, D. (2011). 'Understanding Process Tracing'. *PS: Political Science and Politics*, 44(4): 823–830. https://doi.org/10.1017/S1049096511001429.
Cristino, M.R. (2021). 'The Philippines Passes the 2 Million Mark as COVID-19 Cases Surge in Southeast Asia', *The Conversation*. 9 September. Available at: https://theconversation.com/the-philippines-passes-the-2-million-mark-as-covid-19-cases-surge-in-southeast-asia-167186 (accessed 5 November 2021).
De Jesus, E.C., and M. Dayrit (2021). 'Introduction: Responding to COVID-19'. In E.C. de Jesus, M.M. Dayrit, and I.S. Baysic (eds),*Countering COVID-19: Cases in Crisis Response*. Quezon City: Ateneo de Manila University Press/Bughaw.
De Leon, M. (2020). 'Man in Private Village Assaulted, Nearly Arrested without Warrant by Makati Police', Rappler. 27 April. Available at: www.rappler.com/nation/259129-man-private-village-assaulted-nearly-arrested-without-warrant-makati-police?fbclid=IwAR1N5zf2HhZSOvfz1iUJacQW8QGQDD6pe4GiYHRGEKWmjHVQxX50fILPFx0 (accessed 1 May 2020).
Del Castillo, F.A. (2021). 'Negative COVID-19 Excess Mortality in the Philippines: Outcome of Public Health Measure or Product of Incomplete Data?'. *Journal of Public Health*, June: fdab203. https://doi.org/10.1093/pubmed/fdab203.

Dela Peña, K. (2021). 'Corruption Scandals under Duterte: From Whiff to Helplessness', Inquirer.net. 16 September. Available at: https://newsinfo.inquirer.net/1488894/corruption-scandals-under-duterte-from-whiff-to-helplessness (accessed 4 October 2021).

Diamond, L. (2020). 'Democracy versus the Pandemic: The Coronavirus Is Emboldening Autocrats the World Over', *Foreign Affairs*. 13 June. Available at: www.foreignaffairs.com/articles/world/2020-06-13/democracy-versus-pandemic (accessed 4 July 2020).

Dizon, N. (2020). 'Duterte and His Generals: A Shock and Awe Response to the Pandemic', Rappler. 31 July. Available at: www.rappler.com/newsbreak/in-depth/duterte-shock-and-awe-coronavirus-pandemic-responsegenerals (accessed 11 September 2020).

Dobbs, K.L. (2022). 'Falling Flat? The Impact of State Legitimacy, Capacity, and Political Trust on Flattening the Curve of COVID-19'. *Medical Research Archive* 10(4): 1–16. Available at: https://esmed.org/MRA/mra/article/view/2805/193546111 (accessed 15 June 2022). https://doi.org/10.18103/mra.v10i5.2805.

DOH (Department of Health) (2020). 'COVID Daily Testing Increases, Numbers to Improve Further to 10k'. DOH, 20 April'. Available at: https://doh.gov.ph/doh-press-release/percent20COVID-DAILY-TESTING-CAPACITY-INCREASES-NUMBERS-TO-IMPROVE-FURTHER-TO-10K (accessed 16 May 2020).

Espia, J.C., W. Gera, and R.A. Hall (2021). 'Local Adaptations to Central Government Shortcomings: COVID-19 Responses in the Cities of Iloilo and Cebu, Philippines'. *Contemporary Southeast Asia: A Journal of International and Strategic Affairs*, 43(1): 53–62.

Fukuyama, F. (2020). 'The Pandemic and Political Order: It Takes a State'. *Foreign Affairs*, 99(4): 26–32.

Gisselquist, R.M., and A. Vaccaro (2021). 'COVID-19 and the State'. WIDER Working Paper 80/2021. Helsinki: UNU-WIDER. Available at: www.wider.unu.edu/publication/covid-19-and-state www.wider.unu.edu/publication/covid-19-and-state (accessed 6 October 2021). https://doi.org/10.35188/UNU-WIDER/2021/018-4.

Greer, S.L., E.J. King, E.M. da Fonseca, and A. Peralta-Santos (2020). 'The Comparative Politics of COVID-19: The Need to Understand Government Responses'. *Global Public Health*, 15(9): 1413–1416. https://doi.org/10.1080/17441692.2020.1783340.

Greer, S.L., E.J. King, E.M. da Fonseca, and A. Peralta-Santos (eds) (2021). *The Comparative Politics and Policy of COVID 19*. Ann Arbor, MI: University of Michigan Press. https://doi.org/10.3998/mpub.11927713.

Gregorio, X. (2020). 'Duterte Tells Police, Military to Shoot Unruly Quarantine Violators', CNN Philippines. 1 April. Available at: www.cnnphilippines.com/news/2020/4/1/Rodrigo-Duterte-police-military-shoot-unruly-quarantine-violators.html (accessed 12 June 2020).

Gutierrez, J. (2020). '"Will We Die Hungry?": A Teeming Manila Slum Chafes Under Lockdown', *The New York Times*. 15 April. Available at: www.nytimes.com/2020/04/15/world/asia/manila-coronavirus-lockdown-slum.html (accessed 3 July 2020).

Hall, R.A. (2022). 'Camouflage in the Streets: Emergency Powers, the Military, and the Philippines' COVID-19 Pandemic Response'. *Philippine Political Science Journal*, 43: 168–191.

Hall, R.A. (2023). 'Introduction'. In R. Hall (ed.), *Lockdowns and Lowdown: The Politics of the Philippines' COVID-19 Pandemic Response*. Quezon City: Ateneo de Manila University Press/Bughaw, pp. 1–22.

Hanson, J.K. 2015. 'Democracy and State Capacity: Complements or Substitutes?'. *Studies in Comparative International Development*, 50(3): 304–330. https://doi.org/10.1007/s12116-014-9173-z.

Hanson, J.K. 2018. 'State Capacity and the Resilience of Electoral Authoritarianism: Conceptualizing and Measuring the Institutional Underpinnings of Autocratic Power'. *International Political Science Review*, 39(1): 17–32. https://doi.org/10.1177/0192512117702523.

Hapal, K. (2021). 'The Philippines' COVID-19 Response: Securitising the Pandemic and Disciplining the Pasaway'. *Journal of Current Southeast Asian Affairs*, 40(2): 224–244. https://doi.org/10.1177/1868103421994261.

Hartley, K., S. Bales, and A.S. Bali. (2021). 'COVID-19 Response in a Unitary State: Emerging Lessons from Vietnam'. *Policy Design and Practice*, 4(1): 152–168. https://doi.org/10.1080/25741292.2021.1877923.

Hartley, K., and D.S.L. Jarvis (2020). 'Policy-Making in a Low-Trust State: Legitimacy, State Capacity, and Responses to COVID-19 in Hong Kong'. *Policy and Society*, 39(3): 403–423. https://doi.org/10.1080/14494035.2020.1783791.

Hutchcroft, P.D., and W. Gera (2022). 'Strong-Arming, Weak Steering: Central–Local Relations in the Philippines in the Era of the Pandemic'. *Philippine Political Science Journal*, 43(2): 123–167. https://doi.org/10.1163/2165025x-bja10037.

Jansen R.S. (2011). 'Populist Mobilization: A New Theoretical Approach to Populism'. *Sociological Theory*, 29(2): 75–96. https://doi.org/10.1111/j.1467-9558.2011.01388.x.

Katsambekis, G., and Y. Stavrakakis (eds) (2020). 'Populism and the Pandemic: A Collaborative Report'. *POPULISMUS Interventions*, 7 (special edition).

Kenny P.D. (2017). *Populism and Patronage: Why Populists Win Elections in Asia, and Beyond*. Oxford: Oxford University Press. https://doi.org/10.1093/oso/9780198807872.003.0009.

Khemani, S. (2019). 'What Is State Capacity?' Policy Research Working Paper 8734. Washington, DC: World Bank Group. Available at: https://openknowledge.worldbank.org/handle/10986/31266 (accessed 9 September 2020).

Kjellberg, F. (1995). 'The Changing Values of Local Government'. *The Annals of the American Academy of Political Science*, 540: 40–50. https://doi.org/10.1177/0002716295540000004.

Kleinfeld, R. (2020). 'Do Authoritarian or Democratic Countries Handle Pandemics Better?' Carnegie Endowment for International Peace, 31 March. Available at: https://carnegieendowment.org/2020/03/31/do-authoritarian-or-democratic-countries-handle-pandemics-better-pub-81404 (accessed 21 May 2020).

Kusaka, W. (2020). 'Duterte's Disciplinary Quarantine: How a Moral Dichotomy Was Constructed and Undermined'. *Philippine Studies: Historical and Ethnographic Viewpoints*, 68(3): 423–442. https://doi.org/10.1353/phs.2020.0027.

Lasco, G. (2020). 'Medical Populism and the COVID-19 Pandemic'. *Global Public Health*, 15(10): 1417–1429. https://doi.org/10.1080/17441692.2020.1807581.

Li, G. (2021). 'China Falls from Top Spot in Nikkei COVID Recovery Ranking', Asian Nikkei. 6 October. Available at: https://asia.nikkei.com/Spotlight/Coronavirus/COVID-19-Recovery-Index/China-falls-from-top-spot-in-Nikkei-COVID-recovery-ranking (accessed 3 November 2021).

Lührmann, A., A.B. Edgell, and S.F. Maerz (2020). 'Pandemic Backsliding: Does Covid-19 Put Democracy at Risk?'V-Dem Institute Policy Brief 23. Gothenburg: Varieties of Democracy Institute, University of Gothenburg. Available at: www.v-dem.net/media/filer_public/52/eb/52eb913a-b1ad-4e55-9b4b-3710ff70d1bf/pb_23.pdf (accessed 17 September 2020).

Magsambol, B. (2021). 'Philippines Reaches Grim Milestone of 2 Million COVID-19 Cases', Rappler. 1 September. Available at: www.rappler.com/nation/coronavirus-cases-philippines-september-1-2021 (accessed 4 September 2021).

Mangosing, F. (2020). 'Ex-Soldier Shot Dead by Cop in QC Laid to Rest with Military Honors', Inquirer.net. 26 April. Available at: https://newsinfo.inquirer.net/1264964/ex-soldier-shot-dead-by-cop-in-qc-laid-to-rest-with-military-honors (accessed 16 May 2020).

Mann, M. (1984). 'The Autonomous Power of the State: Its Origins, Mechanisms, and Results'. *Archives Europeennes de Sociologie/European Journal of Sociology/Europaisches Archiv Fur Soziologie*, 25(2): 185–213. https://doi.org/10.1017/S0003975600004239.

Mao, Y. (2021). 'Political Institutions, State Capacity, and Crisis Management: A Comparison of China and South Korea'. *International Political Science Review*, 42(3): 316–332. https://doi.org/10.1177/0192512121994026.

Mendoza, R.U. (2021). 'The Philippine Economy under the Pandemic: From Asian Tiger to Sick Man Again?', Brookings. 2 August. Available at: www.brookings.edu/blog/order-from-chaos/2021/08/02/the-philippine-economy-under-the-pandemic-from-asian-tiger-to-sick-man-again (accessed 23 September 2021).

Meyer, B. (2020). *Pandemic Populism: An Analysis of Populist Leaders' Responses to Covid-19*. London: Tony Blair Institute for Global Change. Available at: https://institute.global/policy/pandemic-populism-analysis-populist-leaders-responses-covid-19 (accessed 3 November 2020).

Migdal, J.S. (1988). *Strong Societies and Weak States: State–Society Relations and State Capabilities in the Third World*. Princeton, NJ: Princeton University Press. https://doi.org/10.1515/9780691212852.

Moffit, B. (2016). *The Global Rise of Populism*. Stanford, CA: Stanford University Press.

Mudde, C. (2015). 'The Problem with Populism', *Guardian*. 17 February. Available at: www.theguardian.com/commentisfree/2015/feb/17/problem-populism-syriza-podemos-dark-side-europe (accessed 21 August 2020).

Navarro, S., M.H. Yusingco, and S.V. Sison (2020). 'Interrogating the Centralization–Decentralization Tension in the Philippines in the Midst of the COVID-19 Pandemic'. Working paper. https://doi.org/10.2139/ssrn.3721883.

O'Donnell, G. (1994). 'Delegative Democracy'. *Journal of Democracy*, 5(1): 55–69. https://doi.org/10.1353/jod.1994.0010.

Olanday, D., and J. Rigby (2020). 'Inside the World's Longest and Strictest Coronavirus Lockdown in the Philippines', *The Telegraph*. 11 July. Available at: www.telegraph.co.uk/global-health/science-and-disease/insideworlds-longest-strictest-coronavirus-lockdown-philippines (accessed 29 August 2020).

Patag, K.J. (2020). 'NBI Going After Social Media Users Who Criticize Government, Too', *Philippine Star*. 2 April. Available at: www.philstar.com/headlines/2020/04/02/2005013/diokno-nbi-going-after-social-media-users-who-criticize-governmenttoo (accessed 19 May 2020).

Pernia, R.A. (2022). 'Explaining the High Political Trust in the Philippines: The Role of Citizen's Health and Political Values'. *Philippine Political Science Journal*, 43: 191–222.

Pulse Asia (2020). 'The National Administration and the President's Handling of the COVID-19 Pandemic', Pulse Asia Research Inc. 8 October. Available at: www.pulseasia.ph/september-2020-nationwide-survey-on-the-national-administration-and-the-presidents-handling-of-the-covid-19-pandemic (accessed 9 October 2020).

Ramos, C.M. (2020). 'MECO Exec Apologizes to Taiwan over OFW Deportation Issue', Inquirer.net. 29 April. Available at: https://globalnation.inquirer.net/187323/meco-exec-apologizes-to-taiwan-over-ofw-deportation-issue (accessed 13 May 2020).

Ranada, P. (2020). '56,000 Words on the Virus: Duterte's Crisis Messaging All Bluster, Little Science', Rappler. 6 May. Available at: www.rappler.com/newsbreak/in-depth/duterte-crisis-messaging-bluster-little-science-words-coronavirus (accessed 10 May 2020).

Romero, D., and E. Baculinao (2020). 'First Coronavirus Death Outside China Reported in Philippines', NBC News. 2 February. Available at: www.nbcnews.com/news/world/first-coronavirus-death-outside-china-reported-philippines-n1128371 (accessed 22 October 2020).

Serhan, Y. (2020). 'The Pandemic Isn't a Death Knell for Populism', *The Atlantic*. 22 August. Available at: www.theatlantic.com/international/archive/2020/08/populism-will-survive-the-pandemic/615358 (accessed 4 September 2020).

Serikbayeva, B., K. Abdulla, and Y. Oskenbayev. (2020). 'State Capacity in Responding to COVID-19'. Munich: University Library of Munich. Available at: https://ideas.repec.org/p/pra/mprapa/101511.html (accessed 6 October 2021).

Teehankee, J.C. (2017). 'Was Duterte's Rise Inevitable?'. In N. Curato (ed.), *A Duterte Reader: Critical Essays on Rodrigo Duterte's Early Presidency*. Quezon City: Ateneo de Manila University Press/Bughaw, pp. 37–56.

Teehankee, J.C. (2020a). 'Duterte's COVID-19 Powers and the Paradox of the Philippine Presidency'. *CSEAS Newsletter*, 78 (28 April). Available at: https://covid-19chronicles.cseas.kyoto-u.ac.jp/post-007-html (accessed 28 April 2020).

Teehankee, J.C. (2020b). 'Rodrigo Duterte's War on Many Fronts', East Asia Forum. 9 August. Available at: www.eastasiaforum.org/2020/08/09/rodrigo-dutertes-war-on-many-fronts (accessed 9 August 2020).

Teehankee, J.C. (2021). 'The Philippines in 2020: COVID-19 Pandemic Threatens Duterte's Populist Legacy'. *Asian Survey*, 61(1): 130–137. https://doi.org/10.1525/AS.2021.61.1.130.

Teehankee, J.C. (2022). 'The Philippines in 2021: Twilight of the Duterte Presidency'. *Asian Survey*, 62(1): 126–136. https://doi.org/10.1525/as.2022.62.1.12.

Teehankee, J.C., and C.A.A. Calimbahin (2020). 'Mapping the Philippines' Defective Democracy'. *Asian Affairs: An American Review*, 47(2): 97–125. https://doi.org/10.1080/00927678.2019.1702801.

Teehankee, J.C., and Y. Kasuya (2020). 'The 2019 Midterm Elections in the Philippines: Party System Pathologies and Duterte's Populist Mobilization'. *Asian Journal of Comparative Politics*, 5(1): 69–81. https://doi.org/10.1177/2057891119896425.

Teehankee, J.C., and M.R. Thompson (2016). 'Electing a Strongman'. *Journal of Democracy*, 27(4): 125–134. https://doi.org/10.1353/jod.2016.0068.

Thompson, M.R. (2019). 'The Rise of Illiberal Democracy in the Philippines: Duterte's Early Presidency'. In I. Deinla and B. Dressel (eds), *From Aquino II to Duterte (2010–2018): Change, Continuity—and Rupture*. Singapore: ISEAS-Yusof Ishak Institute, pp. 39–61.

Thompson, M.R. (2020). 'The COVID-19 Pandemic, the "War on Drugs", and Duterte's Brute Force Governance in the Philippines'. *Panorama: Insights into Asian and European Affairs*, 1: 45–54.

Urbinati, N. (2020). 'The Pandemic Hasn't Killed Populism', *Foreign Affairs*. 6 August. Available at: www.foreignaffairs.com/print/node/1126370 (accessed 16 September 2020).

Vu, K., P. Nguyen, and J. Pearson (2020). 'After Aggressive Mass Testing, Vietnam Says it Contains Coronavirus Outbreak', Reuters. 30 April. Available at: www.reuters.com/article/us-health-coronavirus-vietnam-fight-insi-idUSKBN22B34H (accessed 1 November 2020).

5

Local Governance and COVID-19's Health Impact

Evidence from Vietnam

Duc Anh Dang and Anh Tran

5.1 Introduction

More developed countries could mitigate the adverse effects of a health crisis by better preparing for it through having adequate responses and preventative infrastructure. However, the appearance and evolution of the COVID-19 pandemic show that some developing countries with limited resources and inferior healthcare capacities could respond well and control the spread of the pandemic better than many developed countries with higher capacity. The natural question is: what aspects of a state, such as legitimacy and capacity, may contribute to these successes?

In theory, state legitimacy should encourage individuals to trust, support, and participate with the government, resulting in increased compliance with laws and regulations (UNDP et al. 2021). In the case of the COVID-19 pandemic, state legitimacy assists translating tight measures into efficient pandemic control (Mizrahi et al. 2021; Liang et al. 2020). Previous research has shown that state capacity has a favourable impact on development outcomes under a variety of regime types and that high state capacity can aid non-democratic regimes in succeeding and gaining legitimacy (Hanson 2015; Knutsen 2013). It also stresses the importance of state capability in developing, adopting, and fulfilling state tasks and policies in the event of a pandemic (Persson and Povitkina 2017). The greater the state capacity to provide adequate health infrastructure to assess risks and health system resources to respond to a health crisis, the lower the rates of infection and mortality (Serikbayeva et al. 2021). In this context, we can use the terms state capacity and governance capacity interchangeably, based on Fukuyama's (2013) definition of governance as 'a government's ability to make and enforce rules, and to deliver services, regardless of whether that government is democratic or not' (cited in Serikbayeva et al. 2021: 921–922). This relationship is more likely to exist in Vietnam, an authoritarian country where the party-state dominates society (Shanks et al. 2004; Kleinen 2015).

Duc Anh Dang and Anh Tran, *Local Governance and COVID-19's Health Impact*. In: *How States Respond to Crisis*.
Edited by: Rachel M. Gisselquist and Andrea Vaccaro, Oxford University Press. © UNU-WIDER (2025).
DOI: 10.1093/9780198907237.003.0005

The objective of this study is to examine the relationship between the effectiveness of the local governance and COVID-19's health impacts in Vietnam. Vietnam offers an attractive setting to study when it has limited resources but has low confirmed COVID-19 cases and deaths (Abuza 2021). By using the Provincial Governance and Public Administration Performance Index (PAPI) and COVID-19 data at provincial levels in 2019, this chapter will describe the evolution of COVID-19 and the responses of the Vietnamese state in preparing and confronting the pandemic. It also examines the relationship between the effectiveness of local governance—especially in terms of its capacity in providing public healthcare services and legitimacy understood as citizen participation, transparency, and accountability—and pandemic health outcomes (measured by the number of confirmed cases and deaths).

The key findings of the study are as follows. Vietnam has been able to weather the COVID-19 pandemic due to improved governance. The findings suggest that increased governance effectiveness is significantly associated with decreased infection rates. Particularly, increased transparency is significantly associated with fewer confirmed cases.[1] For the impact of the level of participation, we find that provinces that have higher-quality village head elections, or where people have more opportunities for participation, especially participation in formal and informal associations, and have voted in the National Assembly election, tend to have fewer confirmed cases. At the same time, the findings show the importance of health system capacity in the battle against COVID-19.

The remainder of the chapter is structured as follows. Section 5.2 briefly describes the outbreak of COVID-19 in Vietnam and its response. This is followed by Section 5.3, which provides a more detailed discussion of the governance capacities that have facilitated Vietnam's efforts to manage the COVID-19 pandemic and imperfections of current administrative decentralization, and how these affected its COVID-19 policy responses. Section 5.4 discusses the data together with the descriptive analysis, and then presents the empirical model. Section 5.5 provides the estimation results. Section 5.6 concludes.

5.2 Overview of COVID-19 in Vietnam and its responses

As a neighbouring country to China, Vietnam has been extremely cautious and responded immediately after COVID-19 was discovered in China. When the first COVID-19 cases in Vietnam were confirmed in January 2020, the government began to take preventative steps, such as tightening entry-screening procedures and extending the Lunar New Year break for schools (Dang 2022). In January 2020, the Vietnamese government immediately announced the first National Response

[1] This result is consonant with other previous studies such as Serikbayeva et al. (2021), who found that state effectiveness reduces the number of COVID-19 deaths.

Plan and formed the National Steering Committee (NSC) to implement this plan. The NSC is central to the governance and oversight of the COVID-19 response, strengthening inter-provincial cooperation and delegating responsibility for the response elements to various central ministries (Hartley et al. 2021).

The NSC is chaired by Deputy Prime Minister Vu Duc Dam, and it manages four sub-committees in technical and logistical areas, with high-level involvement from 14 line ministries, the National Assembly, the media, and information technology businesses. Each ministry and level of government—central, provincial, district, and commune—has specific tasks and responsibilities outlined in the plan. The prime minister and deputy prime minister were able to spearhead a whole-of-society strategy to combat COVID-19 thanks to the swift mobilization of financial and human resources, based on the idea of 'protecting people's health first' (WHO 2020).

As the number of cases could increase and the virus could spread further in Vietnam, Vietnam carried out a targeted three-week quarantine while developing a broader quarantine and quarantine policy to control COVID-19. The government knew it was important to limit viral transmission as quickly as possible to protect the country's economy when the first wave of the outbreak began in early March (Figure 5.1), thanks to an imported case from the United Kingdom. Vietnam closed its borders and halted international flights from mainland China in February, gradually expanding this to the United Kingdom, Europe, the United States, and finally the rest of the world in March, imposing a 14-day mandatory

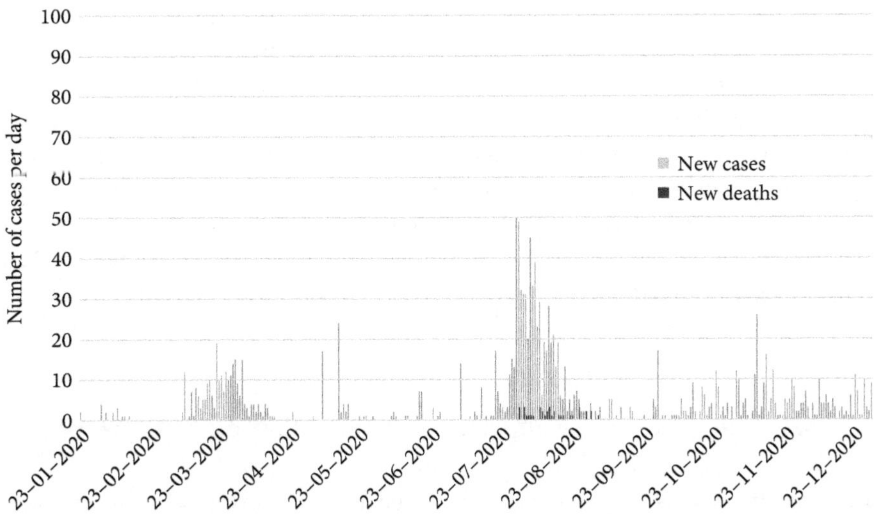

Figure 5.1 Evolution of new COVID-19 confirmed cases and deaths in 2020.

Note: COVID-19 = coronavirus disease.

Source: Authors' compilation based on data from the COVID-19 Data Repository by the Center for Systems Science and Engineering (CSSE) at Johns Hopkins University.

quarantine on all visitors, including Vietnamese nationals. This allowed authorities to keep track of COVID-19 cases imported from other countries and prevent additional local transmission, which may have spread to the rest of the community. Even though there was never a nationwide lockdown, the country was subjected to stringent physical separation measures. On 1 April 2020, the prime minister issued a countrywide two-week physical distancing order, which was extended by a week in large cities and hotspots, advising people to stay at home, closing non-essential enterprises, and restricting public transit. After two weeks without a locally reported case, schools and businesses were permitted to resume operations, and individuals were able to return to their daily routines by early May (Malhotra 2020).

As of July 2020, there had been no additional COVID-19 incidents in Vietnam caused by local transmission for more than three months. The country entered its second wave of illness when the ministry of health announced additional cases in Da Nang. On 28 July, the city of Da Nang was shut down for 15 days. Hundreds of illnesses linked to Da Nang were recorded around the country, with the first death on 31 July. In less than two months, Vietnam had successfully controlled the epidemic for the second time, employing the same strategies as in the previous outbreak, and had resumed practically all economic operations. People who were infected abroad and were quarantined by the authorities were the cases in late 2020 (Dang 2022).

The government's commitment had remained the same in 2021, and it made efforts to achieve dual objectives of disease control and economic development. However, the fourth COVID-19 wave, which began in May 2021, resulted in the greatest increase in locally transmitted infections since the start of the pandemic (Figure 5.2). By late May, new highly contagious coronavirus variants were causing hundreds of positive cases per day, a low incidence rate by international standards but the highest in Vietnam's history. As a result, authorities in the affected areas, as well as those in the country's three major cities—Ho Chi Minh City, Hanoi, and Da Nang—imposed severe mobility restrictions. As a result of the outbreak, several companies and industrial zones in the Bac Giang and Bac Ninh provinces, two important industrial centres in Vietnam's north, were forced to close (Ngoc 2021). As of 31 July, all-time total infections stood at 145,686 cases and 1,306 deaths.

5.3 The governance effectiveness in combating COVID-19

Because Vietnam is a one-party state, all government institutions at all levels are subordinate to the Vietnamese Communist Party. Decisions that can be taken by a single agency tend to be implemented quickly. Vietnamese institutions have often demonstrated an impressive capacity to mobilize and achieve

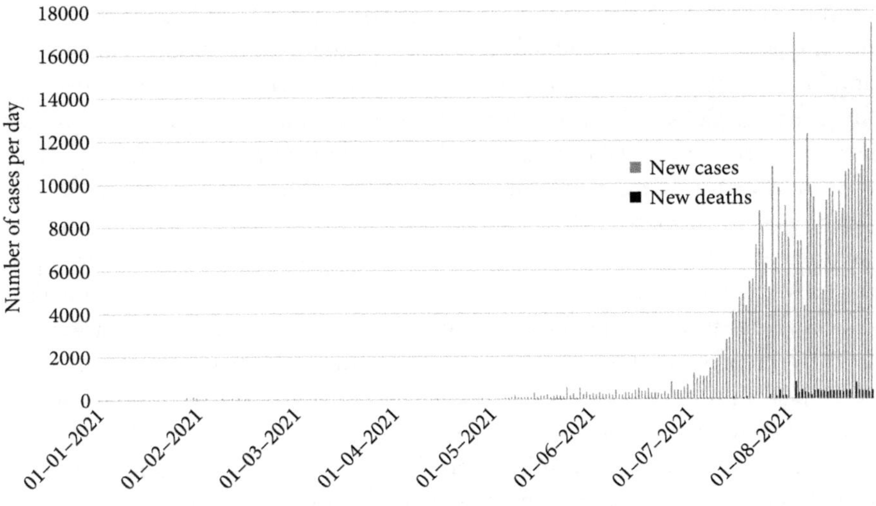

Figure 5.2 Evolution of new COVID-19 confirmed cases and deaths in 2021.

Note: COVID-19 = coronavirus disease.
Source: Authors' compilation based on data from the COVID-19 Data Repository by the Center for Systems Science and Engineering (CSSE) at Johns Hopkins University.

targets—strong governance leadership with effective multi-sectoral collaboration and coordination and successful mobilization of national resources using a whole-of-society approach (Malesky et al. 2014). For example, Vietnam acted quickly in early 2020 in response to the first signs of the coronavirus pandemic. National borders were closed and a testing and quarantine system was immediately put in place. Under the strong leadership of the government and effective multi-sectoral coordination and collaboration, a strategic approach to controlling and detecting COVID-19 has been successfully and rapidly implemented. Recent examples in 2021 include the supply and distribution of vaccines, as well as the deployment of medical equipment and health workers from central hospitals and provinces to virus hotspots. These were decisions that did not necessitate the alignment of the authority structure's fragments. The government drew lessons from previous epidemics and pandemics and acted on scientific evidence and expert advice (Pincus 2021).

Given the pandemic's complexity and multiple consequences, governments had to adapt quickly and ensure adequate coordination capacity was in place. Although the central government's standards and rules governing isolation and movement between provinces are clear and consistently enforced, the ability to tailor the response to local conditions would be preferable. This could be seen in the first COVID-19 waves in 2020 and the first half of 2021 (Pincus 2021). The central government's clear vision of 'people's safety first', which was accepted as the national consensus, as well as its rules on quarantine, social distancing, and movement between provinces, free testing and treatment, and support for people in quarantine centres and affected by the pandemic were widely understood and followed by local governments and people. This helped Vietnam contain the first waves of COVID-19 at relatively low levels of infection and made a robust economic recovery possible, building public trust in government. This high level of trust in turn made the government's responses more effective. More than 90 per cent of Vietnamese respondents between May 2020 and May 2021 believed the government was handling the situation 'very' or 'somewhat' well, according to the COVID-19 behaviour tracker, which was created by YouGov (2021), a British data analytics firm, and Imperial College London. Even when the worst wave of COVID-19 infections hit Vietnam in May 2021, roughly 83 per cent of Vietnamese respondents polled said they trusted the government's pandemic response, which was well above that of comparable data in Southeast Asia (Nguyen 2021).

Moreover, rather than controlling the flow of information, Vietnamese authorities chose to apply a more flexible strategy by prioritizing transparency and allowing information sharing. Vietnam is a fully authoritarian state, a type of regime that is not always transparent. The state is aware, however, that in matters of public health, transparency and communication are critical, and it gained legitimacy through its performance (Abuza 2020). Transparency efforts have also helped to alleviate scepticism about the state's reporting on COVID-19. Information on the COVID-19 pandemic, scenarios, and government policy interventions was disseminated in an open, diverse, and timely manner, followed by widespread policy consultation. The ministry of health has made all reported cases public, allowing for more in-depth analysis by data scientists and bloggers, as well as support from public health experts (Nguyen and Malesky 2020). Vietnam was credited with turning the tide of public mistrust into firm confidence by handling the pandemic transparently and effectively. This transparency aims to boost the trust of people and businesses in the fight against the pandemic, especially in policy responses, to achieve the dual goal of pandemic containment and economic recovery. This approach showed how Vietnam combined democratic principles with authoritarian practices in a way that publicly promoted government legitimacy (Hartley et al. 2021).

However, the pandemic has also highlighted challenges in governance that call for reform in preparation for future crises. When the pandemic was out of control in July 2021, leading to a lockdown in many provinces, the decentralization system between the central and local governments showed weaknesses. The current local administration has two functions—organizing and ensuring the enforcement of the law in the community and determining local issues. It expresses a fundamental principle that policies and laws should be created by central agencies and that local governments are responsible for organizing their implementation under the supervision of higher government agencies (the structure of Vietnamese administration is illustrated in Figure 5.3). In addition, the authority of local governments is determined on the basis of the division of authority between central and

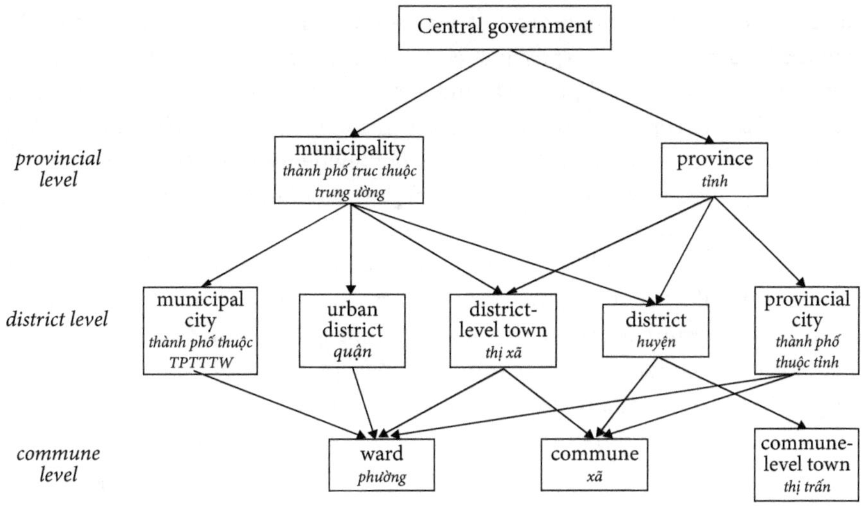

Figure 5.3 Vietnamese administrative structure.

Source: Authors' compilation.

local government agencies and between different levels of local government. This provision aims to create a space for local initiatives and self-responsibility and the effective control of power (Vietnam Law and Legal Forum 2017). This means provinces may have policies that, to some extent, conflict with those issued by the central government.

During the first waves, the system's shortcomings were exposed when several provinces implemented differing restrictions for mobility (travel and transportation), creating some supply-chain interruptions. The various COVID-19 policies are implemented by local governments, sometimes in defiance of central government or health ministry directives (Tran 2021). The expenses became more obvious in the fourth wave of the Delta variety, when the magnitude of new cases and deaths was substantially higher, putting the health system under strain. They are primarily the result of disagreements between different levels of government on how to combat the virus while also achieving economic growth. Local governments implemented a variety of social distancing, testing, and quarantine regimes, which were usually inconsistent and changed. People and businesses were perplexed by the shifts and disparities between locations. Despite the criteria for applying social distancing measures, local authorities quarantined entire villages in several cases where there were no active cases (Government of Vietnam 2021). Local authorities were cautious because they feared punishment for rising case levels—not for extreme control measures that violated central government rules.

Local authorities' conservatism was evident in local travel and transportation restrictions within and between provinces, as well as related testing and quarantine rules. Local governments issued inconsistent travel permit rules—rules that were frequently changed in unpredictable ways—and related test requirements. The increased number of checkpoints and roadblocks disrupted supply networks, especially those of critical products and export goods, as well as increasing testing costs for enterprises. Despite efforts to create 'green routes' or 'bubbles' or to apply standard requirements for air travellers (evidence of two vaccinations or a negative test and no symptoms, as well as following ministry of health quarantine requirements based on the risk level of departure locations), local authorities, fearful of being held responsible for the local case count, imposed harsher conditions that did not follow central government directives. Furthermore, the direction of the central government has been uncertain at times, and laws and regulations have been slowly disseminated, leaving room for interpretation and the implementation of tighter restrictions and requirements at the local level. The strategy shifted from 'zero COVID' to 'safe and flexible adaptation and effective control of the COVID-19 pandemic', but the 'new normal' precondition of vaccination rates approaching community immunity and safety standards and rules (such as for goods and passenger transportation or for businesses to operate safely in the new normal) were vague, complicated, or delayed. As a result, there was a race to the bottom that did not contribute to the national goals of COVID-19 control while safeguarding the economy and livelihoods (Pincus 2021).

5.4 Data description

5.4.1 Measure of pandemic outcomes

We use two indicators that have been frequently employed in the literature to measure the health effects of the pandemic: confirmed COVID-19 cases (i.e. infections) and deaths. These data have been published and updated daily by the ministry of health. Confirmed COVID-19 cases and deaths measure respectively the total number of cases and deaths linked to COVID-19 as of 31 July 2021. We chose this cut-off date because it is before Vietnam implemented widespread lockdowns in many provinces, especially in the south due to the spread of the Delta variant. We also normalized the cases and deaths by the local population to account for between-province differences in population. Figure 5.4 illustrates the spread of COVID-19 over the country in July 2021. We can observe that economic centres with a high population density, such as Da Nang, Hanoi, Ho Chi Minh City, and surrounding areas, tend to have more infections (adjusted by the population). Regions with a low population density, such as the Northern Midland and Mountains, the Central Coast, and the Central Highlands, have fewer infections.

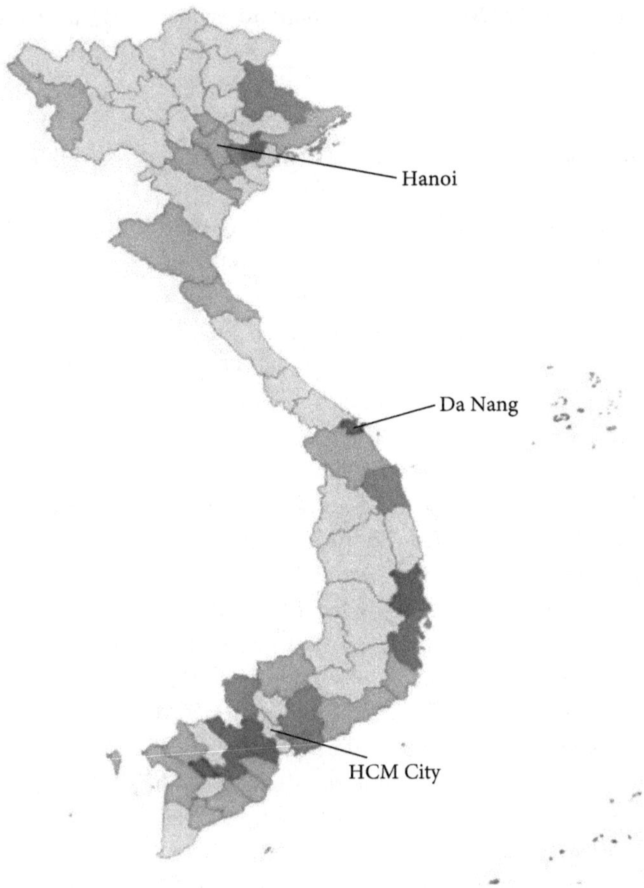

Figure 5.4 Accumulated COVID-19 confirmed cases in provinces by 31 July 2021.

Note: Lighter colours mean a lower level of confirmed cases per 100,000 citizens.
Source Authors' illustration based on Vietnam's ministry of health data. Map created using ArcGIS.

As mentioned in Gisselquist and Vaccaro (2021), the published numbers of confirmed cases may underestimate the actual numbers of infections due to incomplete testing and incomplete testing sensitivity. The number of confirmed deaths is also likely to be underestimated as there are deaths from other diseases not recorded as being caused by COVID-19. However, these measures are commonly used in many studies on COVID-19. For instance, Ferraresi et al. (2020) have used the number of confirmed cases as a measure of COVID-19 health outcomes. Similarly, this measure is used in the studies by Polo (2020) and Qiu et al. (2020). For the number of confirmed deaths, it has been used in Cheibub et al.

(2020), Sebhatu et al. (2020), and Vadlamannati et al. (2021) as a measure of COVID-19 health outcomes.

5.4.2 Measures of effectiveness of local governance

To measure the effectiveness of the local governance, we used PAPI in 2019. This index is created by surveying citizens' opinions on the quality of governance and public services at the local level. This survey has been annually implemented since 2010 by the United Nations Development Program and Vietnam Fatherland Front (UNDP et al. 2012). The survey uses a clustered sampling approach to provide representative citizens' responses to the quality of governance at all levels of the Vietnamese government from the province level to the village. The sample includes all 63 provinces.[2]

Although PAPI is designed to measure overall provincial performance, it is first scored at the individual level and then an unweighted index is calculated by averaging respondent scores (with a score ranging from 10 to 60) and six individual sub-indices (with scores ranging from 1 to 10). The six sub-indices include the following: (1) participation, a measure of the citizens' knowledge, opportunities for participating in local elections, and quality of leaders; (2) transparency measures citizens' access to information such as local budget and land-use plans; (3) accountability measures the interaction level with local authorities—how local governments respond to citizens' appeals or access to justice services; (4) control of corruption measures the level of corruption in service delivery and other services by local governments and their willingness to fight it; (5) public administrative procedures measure the quality of providing certification services, land certificates, and construction permits; and (6) public services delivery measures the quality of social security, public health services, education, and infrastructure in the locality. In all sub-indices, a better score means a higher quality of local governance (Malesky et al. 2014).

Local governance capacity and legitimacy

We understand local governance effectiveness as a combination of state capacity and state legitimacy at the provincial level. In our conceptual framework, capacity reflects the state's ability to provide public services at the local level and legitimacy reflects the state's ability to ensure citizens' compliance with rules.

The measures of governance capacity are based on the idea that prompt policy responses to the health crisis will rely on local governance capacity

[2] CECODES et al. (2012). The Vietnam Governance and Public Administration. Data available at www.papi.vn.

(Toshkov et al. 2021).[3] In order to take appropriate policy measures to address the health crisis, the state needs to be able to provide adequate health infrastructure or public health services to assess the risks and responses to the health crisis. We take the sub-index of the quality of public healthcare and the number of hospital beds per 100,000 people as proxies for local governance capacity.

Legitimacy in the context of COVID-19 can be defined as 'the ability of leaders to win compliance with new public health orders because people share a widespread belief that everyone is complying' (Stuti 2020: 1). We use some potential PAPI dimensions that could impact compliance to assess whether the quality of local governance enhanced compliance. Performance in some PAPI categories could play an influence and is likely to boost citizen trust in local governance, potentially leading to more compliance with social distancing or lockdown regulations. For example, because of the familiarity of participation in local affairs and readiness to obey laws, good performance in participation at local levels could boost citizen compliance. As citizens have a better understanding of local decision-making processes, they may have more faith in local governance and enhancing state legitimacy. Different dimensions of accountability, such as the share of citizens contacting the People's Council successfully or the share of successful appeals of citizens, may also affect compliance because proof of better accountability by local officials may improve willingness to follow their rules (UNDP et al. 2021).

Table 5.1 presents the main variables of our analysis and provides summary statistics for them. For instance, the average score for quality of public healthcare is as high as 1.99, equivalent to 80 per cent of the maximum score, showing that local citizens feel comfortable with the capacity of the state in providing basic health services. On average, 52 per cent of citizens have participated in formal associations; however, only 17 per cent of them have been involved in informal associations. Further, 15 per cent of people have searched for information on state policy and legislation and 14 per cent of people thought that the information they received was useful and reliable; 63 per cent of people were involved in elections and 85 per cent of these participated in village chief elections; and 91 per cent of citizens can successfully contact the People's Council. On average, 21 per cent of citizens' appeals have been satisfactorily answered.

5.5 The relationship between local governance effectiveness and COVID-19's health impacts

To assess the relationship between governance effectiveness and COVID-19 health outcomes, we regress health outcomes on selected proxies (see Table 5.1) of state

[3] Other studies, such as Christensen et al. (2016) and Capano et al. (2020), also discussed governance capacity during crises.

Table 5.1 Descriptive statistics

Variables	N	Mean	SD	Min	Max
Participation					
Opportunities for participation in elections	63	1.44	0.13	1.17	1.81
Participated in formal associations	63	0.52	0.17	0.18	0.83
Participated in informal associations	63	0.17	0.08	0.01	0.39
Voted in People's Council election	63	0.53	0.08	0.34	0.74
Voted in last National Assembly election	63	0.46	0.09	0.27	0.64
Village chief elected	63	0.85	0.07	0.68	0.97
Participated in election	63	0.63	0.07	0.44	0.84
Quality of village head elections	63	1.53	0.17	1.05	1.90
Invited to participate	63	0.60	0.16	0.23	0.93
Voted for winner	63	0.92	0.05	0.76	1.00
Transparency					
Access to information	63	0.83	0.07	0.69	1.04
Searched state policy and legislation	63	0.15	0.05	0.07	0.29
Received information of state policy	63	0.13	0.05	0.06	0.27
Information received useful	63	0.14	0.05	0.06	0.28
Information received reliable	63	0.14	0.05	0.05	0.27
Reasonable waiting time for information	63	1.00	0.01	0.98	1.00
Accountability					
Citizens contacted People's Council	63	0.05	0.03	0.01	0.14

Citizens contacted People's Council successfully	63	0.91	0.14	0.34	1.00
Appeals taken by citizens	63	0.24	0.09	0.09	0.49
Successful appeals of citizens	63	0.21	0.08	0.08	0.41
Capacity					
Quality of public healthcare	63	1.99	0.09	1.70	2.21
Ln(hospital beds/100,000 pop.)	63	0.34	1.17	−3.51	1.88
COVID-19					
Ln(deaths/mil. pop.)	63	−8.27	1.62	−9.21	−3.54
Ln(cases/100,000 pop.)	63	−3.56	2.06	−9.21	−0.24
Controls					
Ln(population density)	63	5.72	1.00	3.93	8.39
Ln(GDP per capita)	63	3.94	0.43	3.03	5.04
Ln(population over 60)	63	4.95	0.70	3.25	6.92

Source: Authors' construction.

capacity and legitimacy at the local level in Vietnam. The regression equation is as follows:

$$Cases_i = \alpha + \beta ELG_i + X_i + \varepsilon_i \quad (1)$$

where $Cases_i$ is the accumulative number of COVID-19 cases or deaths in province i in 2020–2021. Our main variable, ELG_i, is the different proxies for local governance effectiveness in province i in 2019. The main variable is lagged by one year to mitigate the problem of endogeneity. The coefficient of interest is β, capturing the relationship between local governance effectiveness and health indicators. The provinces with better capacity in terms of health systems and efficiency in governance are expected to cope and control the spread of COVID-19 better.

X_i are provincial characteristics. They include province economic wealth, population density, and the age structure of a population. Uneven responses to COVID-19 could be caused by variation in local-level wealth, and the spread of COVID-19 is likely to also be influenced by other socioeconomic factors at the local level, such as population density and the senior population. Therefore, we control for ln(provincial GDP per capita), ln(population density), and ln(population over 60) in the regressions. We control for these three factors in the baseline models. In addition to these three factors, in the full models we also control for regional dummies.

Figure 5.5 shows the estimated regression coefficients for the association between participation and COVID-19 cases (top panel) and deaths (bottom panel). The dots in a coefficient plot reflect a predictor's point estimates, while the spikes represent its 95 per cent confidence intervals. For each estimated relationship, we investigate two specifications. The details of the specifications used in the regression model and results can be found in Tables 5.A1 to 5.A5 in the Appendix. The first is a baseline specification, where the independent variables include different categories for the level of participation. As previously mentioned, controls in baseline models include provincial characteristics such as the elderly population, GDP per capita, and population density. These controls allow us to explain the differences in cases and death rates across provinces with varying degrees of governance quality (Serikbayeva et al. 2021). In the full specification, we additionally control for regional dummies, examining the possibility that policy measures may vary within a region.[4]

As shown by Figure 5.5's top panel, provinces where people have more opportunities for participation in elections generally tend to have fewer COVID-19 infections. Since the outcome variable is the natural logarithm of confirmed

[4] Vietnam has been divided into six regions: Northern Midland and Mountain, Red River Delta, Central Coast, Central Highlands, South East, and Mekong River Delta.

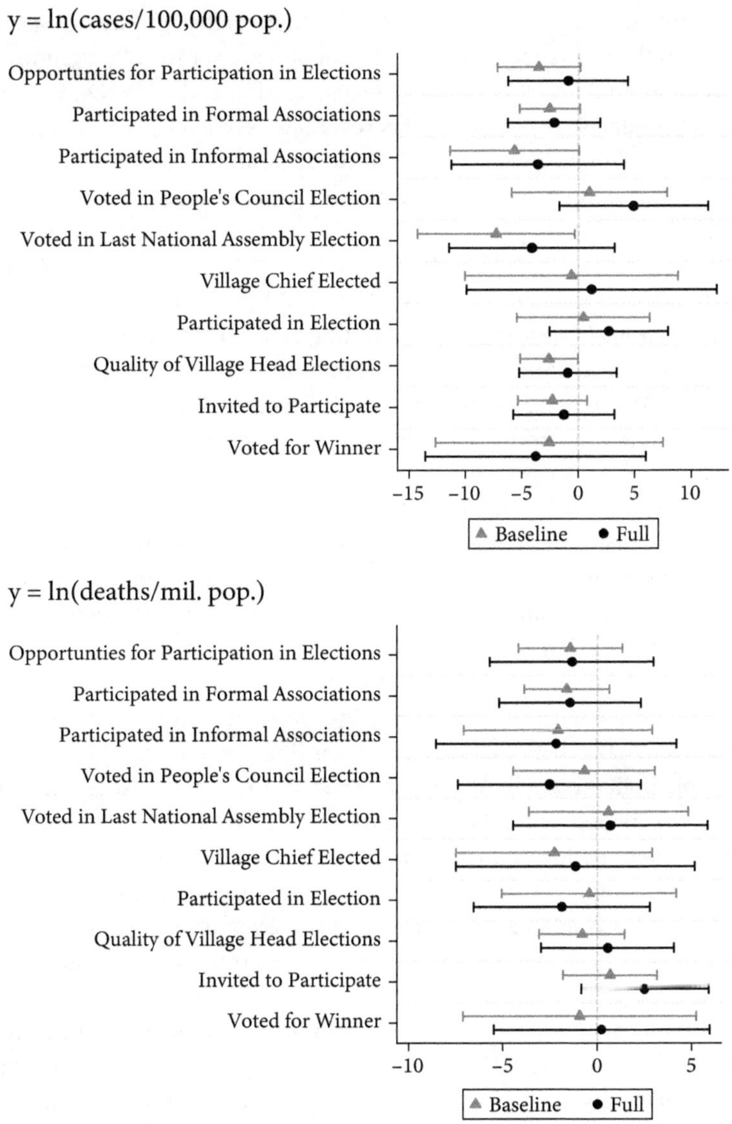

Figure 5.5 Relationship between participation and COVID-19 cases (top panel) and participation and COVID-19 deaths (bottom panel).
Source: Authors' construction.

COVID-19 cases, one standard deviation higher for opportunities for participation in elections will reduce roughly 44 per cent of the predicted number of COVID-19 cases over 100,000 people. In particular, the coefficients are significant at the 90 per cent level for several sub-components, such as participation in formal and informal associations, voting in the National Assembly election, and the quality of village head elections. The other coefficients are not statistically significant. In the full specification, we do not observe statistically significant relationships between different measures of participation and COVID-19 cases. This shows that the effects are not different across regions. We observe statistically non-significant associations between different participation measures and the number of COVID-19 deaths, as shown in the bottom panel in Figure 5.5. These findings suggest that higher participation is not effective in reducing the number of deaths.

Figure 5.6 shows the relationship between the 2019 provincial scores for each dimension of transparency and COVID-19 health outcomes. As seen in the top panel, apart from the last sub-index, waiting time for information, each of the remaining five dimensions has a significant and negative relationship with the number of COVID-19 cases. For example, a one-standard-deviation increase in the score of access to information leads to an approximately 7 per cent lower number of confirmed cases over 100,000 citizens. For the dimension of information received useful, a one-standard-deviation increase in the score led to an 8 per cent decrease in the number of confirmed cases over 100,000 citizens. Similarly, a one-standard-deviation increase in the dimension of reliable information received leads to 7.3 per cent less cases over 100,000 citizens. All this fits with the notion that improvements in governance effectiveness lead to more desirable health impacts. These findings are also consonant with the previous studies showing that transparency increases trust in local governance. For example, Vu (2021) demonstrates there is a link between public trust in governance and policy compliance. Public trust in local governance increases the likelihood that people will follow policies and regulations during the COVID-19 epidemic, thereby reducing infections and deaths. When we control for regional dummies, the estimates are almost the same, and most remain statistically significant at the 90 per cent level. As seen in Figure 5.6's bottom panel, we do not find strong evidence of an inverse relationship between transparency and COVID-19 deaths.

The top panel in Figure 5.7 shows the relationship between different dimensions of accountability and COVID-19 cases. The estimates are inverse and significant in some dimensions, including appeals taken by citizens and successful appeals of citizens. The results indicate that improvements in these two dimensions will reduce the number of infections. When we add the regional dummies into the models, the relationship between accountability and COVID-19 cases becomes inverse for all dimensions of accountability, but significant (at the 90 per cent level) only for appeals taken by citizens. The regression estimates of the relationships between different dimensions of accountability and COVID-19 deaths show that none of the dimensions significantly predicts COVID-19, as illustrated in Figure 5.7's bottom panel.

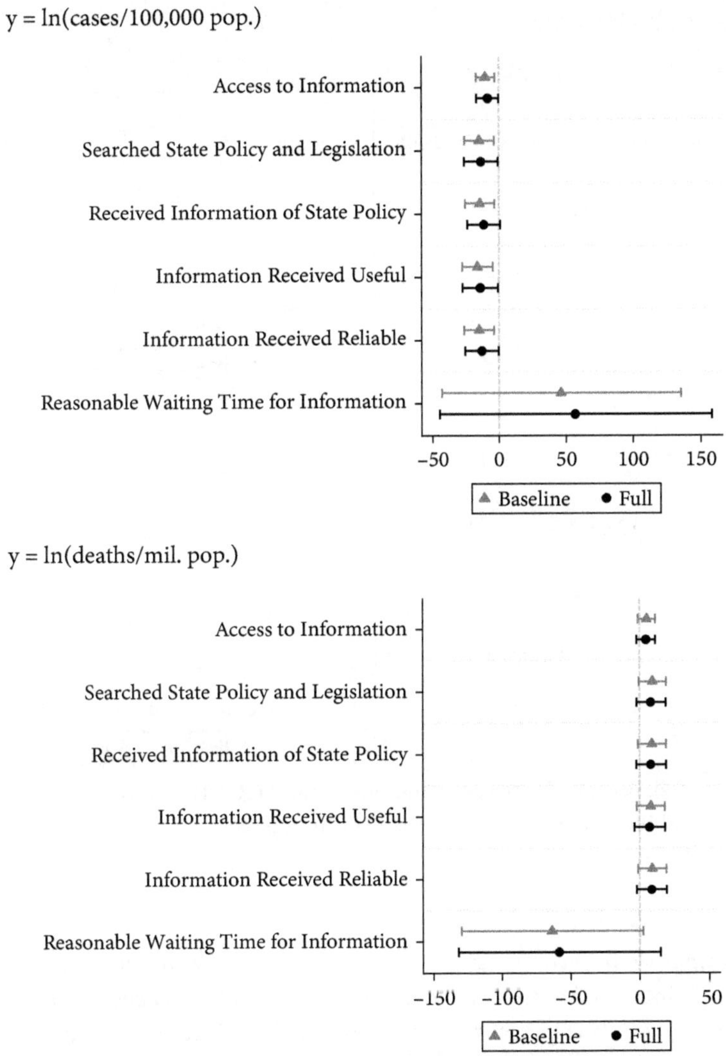

Figure 5.6 Relationship between transparency and COVID-19 cases (top panel) and transparency and COVID-19 deaths (bottom panel).
Source: Authors' construction.

A strong and effective public health infrastructure is required to respond to any health crisis, such as pandemics. It is also needed to tackle ongoing concerns, such as the prevention and management of communicable and non-communicable diseases (Pandey et al. 2021). Nguyen and Malesky (2020) argued that the standard of care in Vietnamese hospitals has steadily improved. Vietnamese citizens should therefore no longer be concerned about the costs of COVID-19

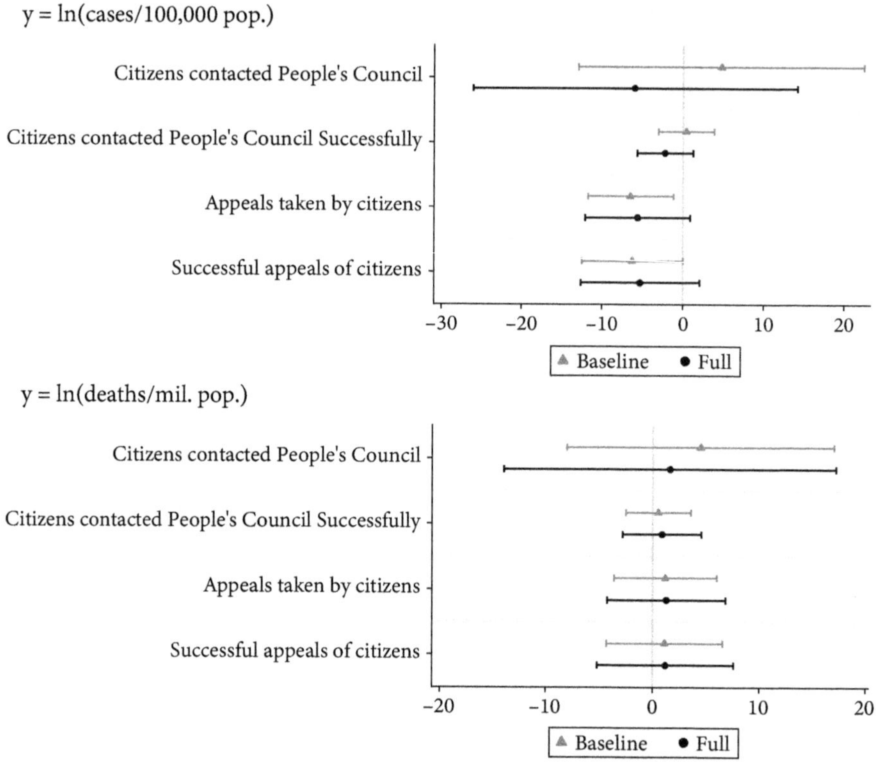

Figure 5.7 Relationship between accountability and COVID-19 cases (top panel) and accountability and COVID-19 deaths (bottom panel).
Source: Authors' construction.

tests (formal or informal), associated hospitalization, and centralized quarantine, which increased their willingness to comply with extensive contact tracing and strict quarantine measures. The top panel in Figure 5.8 shows that the estimated coefficient on governance capacity, which is proxied by ln(number of hospital beds per 100,000 people), is statistically significant at the 90 per cent level and negative, meaning that better health infrastructure is significantly associated with lower infection rates. The coefficient is not significant when we control for regional dummies, but the magnitude is similar. The coefficients on quality of public healthcare are negative, appearing to suggest that the higher perception of citizens on the quality of public healthcare will lower COVID-19 confirmed cases, but the effect is statistically non-significant. For the association between governance capacity and deaths from COVID-19, the slope coefficients are not statistically significant (Figure 5.8, bottom panel).

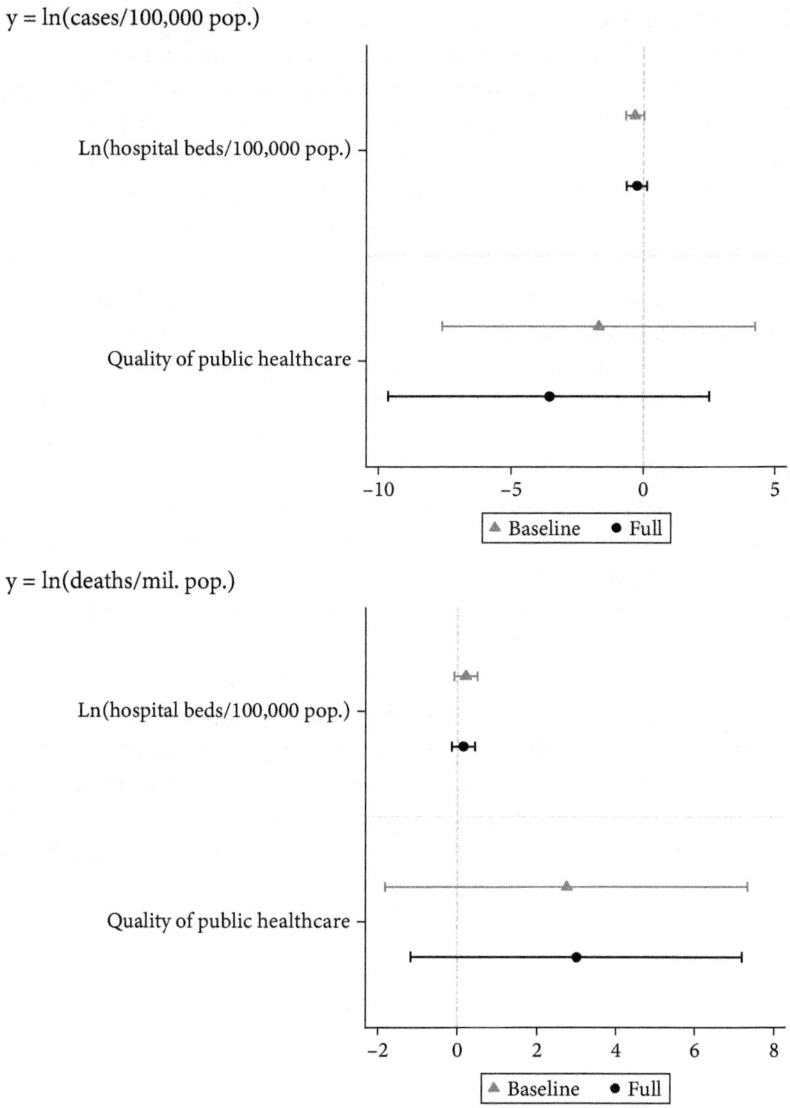

Figure 5.8 Relationship between capacity and COVID-19 cases (top panel) and capacity and COVID-19 deaths (bottom panel).
Source: Authors' construction.

5.6 Conclusion

In this chapter, we investigated the various aspects of governance effectiveness in explaining the variation in COVID-19 confirmed cases and death levels in Vietnam. We use PAPI in 2019 to measure the effectiveness of the local governance and examine its relationship with health outcomes such as confirmed cases and deaths. One of the major findings suggests that health system capacity is critical in the fight against COVID-19. The effect of transparency, which is consistently negative and statistically significant across all model specifications, shows that increased transparency is significantly associated with lower confirmed rates. For the impact of the level of participation, we find that provinces that have higher-quality village head elections or where people have more opportunities for participation tend to have lower infected cases, especially those where people participate in formal and informal associations and have voted in the National Assembly election. Although the results may not imply causality, the statistical correlation between local governance effectiveness and health indicators, controlling for other factors, provides evidence that good governance is importance in dealing with a crisis (UNDP et al. 2021).

The empirical findings of the study have some implications. The first is to increase governance effectiveness by increasing transparency and accountability at all levels. These characteristics are the result of a long-term investment in the quality and credibility of institutions. The second is the importance of having capable governance. While policy implementation characteristics influence policy outcomes, it is critical to facilitate the accumulation of governance capacity. The COVID-19 experience emphasizes the need to strengthen the effective public health system with adequate investments in trained personnel and infrastructure (Serikbayeva et al. 2021). Gaps in healthcare infrastructure and resource distribution across jurisdictions should be evaluated and adjusted as needed. It is also necessary to create effective mechanisms for leveraging the private health sector's capacity.

Appendix

Table 5.A1 The relationship between participation and COVID-19 cases

VARIABLES	(1)	(2)	(3)	(4)	(5)	(6)	(7)	(8)	(9)	(10)
	y = ln(cases/100,000 pop.)									
Opportunities for participation in elections	−3.391* (1.870)									
Participated in formal associations		−2.493* (1.317)								
Participated in informal associations			−5.566* (2.784)							
Voted in People's Council election				1.357 (3.415)						
Voted in last National Assembly election					−6.968* (3.527)					
Village chief elected						−0.345 (4.613)				
Participated in election							0.154 (2.810)			
Quality of village head elections								−2.417* (1.220)		
Invited to participate									−2.202 (1.486)	
Voted for winner										−2.748 (5.002)
Regional dummies	No	No	No	No	No	No	No	No	No	No
Observations	63	63	63	63	63	63	63	63	63	63
R2	0.127	0.123	0.133	0.085	0.150	0.082	0.082	0.121	0.111	0.087

VARIABLES	(11)	(12)	(13)	(14)	(15)	(16)	(17)	(18)	(19)	(20)
Opportunities for participation in elections	−0.894 (2.567)									
Participated in formal associations		−2.146 (1.998)								
Participated in informal associations			−3.562 (3.637)							
Voted in People's Council election				4.523 (3.052)						
Voted in last National Assembly election					−4.068 (3.607)					
Village chief elected						1.126 (5.389)				
Participated in election							2.696 (2.510)			
Quality of village head elections								−0.849 (1.961)		
Invited to participate									−1.269 (2.120)	
Voted for winner										−3.741 (4.853)
Regional dummies	Yes	Yes	Yes	Yes	Yes	Yes	Yes	Yes	Yes	Yes
Observations	63	63	63	63	63	63	63	63	63	63
R2	0.275	0.285	0.284	0.299	0.293	0.274	0.281	0.275	0.279	0.281

Note: Robust standard errors in parentheses; $^{*}p < 0.10$, $^{**}p < 0.05$, $^{***}p < 0.01$. Constant coefficient measured but not reported. Estimates for control variables are not reported. Control variables include ln(population density), ln(population over 60), ln(GDP per capita), and regional dummies. Regional dummies include indicators for the Red River Delta, Central Coast, Central Highlands, Southeast, and Mekong River Delta.
Source: Authors' calculations.

Table 5.A2 The relationship between participation and COVID-19 deaths

VARIABLES	(1)	(2)	(3)	(4)	(5)	(6)	(7)	(8)	(9)	(10)
	y = ln(deaths/mil. pop.)									
Opportunities for participation in elections	−1.329 (1.374)									
Participated in formal associations		−1.566 (1.125)								
Participated in informal associations			−1.974 (2.527)							
Voted in People's Council election				−0.191 (1.850)						
Voted in last National Assembly election					0.849 (2.126)					
Village chief elected						−1.978 (2.638)				
Participated in election							−0.760 (2.311)			
Quality of village head elections								−0.618 (1.115)		
Invited to participate									0.775 (1.244)	
Voted for winner										−1.147 (3.176)
Regional dummies	No	No	No	No	No	No	No	No	No	No
Observations	63	63	63	63	63	63	63	63	63	63
R2	0.163	0.178	0.162	0.152	0.153	0.159	0.153	0.156	0.158	0.153

VARIABLES	(11)	(12)	(13)	(14)	(15)	(16)	(17)	(18)	(19)	(20)
Opportunities for participation in elections	−1.161 (2.084)									
Participated in formal associations		−1.376 (1.823)								
Participated in informal associations			−2.008 (3.106)							
Voted in People's Council election				−2.104 (2.243)						
Voted in last National Assembly election					0.802 (2.540)					
Village chief elected						−0.968 (3.168)				
Participated in election							−1.910 (2.331)			
Quality of village head elections								0.693 (1.606)		
Invited to participate									2.539 (1.625)	
Voted for winner										0.165 (2.844)
Regional dummies	Yes	Yes	Yes	Yes	Yes	Yes	Yes	Yes	Yes	Yes
Observations	63	63	63	63	63	63	63	63	63	63
R2	0.296	0.300	0.297	0.301	0.293	0.293	0.298	0.294	0.328	0.292

Note: Robust standard errors in parentheses; $^{*}p < 0.10$, $^{**}p < 0.05$, $^{***}p < 0.01$. Constant coefficient measured *but* not reported. Estimates for control variables are not reported. Control variables include ln(population density), ln(population over 60), ln(GDP per capita), and regional dummies. Regional dummies include indicators for the Red River Delta, Central Coast, Central Highlands, Southeast, and Mekong River Delta.
Source: Authors' calculations.

Table 5.A3 The relationship between transparency and COVID-19 cases and transparency and COVID-19 deaths

VARIABLES	(1)	(2)	(3)	(4)	(5)	(6)	(7)	(8)	(9)	(10)	(11)	(12)
	y = ln(cases/100,000 pop.)											
Access to information	−10.11*** (3.383)						−7.783* (4.044)					
Searched state policy and legislation		−14.60*** (5.391)						−11.84* (6.220)				
Received information of state policy			−14.22** (5.526)						−10.21 (6.325)			
Information received useful				−15.83*** (5.608)						−12.60* (6.660)		
Information received reliable					−14.62*** (5.396)						−11.40* (6.251)	
Reasonable waiting time for information						45.07 (44.94)						56.79 (50.09)
Regional dummies	No	No	No	No	No	No	Yes	Yes	Yes	Yes	Yes	Yes
Observations	63	63	63	63	63	63	63	63	63	63	63	63
R2	0.201	0.201	0.192	0.180	0.197	0.180	0.332	0.333	0.315	0.333	0.323	0.302

VARIABLES	(13)	(14)	(15)	(16)	(17)	(18)	(19)	(20)	(21)	(22)	(23)	(24)
	y = ln(deaths/mil. pop.)											
Access to information	3.890 (2.963)						3.987 (3.264)					
Searched state policy and legislation		7.277 (4.639)						6.990 (4.873)				
Received information of state policy			6.812 (4.784)						7.040 (5.130)			
Information received useful				6.101 (4.821)						6.163 (5.297)		
Information received reliable					6.985 (4.838)						7.382 (5.181)	
Reasonable waiting time for information						-63.65^{*} (33.12)						−58.36 (36.25)
Regional dummies	No	No	No	No	No	No	Yes	Yes	Yes	Yes	Yes	Yes
Observations	63	63	63	63	63	63	63	63	63	63	63	63
R2	0.181	0.196	0.188	0.180	0.188	0.217	0.317	0.326	0.324	0.315	0.326	0.341

Note: Robust standard errors in parentheses; $^{*}p < 0.10$, $^{**}p < 0.05$, $^{***}p < 0.01$. Constant coefficient measured but not reported. Estimates for control variables are not reported. Control variables include ln(population density), ln(population over 60), ln(GDP per capita), and regional dummies. Regional dummies include indicators for the Red River Delta, Central Coast, Central Highlands, Southeast, and Mekong River Delta.
Source: Authors' calculations.

Table 5.A4 The relationship between accountability and COVID-19 cases and accountability and COVID-19 deaths

VARIABLES	(1)	(2)	(3)	(4)	(5)	(6)	(7)	(8)
					y = ln(cases/100,000 pop.)			
Contacted People's Council	5.432				−5.948			
	(8.849)				(9.947)			
Contact People's Council successfully		0.441				−2.171		
		(1.712)				(1.733)		
Appeals taken by citizens			−5.915**				−5.496*	
			(2.722)				(3.146)	
Successful actions of citizens				−5.607*				−5.126
				(3.199)				(3.548)
Regional dummies	No	No	No	No	Yes	Yes	Yes	Yes
Observations	63	63	63	63	63	63	63	63
R2	0.083	0.083	0.140	0.123	0.279	0.289	0.317	0.303

VARIABLES	(9)	(10)	(11)	(12)	(13)	(14)	(15)	(16)
				y = ln(deaths/mil. pop.)				
Contacted People's Council	5.316 (6.249)				1.630 (7.589)			
Contact People's Council successfully		0.601 (1.528)				0.835 (1.831)		
Appeals taken by citizens			1.588 (2.353)				1.400 (2.689)	
Successful actions of citizens				1.610 (2.656)				1.360 (3.089)
Regional dummies	No	No	No	No	Yes	Yes	Yes	Yes
Observations	63	63	63	63	63	63	63	63
R2	0.161	0.154	0.159	0.157	0.292	0.295	0.296	0.295

Note: Robust standard errors in parentheses; * $p < 0.10$, ** $p < 0.05$, *** $p < 0.01$. Constant coefficient measured but not reported. Estimates for control variables are not reported. Control variables include ln(population density), ln(population over 60), ln(GDP per capita), and regional dummies. Regional dummies include indicators for the Red River Delta, Central Coast, Central Highlands, Southeast, and Mekong River Delta.
Source: Authors' calculations.

Table 5.A5 The relationship between capacity and COVID-19 cases and capacity and COVID-19 deaths

VARIABLES	(1)	(2)	(3)	(4)	(5)	(6)	(7)	(8)
	y = ln(cases/100,000 pop.)				y = ln(deaths/mil. pop.)			
Ln(number of beds/100,000 pop.)	−0.328*		−0.255		0.213		0.155	
	(0.180)		(0.195)		(0.146)		(0.142)	
Quality of public healthcare		−1.680		−3.565		2.759		3.011
		(2.958)		(3.025)		(2.282)		(2.079)
Regional dummies	No	No	Yes	Yes	No	No	Yes	Yes
Observations	63	63	63	63	63	63	63	63
R2	0.130	0.095	0.295	0.295	0.196	0.192	0.307	0.319

Note: Robust standard errors in parentheses; *$p < 0.10$, **$p < 0.05$, ***$p < 0.01$. Constant coefficient measured but not reported. Estimates for control variables are not reported. Control variables include ln(population density), ln(population over 60), and ln(GDP per capita). Regional dummies include indicators for the Red River Delta, Central Coast, Central Highlands, Southeast, and Mekong River Delta.
Source: Authors' calculations.

References

Abuza, Z. (2020). 'Explaining Successful (and Unsuccessful) COVID-19 Responses in Southeast Asia', *The Diplomat*. Available at: https://thediplomat.com/2020/04/explaining-successful-and-unsuccessful-covid-19-responses-in-southeast-asia (accessed 28 February 2022).

Abuza, Z. (2021). 'What Explains Vietnam's Current COVID-19 Struggles?', *The Diplomat*. Available at: https://thediplomat.com/2021/06/what-explains-vietnams-current-covid-19-struggles (accessed 28 February 2022).

Capano, G., M. Howlett, D.S.L. Jarvis, M. Ramesh, and N. Goyal (2020). 'Mobilizing Policy (In)capacity to Fight COVID-19: Understanding Variations in State Responses'. *Policy and Society*, 39(3): 285–308. https://doi.org/10.1080/14494035.2020.1787628.

Cheibub, J.A., J.Y.J. Hong, and A. Przeworski (2020). 'Rights and Deaths: Government Reactions to the Pandemic'. *SSRN* (7 July). https://doi.org/10.2139/ssrn.3645410.

Christensen, T., P. Lægreid, and L.H. Rykkja (2016). 'Organizing for Crisis Management: Building Governance Capacity and Legitimacy'. *Public Administration Review*, 76(6): 887–897. https://doi.org/10.1111/puar.12558.

Dang, D.A. (2022). 'COVID-19 in Vietnam'. In L.Y. Ing and C. Basri (eds), *COVID-19 in Indonesia: Impacts on the Economy and Ways to Recovery, 2022*. Abingdon: Routledge, pp. 225–246. www.routledge.com/COVID-19-in-Indonesia-Impacts-on-the-Economy-and-Ways-to-Recovery/Ing-Basri/p/book/9781032153353.

Ferraresi, M., C. Kotsogiannis, L. Rizzo, and R. Secomandi (2020). 'The "Great Lockdown" and Its Determinants'. *Economics Letters*, 197: 109628. https://doi.org/10.1016/j.econlet.2020.109628.

Fukuyama, F. (2013). 'What Is Governance?'. *Governance*, 26(3): 347–368. https://doi.org/10.1111/gove.12035.

Gisselquist, R.M., and A. Vaccaro (2021). 'COVID-19 and the State'. WIDER Working Paper 2021/80. Helsinki: UNU-WIDER. https://doi.org/10.35188/UNU-WIDER/2021/018-4.

Government of Vietnam (2021). 'COVID-19 Response Policy Must Be Synchronously Implemented Nationwide'. Available at: https://moit.gov.vn/en/news/ministerial-leaders-activities/covid-19-response-policy-must-be-synchronously-implemented-nationwide.html (accessed 28 February 2022).

Hanson, J. (2015). 'Democracy and State Capacity: Complements or Substitutes?'. *Studies in Comparative International Development*, 50(3), 304–330. https://doi.org/10.1007/s12116-014-9173-z.

Hartley, K., S. Bales, and A.S. Bali (2021). 'COVID-19 Response in a Unitary State: Emerging Lessons from Vietnam'. *Policy Design and Practice*, 4(1): 152–168. https://doi.org/10.1080/25741292.2021.1877923.

Kleinen, J. (2015). *Vietnam: One-Party State and the Mimicry of the Civil Society*. Pathumwan, Thailand: Research Institute on Contemporary Southeast Asia. Available at: https://books.openedition.org/irasec/1032 (accessed 13 May 2022).

Knutsen, C.H. (2013). 'Democracy, State Capacity, and Economic Growth'. *World Development*, 43: 1–18. https://doi.org/10.1016/j.worlddev.2012.10.014.

Liang, L.L., C.H. Tseng, and H.J. Ho (2020). 'Covid-19 Mortality Is Negatively Associated with Test Number and Government Effectiveness'. *Scientific Reports*, 10: 12567. https://doi.org/10.1038/s41598-020-68862-x.

Malesky, E., C. Nguyen, and A. Tran (2014). 'The Impact of Recentralization on Public Services: A Difference-in-Differences Analysis of the Abolition of Elected Councils in

Vietnam'. *American Political Science Review*, 108(1): 144–168. https://doi.org/10.1017/S0003055413000580.

Malhotra, K. (2020). 'The Key to Vietnam's Successful COVID-19 Response: A UN Resident Coordinator Blog', UN News. 29 August. Available at: https://news.un.org/en/story/2020/08/1070852 (accessed 24 April 2021).

Mizrahi, S., E. Vigoda-Gadot, and N. Cohen (2021). 'How Well Do They Manage a Crisis? The Government's Effectiveness During the COVID-19 Pandemic'. *Public Administration Review*, 81(6): 1120–1130. https://doi.org/10.1111/puar.13370.

Ngoc, M. (2021). 'Fourth Covid-19 Outbreak Puts Pressure on Vietnam Strategic Sectors'. Available at: http://hanoitimes.vn/fourth-covid-19-outbreak-puts-pressure-on-vietnam-strategic-sectors-wb-317724.html (accessed 24 February 2022).

Nguyen, D.A.L. (2021). 'Restoring Public Trust in Vietnam's Pandemic Response: A Bumpy Road Ahead'. *Perspective*, 151. Singapore: ISEAS, Yusok Ishak Institute. Available at: www.iseas.edu.sg/wp-content/uploads/2021/10/ISEAS_Perspective_2021_151.pdf (accessed 13 May 2022).

Nguyen, T.M., and E. Malesky (2020). 'Reopening Vietnam: How the Country's Improving Governance Helped It Weather the COVID-19 Pandemic'. Available at: www.brookings.edu/blog/order-from-chaos/2020/05/20/reopening-vietnam-how-the-countrys-improving-governance-helped-it-weather-the-covid-19-pandemic (accessed 13 May 2022).

Pandey, A., A. Prakash, and R. Agur (2021). 'Determinants of COVID-19 Pandemic in India: An Exploratory Study of Indian States and Districts'. *Journal of Social and Economic Development*, 23: 248–279. https://doi.org/10.1007/s40847-021-00154-0.

Persson, T.A., and M. Povitkina (2017). '"Gimme Shelter": The Role of Democracy and Institutional Quality in Disaster Preparedness'. *Political Research Quarterly*, 70(4): 833–847. https://doi.org/10.1177/1065912917716335.

Pincus, J. (2021). 'Strong Central Government Leadership and Coordination: The Key to Successfully Combat the Covid Pandemic and Ensure Socio-Economic Recovery'. Unpublished manuscript.

Polo, S.M.T. (2020). 'A Pandemic of Violence? The Impact of Covid-19 on Conflict'. *Peace Economics, Peace Science and Public Policy*, 26(3): 1–13. https://doi.org/10.1515/peps-2020-0050.

Qiu, Y., X. Chen, and W. Shi (2020). 'Impacts of Social and Economic Factors on the Transmission of Coronavirus Disease 2019 (COVID-19) in China'. *Journal of Population Economics*, 33(4): 1127–1172. https://doi.org/10.1007/s00148-020-00778-2.

Sebhatu, A., K. Wennberg, S. Arora-Jonsson, and S.I. Lindberg (2020). *Explaining the Homogeneous Diffusion of Covid-19 Policies among Heterogeneous Countries*. V-Dem Working Paper 2020/104. Gothenburg: The V-Dem Institute. https://doi.org/10.2139/ssrn.3672976.

Serikbayeva, B., K. Abdulla, and Y. Oskenbayev (2021). 'State Capacity in Responding to COVID-19'. *International Journal of Public Administration*, 44(11–12): 920–930. https://doi.org/10.1080/01900692.2020.1850778.

Shanks, E., C. Luttrell, T. Conway, V. Manh Loi, and J. Ladinsky (2004). *Understanding Pro-Poor Political Change: The Policy Process—Vietnam*. London: Overseas Development Institute. Available at: https://odi.org/en/publications/understanding-pro-poor-political-change-the-policy-process-vietnam.

Stuti, K. (2020). *An Opportunity to Build Legitimacy and Trust in Public Institutions in the Time of COVID-19*. Research and Policy Briefs 148256. Washington, DC: The World Bank. Available at: https://openknowledge.worldbank.org/handle/10986/33715.

Toshkov, D., B. Carroll, and K. Yesilkagit (2021). 'Government Capacity, Societal Trust or Party Preferences: What Accounts for the Variety of National Policy Responses to the COVID-19 Pandemic in Europe?'. *Journal of European Public Policy*, 29(7): 1009–1028. https://doi.org/10.1080/13501763.2021.1928270.

Tran, T.K. (2021). 'Making the Right Decisions for the Nation's Good', *Vietnam News*. Available at: https://vietnamnews.vn/opinion/1059987/making-the-right-decisions-for-the-nations-good.html (accessed 28 February 2022).

UNDP (United Nations Development Programme) (with Cecodes, the Vietnam Fatherland Front, and Commission on People's Petitions for the Standing Committee of the National Assembly) (2012). *The Vietnam Provincial Governance and Public Administration Performance Index (PAPI) 2011: Measuring Citizens' Experiences*. Ha Noi, Vietnam: UNDP. Available at: https://papi.org.vn.

UNDP (with Cecodes, the Vietnam Fatherland Front, RTA Analytics) (2021). *PAPI 2020: The Vietnam Provincial Governance and Public Administration Performance Index—Measuring Citizens' Experiences*. Ha Noi, Vietnam: UNDP. Available at: https://papi.org.vn.

Vadlamannati, K.C., A. Cooray, and I. de Soysa (2021). 'Health-System Equity, Egalitarian Democracy and COVID-19 Outcomes: An Empirical Analysis'. *Scandinavian Journal of Public Health*, 49(1): 104–113. https://doi.org/10.1177/1403494820982106.

Vietnam Law and Legal Forum (2017). 'Current Local Administration System in Vietnam'. Available at: https://vietnamlawmagazine.vn/current-local-administration-system-invietnam-6058.html (accessed 13 May 2022).

Vu, V.T. (2021). 'Public Trust in Government and Compliance with Policy during COVID-19 Pandemic: Empirical Evidence from Vietnam'. *Public Organization Review*, 21: 779–796. https://doi.org/10.1007/s11115-021-00566-w.

WHO (2020). 'Vietnam COVID-19 Situation Report #1'. Available at: www.who.int/docs/default-source/wpro—documents/countries/viet-nam/covid-19/vnm-moh-who-covid-19-sitrep1.pdf?sfvrsn=87a79f0_2 (accessed 13 May 2022).

YouGov (2021). 'COVID-19: Government Handling and Confidence in Health Authorities'. Available at: https://today.yougov.com/topics/international/articles-reports/2020/03/17/perception-government-handling-covid-19 (accessed 24 February 2022).

PART IV
LATIN AMERICA

6

Decentralization, State Capacity, and Inequality

Explaining COVID-19 Outcomes in Bolivia

Calla Hummel, V. Ximena Velasco Guachalla, Jami Nelson-Nuñez, and Carew Boulding

6.1 Introduction

On 10 March 2020, the Bolivian government identified two COVID-19 cases in Bolivians returning from Italy (Ministerio de Salud y Deportes 2020).[1] The national government responded with one of the world's strictest lockdowns on 22 March 2020. However, low state capacity and low government legitimacy from a pre-existing political crisis stymied the national government's response (Escalera-Antezana et al. 2020; Velasco Guachalla, Hummel, Nelson-Nuñez, and Boulding 2021a). After two months of centralized government response, Bolivia's national government delegated COVID-19 policy decisions to decentralized subnational governments, which responded to the pandemic in different ways, with some following the national government's directives, most selectively complying, and some resisting (Velasco Guachalla, Hummel, Nelson-Nuñez, and Boulding 2021b).

In this case study of Bolivia's pandemic experience, we analyse original daily data on COVID-19 cases, deaths, movements, and policies at the subnational level from Bolivia's nine departments. The data span a year from 10 March 2020 to 10 March 2021. We find important variation across departments, with some experiencing much higher cases and deaths per 100,000 residents than others. We discuss some of the variables that contributed to the country's COVID-19 experience and response, including state capacity, legitimacy, decentralization, pre-existing health resources, infrastructure, geography, partisanship, and public health policies. This chapter contributes to the literature on COVID-19 policies and experiences by developing a quantitative case study that examines subnational variation in a

[1] The authors are grateful for the support of the Grupo de Investigación del Observatorio para la Contención de COVID-19 en América Latina at the University of Miami (http://observcovid.miami.edu), especially the help of Felicia Knaul, Michael Touchton, and Héctor Arreola. Any errors are the authors'.

Calla Hummel et al., *Decentralization, State Capacity, and Inequality*. In: *How States Respond to Crisis*.
Edited by: Rachel M. Gisselquist and Andrea Vaccaro, Oxford University Press. © UNU-WIDER (2025).
DOI: 10.1093/9780198907237.003.0006

decentralized context. Most studies of COVID-19 policies aggregate data at the national level and miss important variation in local responses and experiences (Knaul et al. 2022). In particular, national averages hide subnational inequalities in healthcare, resources, and experiences, as well as the local effects of political polarization around the pandemic.

We discuss how individual factors may have further shaped the experiences of individual citizens. Within the same department, Bolivians with different resources, identities, and jobs had very different experiences. People who were deemed essential workers by local laws and who could not work remotely were probably at a much higher risk of infection than people who could work from home. Similarly, most Bolivians share small homes with several family members and could not socially distance within their household; the small percentage of Bolivians who could stay 2 metres away from potentially infected family members lived a different pandemic. Finally, while healthcare is a constitutional right, healthcare provision in practice is riddled with numerous problems and constraints, leaving Bolivians with limited ability to fully exercise that right during the pandemic. People who could pay for private health services probably had a higher chance of survival, but even private care was hard to find, unreliable, and much more expensive during the pandemic.

We conclude by putting Bolivia in comparative perspective and looking at the challenges that lie ahead. Over 26,000 more Bolivians died in 2020 than in 2019, probably due to a combination of COVID-19, hardship, and delayed treatment for other conditions. This is a 50 per cent increase in mortality over 2019 and potentially one of the largest COVID-19-related death tolls in the world, adjusted for population (Karlinsky and Kobak 2021; Velasco Guachalla, Hummel, Nelson-Nuñez, and Boulding 2021a). The lack of sufficient healthcare capacity is one of the factors that drove this tragedy. Still, national and subnational interventions probably curbed the spread of the virus. While Bolivians had divergent pandemic experiences on the basis of location, occupation, politics, and resources, the difference in experience and the inequality of care was not as pronounced as in other countries, such as neighbouring Brazil or the United States. The Bolivian government expanded the national safety net and invested in health infrastructure, which may help in future crises (Blofield et al. 2020).

6.2 State capacity, infrastructure, and public health in Bolivia

Bolivia is a landlocked, lower-middle-income country of 11 million people (World Bank 2021). A powerful executive leads the government and shapes an extensive bureaucracy that manages the state's natural resources, ambitious social policies, and relationships with one of the most organized civil societies in the world

(Anria 2018; Boulding 2014; Hummel 2021; Toledo Orozco 2022). The Senate and the House of Deputies, known together as the Plurinational Legislative Assembly, legislate in the National Congress. Evo Morales's party, Movement towards Socialism (Movimiento al Socialismo, MAS), had a supermajority in the Plurinational Legislative Assembly until 2020, allowing the party to govern without opposition votes. MAS lost its supermajority in the 2020 elections, and while the party retained a majority in both houses, it needed support from the opposition to pass legislation (Peralta 2020). Finally, while the judiciary is in theory an autonomous and independent institution, in practice the judicial system is highly politicized, with its members often representing partisan viewpoints and agendas (Human Rights Watch 2018; Saavedra Mogro 2017; Velasco Guachalla, Hummel, Nelson-Nuñez, and Boulding 2021a). Bolivia's nine departmental and over 330 municipal governments exercise considerable fiscal and political autonomy under a 1994 decentralization law. These were joined by a small number of indigenous jurisdictions that formed local governments after the 2009 constitutional reform (Faguet 2012; Porto et al. 2018; Zuazo et al. 2012).

In this chapter, we consider three key dimensions of the state established in the literature: authority, defined as the government's ability to provide order within its borders; capacity, defined as the government's ability to provide basic public services; and legitimacy, defined as the government's ability to garner citizens' consent (Ziaja et al. 2019). In studying the Bolivian case, we primarily emphasize the role of the latter two. In this section, we elaborate on Bolivia's state capacity and more briefly on its authority; we focus on legitimacy in the next section. Overall, the Bolivian state exhibits low capacity in comparison with other countries in the Americas (Gray-Molina 2001; Gray-Molina et al. 1999; Hummel 2021). Bolivia ranks at the low end of regional indices for GDP per capita, health spending, education spending, public sector expenditures, military expenditures, industrial production, government statistical capacity, access to public sewers and electrical grids, and other measures that researchers use to measure state capacity (Hendrix 2010; Soifer 2008, 2015). The only measure of capacity on which Bolivia performs reasonably well is homicides (six per 100,000), but this is due more to neighbouring countries' high homicide rates than to any capacity or expertise from the widely derided Bolivian national police force (Zechmeister and Lupu 2019; Our World in Data 2021).

Bolivia has nine departments with their own regional governments: Beni, Chuquisaca, Cochabamba, La Paz, Oruro, Pando, Potosí, Santa Cruz, and Tarija. La Paz, Santa Cruz, and Cochabamba are the largest in population and economic output and host four large cities. The city of La Paz is the administrative and political capital of the country, and the La Paz-El Alto metropolitan area is home to 2 million Bolivians. The La Paz department borders Peru and has a busy international land border and an international airport. The department of Santa Cruz is a wealthy ranching and commerce hub, and its major city houses over 1 million

Bolivians. Santa Cruz borders Brazil and has busy land borders and an international airport. Cochabamba is the only department without an international land border, and its eponymous departmental capital has a population of roughly 600,000. Cochabamba is also an agricultural department and the home district of the MAS Party. The tropical border departments of Beni and Pando are poor and sparsely populated: Pando has only 154,000 people and Beni has fewer than half a million. Both departments border Brazil and rank last out of the departments for GDP per capita. Chuquisaca hosts the country's historic and symbolic capital Sucre, home of the judicial branch, and it is a small and conservative region with below-average GDP. Potosí and Oruro are majority indigenous departments with a mix of agriculture, mining, and commerce, and they share land borders with Chile. Finally, Tarija is a wealthy and conservative agricultural department that cultivates the country's vineyards and borders Argentina and Paraguay.

Governance at all levels of government is characterized by bureaucratic clientelism, where the exchange of perks and privileges for personal, group, and political loyalties takes precedence over merit and efficiency (Calderón and Laserna 1995). Inertia, inefficiency, exaggerated functionary zeal, and improvisation are persistent traits of Bolivia's bureaucracy and public management (Vargas Maldonado 1998). However, national-level indicators hide important subnational variation. Some departments and municipalities are run by experienced politicians and bureaucrats. The nine departments differ significantly in their resources, infrastructure, and state capacity. La Paz and Santa Cruz have adequate hospitals, roads, airports, and other infrastructures, as well as relatively active and experienced departmental governments. Cochabamba, Chuquisaca, Potosí, Oruro, and Tarija have adequate infrastructure and governance in some areas but neglect many rural districts. Pando and Beni have some infrastructure and governance in the largest towns, but state presence is lacking or absent in most places (Acuña et al. 2020).

Bolivia's health infrastructure and public health capacity is limited at the national and subnational levels. The Bolivian Constitution of 2009 (Section II, Article 35) enshrines healthcare as a constitutional right. On paper, the Bolivian state provides free public healthcare to citizens. However, Bolivians regularly note that the few hospitals in the country have long waiting times and require patients to buy their own supplies and medicine, and that doctors at public hospitals routinely ask for bribes to provide care that should be free (Gray-Molina et al. 1999; Zechmeister and Lupu 2019). The Pan American Health Organization (2017) reports that in 2016, the Bolivian government spent about US$400 per person on public health, far below the regional average of US$1,300. Bolivia had 47 general hospitals in the country in 2019 but only 35 functioning intensive care unit (ICU) beds with ventilators (Escalera-Antezana et al. 2020; INE 2021). The department of Pando had no ICU beds and no hospital equipped to treat complex illnesses (Ministerio de Salud y Deportes 2019).

Still, healthcare had improved notably in the decade prior to the pandemic. From 2006 to 2019, Bolivia experienced consistently positive economic growth (Our World in Data 2021). The administration of Evo Morales used surpluses and natural gas rents to fund public spending booms. Popular cash transfer programmes and a universal pension helped millions of Bolivians out of poverty and reduced inequality (Farthing 2019; Niedzwiecki and Anria 2019). This influx of cash helped Bolivia to move up regional development and poverty indices, from last place on many to third or fourth from the bottom (Our World in Data 2021). During this period, important health indicators improved: life expectancy increased from 65 in 2005 to 71.5 in 2019, and child malnutrition fell by half. Cash transfer programmes targeting extreme poverty among families and senior citizens were particularly effective at improving both economic and health indicators.

The Bolivian government repeatedly promised to invest in important but expensive and neglected infrastructures throughout the country, chiefly hospitals, roads, and schools. Between 2010 and 2020, the government started several projects and opened new roads, schools, and hospitals around the country, in some places targeting the most dangerous roads or remote communities. According to the National Institute of Statistics (Instituto Nacional de Estadística, INE), the number of general hospitals increased from 34 in 2006 to 47 in 2019, and the number of hospital beds rose from 10,422 to 14,896 over the same period (INE 2021). Moreover, the ministry of health quadrupled the number of ambulances from 558 to 2,072 in 11 years. These were distributed throughout the country in order to transfer and assist patients in critical condition (Ministerio de Salud y Deportes 2017). At the beginning of 2020, Bolivians had seen GDP per capita and their real incomes nearly triple over the previous 15 years, and life expectancy had increased by six years. Despite these major improvements, there was considerable variation at the municipal level, demonstrating the inequality of economic distribution and the precariousness of local health infrastructures (Candia et al. 2020). Moreover, investment in durable infrastructure and long-term infrastructure projects such as hospitals and a modern transport system lagged behind medium-term projects that could be finished before the next election. More alarming was the large number and cost of government projects, including the construction of hospitals, that were left unfinished or never broke ground (Chambi et al. 2020).

In terms of government authority, Bolivia has been consistently ranked as a poor performer (Ziaja et al. 2019). The lack of authority to enforce its policies severely undermined the government's response to the pandemic, as its security forces were only partially able to enforce lockdown policies. Three factors help us to understand weak enforcement in Bolivia during the pandemic: lack of resources, citizens' adaptability, and corruption. Although police and military personnel were tasked with enforcing lockdown restrictions, they often lacked biosecurity equipment, which in turn led to high rates of confirmed cases and deaths among enforcement ranks (Machicao and Limachi 2020; Página Siete 2021). Additionally, even when enforcement was supplied with the necessary equipment to remain safe and patrol the streets, citizens—in a country where rates of informal work are among the highest in the region (Alaimo et al. 2015; Hummel 2021)—looked for ways to evade enforcement in order to earn a daily income. Anecdotal evidence collected by one of the authors illustrates this dynamic: street market vendors would monitor police presence by either learning patrol times or setting up communication chains to learn of approaching police; they would then adapt their behaviour accordingly, avoiding selling during patrol times and/or picking up their merchandise before the police came by and then returning to their business after the police had gone. Finally, corruption seriously compromises enforcement mechanisms. Corruption is particularly pervasive among the police, and pandemic response is undermined when enforcement is circumvented in exchange for bribes (Orces 2008; Peredo 2019; REDLAD 2020).

6.3 Government legitimacy: a timeline of the pandemic in Bolivia

COVID-19 hit Bolivia in the midst of a political crisis (Velasco Guachalla, Hummel, Nelson-Nuñez, and Boulding 2021a). In November 2019, President Evo Morales resigned and fled the country. Morales and his MAS Party had been in power since 2006, passed a new constitution in 2009, overseen an economic boom and popular social programmes, and easily won elections across the country for years (Anria 2018; Madrid 2012; Niedzwiecki and Anria 2019). Morales and MAS centralized power, ostracized dissidents and young leaders, eliminated term limits, and used state institutions to harass opponents and campaign during elections (Centellas 2018; Farthing 2019; Velasco Guachalla, Hummel, Handlin, and Smith 2021). Morales stepped down after widespread protests and allegations of electoral fraud in the 2019 national elections (Wolff 2020). Supporters denounced Morales's resignation as a coup, while detractors hailed it as the result of a pro-democracy uprising (Anria and Roberts 2019; Arequipa Azurduy 2020; Derpic 2019).

Morales's sudden resignation was followed by the resignation of the rest of the constitutionally named chain of succession. This created a power vacuum that culminated in the appointment of Jeanine Áñez, second vice president of the Chamber of Senators, as interim president (Wolff 2020). The chain of events that started with allegations of electoral fraud and led to the appointment of Áñez as interim president severely damaged the legitimacy of the government and deepened citizens' polarization between MAS supporters and detractors (Velasco Guachalla, Hummel, Nelson-Nuñez, and Boulding 2021b). The Áñez administration exacerbated the political crisis and increased distrust towards her government by sending the military into the streets, allowing the police to fire on protesters, and prosecuting dozens of former MAS officials (Anria and Roberts 2019; Velasco Guachalla, Hummel, Nelson-Nuñez, and Boulding 2021a). Moreover, despite Áñez's initial assurances that she would remain in office only to call the election, she announced her candidacy for president in the national elections that her administration was overseeing (Alanoca Paco 2020). These events further damaged the already frail legitimacy of the government, and would later negatively affect citizen compliance with COVID-19 restriction policies.

It was in the context of a preceding political crisis, weak government legitimacy, and upcoming national and subnational elections that the first two COVID-19 cases were confirmed in the country on 10 March 2020 (Ministerio de Salud y Deportes 2020). On 12 March, the government issued National Emergency Decree 4179, which declared a 'national emergency situation' due to the presence of the novel coronavirus. The same day, the interim president announced further measures including the cancellation of school-teaching, stricter border controls, and the interruption of all flights to and from Europe, and she also launched Bolivia Segura, a national COVID-19 information website with daily case numbers and other information. More emergency decrees came soon after. Supreme Decree 4192 on 16 March limited gatherings of more than 100 people, modified work hours, designated essential workers, and prohibited events in spaces such as bars and clubs. The initial two cases quickly became six in three different departments, and then dozens (Escalera-Antezana et al. 2020). All departments except Beni had confirmed at least one case by the end of March. Supreme Decree 4196 on 17 March instituted a curfew between 5 a.m. and 5 p.m. across Bolivia, prohibited all gatherings, and restricted work hours and public transport. All borders closed on 20 March, leaving many Bolivians stranded abroad, including many at border checkpoints in precarious conditions (Miranda 2020).

On 21 March, Supreme Decree 4199 imposed a strict quarantine. The decree stated that only one person per family could leave a living space once a week, and only to buy supplies near their residence. The decree was first extended to 30 April and later to 31 May. While the use of face masks was initially not mandatory, it became compulsory outside homes on 29 April. Despite the strict national quarantine, thousands of Bolivians left their homes to protest against national or local government decisions (Velasco Guachalla, Hummel, Nelson-Nuñez, and Boulding 2021b). In La Paz, Santa Cruz, Cochabamba, and Beni, protesters decried local and national government measures around the pandemic and demanded the loosening of quarantine restrictions. While a number of protests were motivated by disgruntled citizens unable to earn a living due to movement restrictions, politically motivated demonstrations took place early in the pandemic and throughout 2020. In most departments, at least some people protested against the decision to suspend the May national elections. Amid protests, Supreme Decree 4229 announced that after 11 May, department and municipal governments could set out their own regulations on local work hours, transport, and quarantine. The national government continued to prohibit travel, gatherings, and school attendance, as well as to enforce a nightly curfew, mask use, and social distancing.

The political crisis of 2019 aggravated pre-existing citizen polarization between MAS and anti-MAS camps and negatively impacted generalized trust and support for the interim government. This in turn influenced COVID-19-related policymaking at the national and subnational levels as well as citizen compliance with different lockdown directives. In departments where political authorities and the majority of the electorate were in opposition to the incumbent government, the COVID-19 policy was less restrictive and citizen compliance was lower than in pro-government departments (Velasco Guachalla, Hummel, Nelson-Nuñez, and Boulding 2021a). Moreover, the relationship between the Áñez administration and the MAS-dominated legislature was characterized by conflict and lack of consensus around COVID-19 policy, which on occasion led to health-related policy breaking down along partisan lines at different levels of government (Velasco Guachalla, Hummel, Nelson-Nuñez, and Boulding 2021a).

On 1 June, departments and municipalities allowed people to leave their houses for work, shopping, and exercise. Some departments retained a stricter set of guidelines, such as Santa Cruz, Beni, Tarija, and Potosí. Santa Cruz and Beni were in the midst of horrific first peaks that had started in May and quickly overwhelmed local health systems, leading to shut hospitals and many dead. Despite these outbreaks, departments such as La Paz and Cochabamba let people go back to work and reopened public transport.

After 1 June, COVID-19 cases skyrocketed around the country and overwhelmed the national and local health infrastructure. On 30 June, 20 of the 34 general hospitals across the country were overwhelmed by the large number of COVID-19 patients and sick staff; many hospitals temporarily closed at the height of the outbreak because too many staff were sick (Aguilar 2020). In July, people began dying in the streets in multiple departments, especially La Paz and Cochabamba. On 23 July, the national police reported collecting 86 bodies of confirmed or suspected COVID-19 victims from streets and homes in a single day (Pomacahua 2020).

In light of the escalating crisis, on 23 July the Supreme Electoral Tribunal (Tribunal Supremo Electoral, TSE) announced that presidential elections would be delayed until 18 October (Rosales Melgar 2020). This was the third time elections had been rescheduled, from 3 May to 6 September to 18 October. Subnational elections, suspended in March, had yet to be rescheduled at all. The delay was met with national protests. Protests and blockades spread across the country in the midst of the first COVID-19 peak (Trigo and Kurmanaev 2020).

On 2 August, President Áñez and the ministry of education suspended the rest of the school year because the government could not guarantee distance learning and internet access to most students. All students were passed to enter the next school level, and the government put resources into updating the country's internet connectivity (Ministerio de Educación 2020). The move caused widespread confusion and was widely criticized by parents and students (Tancara Castillo 2020). While schools across the nation abided by the early ending of the school year, protests demanding face-to-face education occurred in various parts of the country until the beginning of 2022. In the end, the decision regarding whether students should retake in-person classes was delegated to subnational governments.

Stress on the national health system appeared early on in the pandemic when hospitals ran out of ventilators as well as technicians to operate them. The toll on healthcare workers and infrastructure worsened during the first peak, when staff in Beni, Santa Cruz, and then the rest of the country became too sick to care for patients and keep facilities open. In September, health statistics quantified the damage: the ministry of health reported that as of 2 September, 80 per cent of personnel in the health system had contracted COVID-19 and 125 doctors had died.

Decree 4314 loosened restrictions on 1 September. Cases declined sharply in September, despite increased transport, work, and circulation. Political parties engaged in a six-week campaign period, with former finance minister Luis Arce and former foreign minister David Choquehuanca leading the polls on the MAS ticket (Velasco Guachalla, Hummel, Nelson-Nuñez, and Boulding 2021a). On 18 October 2020, Arce, Choquehuanca, and MAS won the mandatory in-person presidential election in the first round of voting (Velasco Guachalla, Hummel, Nelson-Nuñez, and Boulding 2021a). Arce assumed the presidency in the first week of November. On 28 November, Arce released Decree 4404, which devolved most COVID-19 policy to departmental and municipal governments as long as they followed (largely unspecified) safety protocols. Masks were still mandatory nationally, and schools remained closed, but all economic activity, gatherings, and transport resumed with safety protocols, as did international travel with polymerase chain reaction tests.

COVID-19 cases started to trend upwards again in December, increasing quickly two weeks after Arce released Decree 4404. All departments and most municipalities tried to reverse the trend by instituting travel restrictions and curfews between 24 December and 2 January, but cases continued to climb into January 2021.

Our research team noted that once the Arce administration began, the information coming out of Bolivia became more upbeat and less informative, and websites such as Bolivia Segura stopped providing regular and reliable health statistics. The first 6,000 doses of the Russian-made Sputnik vaccine arrived on 29 January 2021. Frontline healthcare workers were inoculated in Santa Cruz, La Paz, and Cochabamba over the next few weeks, but President Arce only received his first dose about four months later on 24 May, and Vice President Choquehuanca waited until January 2022 (Ministerio de Salud 2021; Página

Siete 2022). The Arce administration secured millions of vaccine doses from five manufacturers in 2021, but the doses were slow to arrive.

Despite the vaccination campaign, Bolivia experienced two more COVID-19 peaks in the first half of 2021. The second peak started in December 2020, following the repeal of most public health restrictions, and lasted into February 2021. Numbers trended downwards in March before picking up again in April and hitting a third peak that lasted throughout June 2021. The number of confirmed cases was higher in each successive peak, but due to extreme test shortages during the first peak, it is not clear if the total number of cases actually increased. Bolivians found it somewhat easier to access tests in the second and third peaks, although positivity rates were still high at around 40 per cent in the second peak and 25 per cent in the third peak, compared with 60 per cent in the first peak (Our World in Data 2021). These positivity rates are dramatically higher than the World Health Organization guideline of 5 per cent for sufficient testing.

As the pandemic progressed, so did healthcare capacity. The Áñez and Arce administrations built and opened additional hospitals and clinics. The department of Pando received its first hospital, and a number of smaller towns received their first hospitals or clinics. Larger cities such as El Alto and Cochabamba also opened new hospitals to address excess demand on existing infrastructure. The state expanded social assistance programmes, using the data and delivery methods of existing programmes to target vulnerable households and people out of work (Blofield and Filgueira 2020). These measures were imperfect but addressed large gaps in capacity and helped many Bolivians to cope with the pandemic while building future capacity.

6.4 Three hundred and sixty-five days of COVID-19

Our team collected daily data on COVID-19 cases, deaths, policies, and mobile phone mobility for Bolivia's nine departments from 10 March 2020 to 10 March 2021. We collected data from the ministry of health, Bolivia Segura, the departmental health services, the departmental governments, and Google Mobility Reports. We added information from governments', non-governmental organizations', and journalists' reports. We collected background demographic, health, and economic data from the INE and election returns from the TSE. Our data come from these sources unless otherwise specified. In this section we describe patterns of COVID-19 cases and deaths across Bolivia's nine departments. We examine the differences across departments.

Departments entered the pandemic with unequal resources as well as varying institutions and alliances. La Paz, Santa Cruz, and Cochabamba are larger departments whose governments had more resources, experience, and critical healthcare infrastructure than others, while Pando and Beni were especially lacking in resources and infrastructure. The 2019 political crisis had further complicated governance by deepening citizen polarization and eroding government legitimacy. The departmental governments of Santa Cruz and Tarija were allied with the interim government while most were not, and some departments had relatively politically homogeneous populations while others were deeply divided (Velasco Guachalla, Hummel, Nelson-Nuñez, and Boulding 2021b). Table 6.1 describes demographic, public health, and political statistics from the nine departments before and during the pandemic.

When the pandemic began to unfold across Bolivia, officials and ordinary Bolivians reacted quickly. The initial drop in movement across Bolivia was one of the largest drops in the Americas (Hummel et al. 2020; Knaul et al. 2022). However, as the lockdown dragged on, people started to move around, albeit slowly. When local governments reimposed quarantines in response to outbreaks or limited movement at weekends, people obeyed, as we can see in the departmental peaks and troughs over the year.

We witnessed and received anecdotal reports of uneven enforcement across neighbourhoods and cities, and newspapers covered stories of non-compliance. Newspaper stories of non-compliance were often about protests, small parties, or food markets. We do not have enforcement data that would enable us to identify more general patterns. Mobile phone data and newspaper reports suggest that compliance and enforcement were not universal, but that most people followed pandemic regulations most of the time during the first months of the pandemic.

By chance, the first COVID-19 cases were in Oruro, and the first cluster spanned Oruro, Cochabamba, and Santa Cruz. Despite its resources and relatively high local state capacity, Santa Cruz could not assert control over the virus and became the epicentre of the country's pandemic: Santa Cruz accounted for 35 per cent of the country's total case count on 10 March 2021. Conversely, Oruro and Cochabamba contained the initial outbreaks and registered below-average cases and deaths during subsequent outbreaks, despite relatively low local state and healthcare capacity. As the virus spread across the country in the first peak and then in later waves, all departments suffered huge tolls and overloaded their healthcare systems. Still, some departments reported much higher cases and deaths relative to others.

Figure 6.1 charts confirmed COVID-19 cases per 100,000 residents in the nine departments from 10 March 2020 to 10 March 2021. We use cases per 100,000 residents because the overall case tallies simply show the departments with high populations recording more cases; the adjusted numbers demonstrate the risk to a given individual in one department compared with another.

Figure 6.1 shows that Tarija, Santa Cruz, and Pando had the highest case numbers, adjusted for population, over the first year of the pandemic. At the national

Table 6.1 Demographic, public health, and political statistics from Bolivia's nine departments, 2019–2021

Department	Population 2019	GDP per capita 2019	Hospital beds 2019	People per hospital bed	Governor's party 2020	MAS vote share 2019	Cases per 100,000	Confirmed COVID-19 deaths per 100,000
Country totals	11,513,100	3,552	14,481	795		55%	2,192	102
Beni	480,308	2,403	449	1,043	MAS*	34%	2,353	104
Chuquisaca	637,013	3,276	1,388	451	MAS	49%	2,445	114
Cochabamba	2,028,639	3,109	2,463	800	MAS	66%	1,230	78
La Paz	2,926,996	3,988	3,775	764	Sol.bo	68%	2,084	63
Oruro	551,116	3,793	548	982	MAS*	63%	2,133	102
Pando	154,355	2,449	120	1,201	MAS	46%	2,522	143
Potosí	901,555	2,802	788	1,126	MAS	58%	1,533	45
Santa Cruz	3,370,059	3,695	4,166	774	MDS	36%	2,636	158
Tarija	583,330	5,329	784	719	UDA	42%	3,637	93

Note: *The governor changed during the pandemic following protests, but both the former and the new governor were from the MAS Party. UDA = Unidad Departmental Autonomista.
Source: Authors' calculations based on data from INE, TSE, and Bolivia Segura.

level, Bolivia recorded 2,192 cases per 100,000 people (Table 6.1). Tarija had 3,637 cases per 100,000 people, Santa Cruz had 2,636, and Pando had 2,522. In contrast, Cochabamba recorded the lowest caseload at 1,230 confirmed cases per 100,000 people, or one third of Tarija's caseload.

Confirmed deaths from COVID-19 per 100,000 people across Bolivia tell a story similar to Figure 6.1. Santa Cruz, the epicentre of overall cases, recorded the most deaths overall and per capita: 45 per cent of the Bolivians who tested positive for COVID-19 and died were from Santa Cruz. Nationally, Bolivia recorded 104 COVID-19 deaths per 100,000 people in the first year of the pandemic. Santa Cruz recorded 158 deaths per 100,000. The much smaller Pando recorded 144 deaths per 100,000 people, and Chuquisaca reported 114 deaths per 100,000. In comparison, some departments had much lower tolls. Potosí recorded 45 deaths per 100,000 people, less than one third of Santa Cruz's rate, while La Paz recorded 64 deaths per 100,000, and Cochabamba reported 78 per 100,000.

Sadly, the numbers recorded here are an undercount of the true toll. No department had sufficient tests to meet demand during the pandemic, and thus confirmed cases are a significant undercount of actual COVID-19 infections. The Bolivian government only attributed a death to COVID-19 if a person received a positive test result before they died. Amidst a test shortage and delays, these staggering numbers undercount Bolivia's true COVID-19 death toll.

Some might wonder whether these patterns are artefacts of testing and reporting capacity rather than approximate measures of the true distribution of cases and deaths across Bolivia. A few trends suggest that the numbers reflect underlying caseloads rather than testing or reporting capacity. First, La Paz, Santa Cruz, and Cochabamba had the most access to tests and clinics that could analyse the tests, and also had local health departments that were relatively experienced at tracking and reporting infectious diseases. Santa Cruz reported the most cases and deaths, but La Paz and Cochabamba are towards the bottom when we adjust for population; therefore, the higher-capacity departments do not dominate the reported cases or deaths, adjusted for population. Similarly, Pando and Beni had the least access to diagnostic materials and low local statistical and reporting capacity; Tarija and Oruro also had less access and capacity than other departments. Yet Pando and Tarija reported high numbers of cases and deaths. Thus, we know that the reported numbers are lower than the true numbers, but we believe that they reflect the underlying distribution of cases and deaths across the country.

Overall deaths increased dramatically across Bolivia in 2020 and 2021, from COVID-19 as well as other causes. INE data show a dramatic increase in deaths since the beginning of the COVID-19 pandemic. The difference between the pre-pandemic average and the monthly deaths during the pandemic is called 'excess mortality'—deaths in excess of what one would expect under normal conditions.

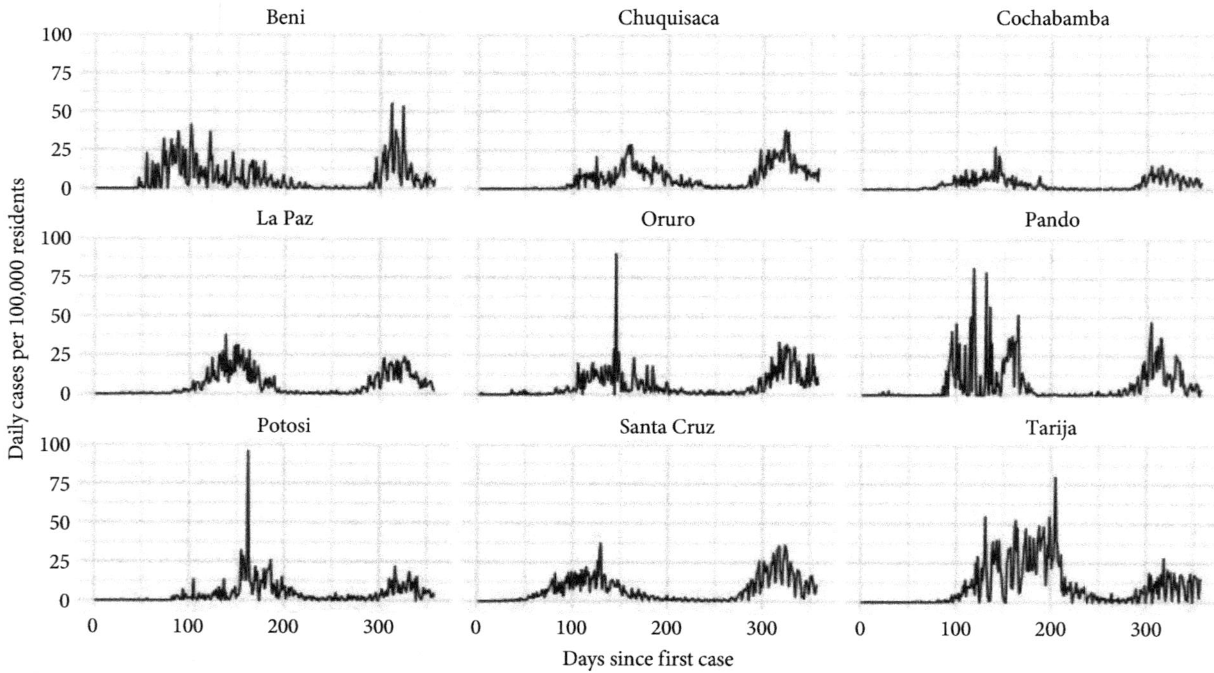

Figure 6.1 Confirmed daily COVID-19 cases per 100,000 residents in Bolivia's nine departments, 10 March 2020 to 10 March 2021.
Source: Authors' illustration based on data from the Bolivian ministry of health.

The excess mortality for Bolivia during the COVID-19 pandemic was astronomical. Bolivia reported over 26,000 more deaths in 2020 than in 2019, an increase of 50 per cent and one of the highest increases in the world (Karlinsky and Kobak 2021). Despite a vaccination campaign, the numbers may be even worse for 2021: Bolivia recorded 35,484 deaths in the first five months of 2021, a 60 per cent increase or 14,087 more deaths than in the same period in 2016 to 2019.

6.5 Discussion

Why were cases and deaths three times higher in some departments than in others? No single variable appears to explain the patterns that we see across Bolivia. We discuss possible political, economic, social, and geographical factors that might account for some of the variation.

6.5.1 Decentralization

Observers have noted that countries with federal structures, such as the United States, Mexico, and Brazil, appear to have fared worse than countries with unitary structures (Knaul et al. 2022). Bolivia's decentralized governance structure is between these two types. The executive has significant autonomy and power to rule through emergency decrees during crises, and the national government supersedes local governments in most instances. However, it is the local governments that implement most policies and projects within their jurisdictions.

Bolivia's decentralized structure appears to have helped the country to respond to COVID-19. The national government swiftly implemented a comprehensive national prevention plan that probably avoided the catastrophic scenarios that unfolded in neighbouring Brazil. Decentralized local governments did not and could not block the central government's policies in the way that federal units did in the United States and Brazil. At most, local governments could protest against national policy, obstruct some implementation, or promote competing local policies. Some local governments did this through initiatives such as distributing chlorine dioxide through pharmacies, but these efforts did not derail the national strategy. Local governments could also respond to outbreaks with their own prevention policies, which many did by imposing mask mandates earlier than the national government, or by locking down cities and towns in response to local outbreaks. It appears that Bolivia's decentralized governance allowed local governments to respond to outbreaks without derailing a comprehensive national response.

6.5.2 Subnational factors

The government was well aware in March 2020 that the country's health system was not prepared for a pandemic. When the government confirmed the first cases, the president, departmental governments, and municipal governments responded immediately with non-pharmaceutical interventions designed to stop transmission, prevent community spread, and contain the initial cases (Hummel et al. 2020; Velasco Guachalla, Hummel, Nelson-Nuñez, and Boulding 2021b). While COVID-19 restrictions did not prevent community spread in Bolivia, they may have slowed and reduced it (Knaul et al. 2022). The per-capita case data suggest that strict policies may have reduced infections: we see peaks in June and December after restrictions loosened, suggesting that policies in prior periods had worked to reduce transmission. Bolivia also recorded fewer cases and deaths per 100,000 people than neighbouring Brazil, which had few restrictions. The departments bordering Brazil—Pando, Beni, and Santa Cruz—had much higher restrictions and much lower cases throughout the pandemic than the Brazilian states they bordered (Touchton et al. 2021). Thus, we would expect departments that maintained strict restrictions throughout the year to have lower cases and deaths per capita than those that did not.

Departmental COVID-19 policies reflected political fault-lines (Hummel et al. 2021). With the controversial and unpopular Áñez administration instituting strict quarantine, some people and politicians who opposed Áñez obstructed the administration's COVID-19 response by spreading misinformation or refusing to comply (Velasco Guachalla, Hummel, Nelson-Nuñez, and Boulding 2021b). Conversely, we found in our earlier research that departments whose governors and electorates were aligned with the administration implemented stricter policies and for a longer period of time than departments that opposed the administration (Velasco Guachalla, Hummel, Nelson-Nuñez, and Boulding 2021b). This politicking and low government legitimacy may have increased transmission in some areas.

We and many others expect pre-existing health infrastructure and capacity to have shaped mortality rates. Where people could access tests, oxygen, assistance, steroids, and ventilators, more people probably survived severe cases and went on to infect fewer other people. We have a pre-pandemic measure of local health capacity in hospital bed numbers from the INE. We can use this measure to approximate local health infrastructure. Thus, we would expect departments with more hospital beds and other health infrastructure to have had fewer deaths than departments with fewer beds and less infrastructure. We can initially evaluate this expectation by comparing mortality rates and hospital beds across departments. Surprisingly, we do not see a clear relationship in the descriptive data that we have. Pando, the department with the weakest health infrastructure before the pandemic, did experience one of the highest case and mortality rates. However, so did

Santa Cruz and Chuquisaca, which had more per-capita hospital beds and other health infrastructures than most departments.

Additionally, health capacity shifted throughout the pandemic as cases rose and fell, supplies arrived or did not, and health workers fell ill in ways our data do not capture. For example, Santa Cruz entered the pandemic with better health infrastructure than most of the country. However, that infrastructure repeatedly collapsed when too many health workers fell ill at once and facilities shut down due to lack of personnel, sending patients to nearby facilities that in turn became overburdened and shut down. We expect that more fine-grained data and sensitive statistical analyses will uncover clearer relationships between health capacity and COVID-19 outcomes.

We expect geography to have influenced the spread of the virus as well. Departments that border Brazil had higher per-capita and overall cases than other departments. Brazil was battered by the pandemic, and state governments were largely on their own in trying to prevent and then treat COVID-19 (Touchton et al. 2021). Beni, Pando, and Santa Cruz share important border crossings with the Brazilian border states of Acre, Rondônia, Mato Grosso, and Mato Grosso do Sul. Acre, Mato Grosso, and Mato Grosso do Sul had the lowest restrictions of Brazil's states, which were already much lower on average than any department in Bolivia (Knaul et al. 2022; Touchton et al. 2021). While border closures helped to insulate Bolivia, shared borders with lax Brazilian states may have increased transmission in Beni, Pando, and Santa Cruz, especially the transmission of more contagious variants. Furthermore, the only department without an international border, Cochabamba, had the lowest caseload per capita of any department and one of the lowest mortality rates. We suspect that Cochabamba's geography may have slowed the spread of the virus.

6.5.3 Individual factors

Within a given department, Bolivians with differing resources, jobs, and families experienced the pandemic in dramatically different ways. The pandemic brought 15 years of economic growth to a halt and unleashed an economic crisis across the country. Unemployment soared (Agencia EFE 2020; Instituto Boliviano de Comercio Exterior 2021; Mamani 2021). The government used the social assistance infrastructure developed during the Morales administration to deliver cash and food assistance to families in need and developed new programmes to send cash to unemployed Bolivians (Blofield et al. 2020, 2021; Velasco Guachalla, Hummel, Nelson-Nuñez, and Boulding 2021b). Social assistance probably prevented a deeper public health and economic crisis, but it was not enough for many Bolivians.

We expect wealthier Bolivians to have lived a different pandemic than most Bolivians. We do not have detailed individual-level data on pandemic experiences yet, but we expect such data will show that wealthier Bolivians had lower rates of infection and lower mortality rates than other Bolivians. We have several reasons for this expectation. First, personal protective equipment, medical attention, and medicines cost money that most Bolivians did not have to hand, despite the government's assurances and the constitutional right to healthcare. Only the wealthiest Bolivians could afford private medical care if beds in public hospitals were not available, although in some places and points in the pandemic even private care was scarce or non-existent. Second, most Bolivians live in homes that are not big enough for family members to socially distance from one another if one person is exposed (Zechmeister and Lupu 2019). Only the wealthiest Bolivians have enough space in their homes to distance themselves from an exposed housemate or family member. Finally, only a few Bolivians have adequate savings to live on during prolonged periods of unemployment, or the financial ability to turn down jobs where they may be exposed to COVID-19.

Similarly, occupation probably influenced how often a person was exposed to COVID-19 (Hummel et al. 2021). Only a minority of jobs in Bolivia can be performed remotely, largely in government, education, and some services. Most people work in agriculture, manufacturing, transport, mining, domestic work, retail, and other services that require in-person work. In 2019, 39 per cent of active workers surveyed categorized themselves as part of service provision and as shop and market vendors (Zechmeister and Lupu 2019). Furthermore, national and local laws declared large swathes of the labour force to be essential workers who could keep working during lockdown; this included people working in agriculture, transport, and many retail and government jobs, as well as healthcare. Many of these workers, particularly in agriculture, transport, and food retail, worked informally and were expected to source and pay for personal protective equipment, as well as to follow social distancing and sanitation protocols; many did not or were not able to do so.

We know that 80 per cent of healthcare workers were diagnosed with COVID-19 in the first six months of the pandemic (Ministerio de Salud y Deportes 2020). Initial reports from the Civil Registry (Servicio de Registro Civil, SERECI) and departmental news coverage suggested that people working in marketplaces and transport contracted COVID-19 at extremely high rates, and that many continued to work while sick, probably passing the virus to co-workers, clients, and their families. For example, research from Universidad Autónoma Gabriel René Moreno in Santa Cruz in June 2020 found that half of the recorded infections in the department's capital were among market and transport workers and their households; this finding was consistent across departments (IIES-JOM 2020;

Ministerio de Salud y Deportes 2020). As a result, we expect that people who worked in markets, retail, transport, food production, and health, as well as their families, were particularly likely to be infected. Conversely, we expect that people who could work remotely had lower risks of infection than people who could not.

6.6 Conclusion

In Bolivia, the COVID-19 pandemic unfolded quickly and with little information. The country entered the pandemic with insufficient hospital beds, ventilators, medical personnel, and other key public health resources. Additionally, Bolivia was reeling from a political crisis that had started in 2019, and an unelected interim president was in charge of the country. Despite or perhaps because of these challenges, the government responded quickly and drastically to the first cases by closing borders and sending the country into lockdown within two weeks.

The data presented in this case study suggest that the response was effective in that it slowed and may have reduced COVID-19 transmission. Bolivians generally obeyed national and local COVID-19 containment laws, particularly in the first few months. However, the response did not prevent the pandemic from taking hold in Bolivia, and by June 2020 thousands of Bolivians were contracting COVID-19 and hundreds were dying from the disease. In an especially grim statistic, the number of people who died in Bolivia increased by 50 per cent in 2020 compared with 2019.

Bolivia started a vaccination campaign in January 2021 with several thousand doses of the Sputnik vaccine. The newly elected Arce government, which assumed power in November 2020 after winning the October 2020 elections, secured millions of doses from five manufacturers in 2021. Bolivia's COVID-19 vaccination rates are similar to its regional peers.

One positive development during the COVID-19 pandemic was that the government made huge investments in the country's healthcare sector and in infrastructure, including internet connectivity. The Morales administration had promised many of these investments for years but under-delivered, in large part because of the necessary time and expense. The pandemic revealed stark deficiencies and pushed both the Áñez and Arce administrations to pump financial and human resources into these areas. Additionally, the government used the impressive social assistance programmes that the Morales administration had developed to reach more Bolivians quickly with cash and food assistance. These were important developments that will help Bolivians now and in the future and can help Bolivia return to sustainable economic growth.

References

Acuña, J., L.E. Andersen, and L. Gonzáles (2020). 'Territorial Data for Pandemics: The Case of COVID-19-Bolivia.' Revista Latinoamericana de Desarrollo Económico, 34: 7–33. https://doi.org/10.35319/lajed.202034424.

Agencia EFE (2020). 'El desempleo se dispara hasta casi el 12% en Bolivia durante la cuarentena.' Available at: www.efe.com/efe/america/economia/el-desempleo-se-dispara-hasta-casi-12-en-bolivia-durante-la-cuarentena/20000011-4329311 (accessed 3 May 2022).

Aguilar, W. (2020). '20 de los 34 hospitales de tercer nivel están colapsados y sin personal', *Los Tiempos*. 30 June. Available at: www.lostiempos.com/actualidad/pais/20200630/20-34-hospitales-tercer-nivel-estan-colapsados-personal (accessed 3 May 2022).

Alaimo, V., M. Bosch, D. Kaplan, C. Pagés, and L. Ripani (2015). 'Jobs for Growth.' Washington, DC: IADB.

Alanoca Paco, J.R. (2020). 'Jeanine Áñez: "He Tomado La Decisión de Presentarme Como Candidata a Las Elecciones Nacionales"', *El Deber*. 24 January. Available at: https://eldeber.com.bo/usted-elige/jeanine-anez-he-tomado-la-decision-de-presentarme-como-candidata-a-las-elecciones-nacionales_163817 (accessed 3 May 2022).

Anria, S. (2018). When Movements Become Parties: The Bolivian MAS in Comparative Perspective. Cambridge: Cambridge University Press.

Anria, S., and K. Roberts (2019). 'Bolivia after Morales', *Foreign Affairs*. 21 November. Available at: www.foreignaffairs.com/articles/bolivia/2019-11-21/bolivia-after-morales (accessed 29 April 2022).

Arequipa Azurduy, M. (2020). 'Polarización a la Boliviana.' In R. Laserna (ed.), Polarización y Conflicto: Midiendo los Riesgos de la Violencia. La Paz: Ceres, pp. 43–52.

Blofield, M., and F. Filgueira (2020). 'Covid-19 and Latin America: Social Impact, Policies and a Fiscal Case for an Emergency Social Protection Floor.' Buenos Aires: Cippec.

Blofield, M., C. Giambruno, and F. Filgueira (2020). 'Policy Expansion in Compressed Time: Assessing the Speed, Breadth and Sufficiency of Post-COVID-19 Social Protection Measures in 10 Latin American Countries.' Santiago: ECLAC.

Blofield, M., J. Pribble, and C. Giambruno (2021). 'Breadth and Sufficiency of Cash Transfer Responses in 12 Latin American Countries.' Seattle, WA: APSA.

Boulding, C. (2014). NGOs, Civil Society, and Political Protest. Cambridge: Cambridge University Press.

Calderón, F., and R. Laserna (1995). Paradojas de la Modernidad: Sociedad y cambios en Bolivia. La Paz: Ceres.

Candia, A.G., I. Egido, and M. Olivera-Villarroel (2020). 'Construyendo resiliencia: Índice de vulnerabilidad del sector salud en Bolivia.' Development Research Working Paper Series 02/2020. La Paz: Instituto de Estudios Avanzados en Desarrollo.

Centellas, M. (2018). 'Bolivia in 2017: Headed into Uncertainty.' Revista de Ciencia Política, 38(2): 155–179. https://doi.org/10.4067/s0718-090x2018000200155.

Chambi, F., M.J. Osorio, and J. Vargas (2020). 'Los Hospitales de Evo Morales que no han Servido en la Pandemia', *Salud con Lupa*. Available at: https://saludconlupa.com/series/la-segunda-ola/los-hospitales-de-evo-morales-que-no-han-servido-en-la-pandemia (accessed 3 May 2022).

Derpic, J.C. (2019). 'Bolivia after Morales: Power Struggles and Shifting Alliances in the Run-Up to New Elections', *LSE Latin America and Caribbean*. 30 November. Available at: https://blogs.lse.ac.uk/latamcaribbean/2019/11/30/bolivia-after-morales-power-struggles-and-shifting-alliances-in-the-run-up-to-new-elections (accessed 1 April 2021).

Escalera-Antezana, J.P., N.F. Lizon-Ferrufino, A. Maldonado-Alanoca, G. Alarcón-de-la-vega, L.E. Alvarado-Arnez, M.A. Balderrama-Saavedra, D.K. Bonilla-Aldana, A.J. Rodríguez-Morales, and LANCOVID (2020). 'Clinical Features of the First Cases and a Cluster of Coronavirus Disease 2019 (COVID-19) in Bolivia Imported from Italy and Spain'. Travel Medicine and Infectious Disease, 35: 101653. http://doi.org/10.1016/j.tmaid.2020.101653.

Faguet, J.P. (2012). Decentralization and Popular Democracy: Governance from Below in Bolivia. Ann Arbor, MI: University of Michigan Press. https://doi.org/10.3998/mpub.175269.

Farthing, L. (2019). 'An Opportunity Squandered? Elites, Social Movements, and the Government of Evo Morales'. Latin American Perspectives, 46(1): 212–229. https://doi.org/10.1177/0094582X18798797.

Gray-Molina, G. (2001). 'Exclusion, Participation and Democratic State-Building'. In J. Crabtree and L. Whitehead (eds), Towards Democratic Viability: The Bolivian Experience. London: Palgrave Macmillan, pp. 63–82.

Gray-Molina, G., E.P. de Rada, and E. Yañez (1999). 'Transparency and Accountability in Bolivia: Does Voice Matter?' IDB Working Paper 113. New York: IDB. http://dx.doi.org/10.2139/ssrn.1814658.

Hendrix, C.S. (2010). 'Measuring State Capacity: Theoretical and Empirical Implications for the Study of Civil Conflict'. Journal of Peace Research, 47(3): 273–285. https://doi.org/10.1177/0022343310361838.

Human Rights Watch (2018). 'World Report 2018: Bolivia'. Available at: www.hrw.org/world-report/2018/country-chapters/bolivia (accessed 3 May 2022).

Hummel, C. (2021). Why Informal Workers Organize. Oxford: Oxford University Press.

Hummel, C., F.M. Knaul, M. Touchton, V.X. Velasco Guachalla, J. Nelson-Nuñez, and C. Boulding (2021). 'Poverty, Precarious Work, and the COVID-19 Pandemic: Lessons from Bolivia'. The Lancet Global Health, 9(5): E579–81. http://dx.doi.org/10.1016/S2214-109X(21)00001-2.

Hummel, C., V.X. Velasco Guachalla, J. Nelson-Nuñez, and C. Boulding (2020). 'Bolivia: Lecciones sobre los primeros seis meses de la pandemia de SARS-CoV-2'. Temas Sociales, 47: 98–129.

IIES-JOM (2020). 'Identificación de Causas Para El Incremento de Casos de COVID-19'. Santa Cruz: Instituto de Investigaciones Económicas y Sociales. Available at: www.iies.uagrm.edu.bo/wp-content/uploads/2020/07/Nota-de-prensa-COVID-19-23-DE-JUNIO-2020-v7.pdf (accessed 6 April 2021).

INE (2021). 'Indicadores de Salud: Registros Administrativos'. Available at: www.ine.gob.bo/index.php/registros-administrativos-salud (accessed 3 May 2022).

Instituto Boliviano de Comercio Exterior (2021). 'Bolivia: Evolución de la tasa de desempleo urbano comparativo trimestral 2016–2021', *Boletin Electronico Bisemanal*, 963. Available at: https://siip.produccion.gob.bo/noticias/files/2021-d6b6a-2desempleo.pdf (accessed 3 May 2022).

Karlinsky, A., and D. Kobak (2021). 'The World Mortality Dataset: Tracking Excess Mortality Across Countries during the COVID-19 Pandemic'. MedRxiv. https://doi.org/10.1101/2021.01.27.21250604.

Knaul, F.M. M.M. Touchton, H. Arreola-Ornelas, R. Calderon-Anyosa, S. Otero-Bahamón, C. Hummel, P. Pérez-Cruz, T. Porteny, F. Patino, R. Atun, P.J. Garcia, J. Insua, O. Mendez, E. Undurraga, C. Boulding, J. Nelson-Nuñez, V.X. Velasco Guachalla, and M. Sanchez-Talanquer (2022). 'Strengthening Health Systems to Face Pandemics: Subnational Policy

Responses to COVID-19 in Latin America'. Health Affairs, 41(3): 454–462. https://doi.org/10.1377/hlthaff.2021.00981.

Machicao, M., and S. Limachi (2020). 'Policía boliviana enfrenta muerte en primera línea de coronavirus', *Reuters*. 29 July. Available at: www.reuters.com/article/salud-coronavirus-bolivia-policia-idLTAKCN24U2V3 (accessed 25 February 2022).

Madrid, R.L. (2012). The Rise of Ethnic Politics in Latin America. Cambridge: Cambridge University Press.

Mamani, L. (2021). 'En 2020 la tasa de desempleo cerro en 8,4% por la pandemia', *Página Siete*. 12 March. Available at: www.paginasiete.bo/economia/2021/3/12/en-2020-la-tasa-de-desempleo-cerro-en-84-por-la-pandemia-287144.html (accessed 3 May 2022).

Ministerio de Educación (2020). 'Gobierno anuncia la clausura de la gestion educativa 2020'. Available at: www.minedu.gob.bo/index.php?option=com_content&view=article&id=4587:gobierno-anuncia-la-clausura-de-la-gestion-educativa-2020&catid=182&Itemid=854 (accessed 3 May 2022).

Ministerio de Salud (2021). 'Presidente Arce recibió la primera vacuna contra el coronavirus en el hospital El Alto Sur'. Available at: www.minsalud.gob.bo/5593-presidente-luis-arce-recibio-la-primera-vacuna-contra-el-coronavirus-en-el-hospital-el-alto-sur (accessed 25 February 2022).

Ministerio de Salud y Deportes (2017). 'Ministerio de Salus entrego 2072 Ambulacias a Bolivia'. Available at: www.minsalud.gob.bo/2975-ministerio-de-salud-entrego-2-072-ambulancias-a-bolivia (accessed 3 May 2022).

Ministerio de Salud y Deportes (2019). 'Ministerio de Salud Implementa Unidad de Terapia Intensiva en el Hospital de Tercer Nivel de Cobija'. Available at: www.minsalud.gob.bo/4295-ministerio-de-salud-implementa-unidad-de-terapia-intensiva-en-el-hospital-de-tercer-nivel-de-cobija (accessed 3 May 2022).

Ministerio de Salud y Deportes (2020). 'Una mujer de 78 anhos es la primera víctima del coronavirus en el país: Ministro de Salud'. Available at: www.minsalud.gob.bo/4012-una-mujer-de-78-anos-es-la-primera-victima-del-coronavirus-en-el-pais-ministro-de-salud (accessed 5 April 2021).

Miranda, B. (2020). 'Coronavirus: El Drama de los 150 Bolivianos atrapados en Chile por el cierre de fronteras (y controversia internacional generado por su situación)', *BBC News Mundo*. 2 April. Available at: www.bbc.com/mundo/noticias-america-latina-52145100 (accessed 5 May 2022).

Niedzwiecki, S., and S. Anria (2019). 'Participatory Social Policies: Diverging Patterns in Brazil and Bolivia'. Latin American Politics and Society, 61(2): 115–137. https://doi.org/10.1017/lap.2018.77.

Orces, D. (2008). 'Victimización por corrupción por la policía'. Revista de Ciencia Política, 28(2): 203–208. https://doi.org/10.4067/S0718-090X2008000200010.

Our World in Data (2021). 'Bolivia: Coronavirus Pandemic'. Available at: https://ourworldindata.org/coronavirus/country/bolivia?country=~BOL (accessed 25 February 2022).

Página Siete (2021). 'Desde diciembre, seis policías fallecieron por la Covid-19 en Bolivia y 231 se contagiaron', *Página Siete*. 8 January. Available at: www.paginasiete.bo/seguridad/2021/1/8/desde-diciembre-seis-policias-fallecieron-por-la-covid-19-en-bolivia-231-se-contagiaron-280523.html (accessed 25 February 2022).

Página Siete (2022). 'Previa limpia y sahumerio, Choquehuanca recibe la primera dosis anticovid', *Página Siete*. 3 January. Available at: www.paginasiete.bo/nacional/2022/1/3/previa-limpia-sahumerio-choquehuanca-recibe-la-primera-dosis-anticovid-319690.html (accessed 25 February 2022).

Pan American Health Organization (2017). 'Health Financing in the Americas'. Washington, DC: Pan American Health Organization. Available at: www.paho.org/salud-en-las-americas-2017/uh-financing.html (accessed 1 April 2021).

Peralta, P.M. (2020). 'Tras dos periodos, el MAS pierde dos tercios en la ALP', *Página Siete*. 24 October. Available at: www.paginasiete.bo/nacional/2020/10/24/tras-dos-periodos-el-mas-pierde-dos-tercios-en-la-alp-272662.html (accessed 3 May 2022).

Peredo, N. (2019). 'Más de 100 policías protagonizaron 24 escándalos en los últimos 10 años', *Los Tiempos*. 28 April. Available at: www.lostiempos.com/actualidad/pais/20190428/mas-100-policias-protagonizaron-24-escandalos-ultimos-10-anos (accessed 25 February 2022).

Pomacahua, P. (2020). 'FELCC hizo levantamiento de 86 cadaveres en un solo día', *Página Siete*. 25 July. Available at: www.paginasiete.bo/seguridad/2020/7/25/felcc-hizo-levantamiento-de-86-cadaveres-en-un-solo-dia-262416.html (accessed 3 May 2022).

Porto, A., M. Garriga, and W. Rosales (2018). 'Medidas de desempeño y eficiencia del gasto en el sector publico descentralizado: El caso de Bolivia'. Revista de Análisis Económico, 33(1): 121–155. https://doi.org/10.4067/S0718-88702018000100121.

REDLAD (2020). 'Pandemia de abuso policial'. Bogotá: REDLAD. Available at: http://redlad.org/wp-content/uploads/2020/12/Informe-Redlad-Pandemia-de-abuso-policial.pdf (accessed 25 February 2022).

Rosales Melgar, A. (2020). 'Bolivia posterga las elecciones hasta el 18 de octubre', *El Deber*. 23 July. Available at: https://eldeber.com.bo/pais/bolivia-posterga-elecciones-hasta-el-18-de-octubre_192191 (accessed 5 May 2022).

Saavedra Mogro, M.A. (2017). 'Los procesos de reforma judicial en Bolivia (1991–2017)'. Revista Juridica Derecho, 5(6): 109–132.

Soifer, H. (2008). 'State Infrastructural Power: Approaches to Conceptualization and Measurement'. Studies in Comparative International Development, 43(3): 231–251. https://doi.org/10.1007/s12116-008-9028-6.

Soifer, H.D. (2015). State Building in Latin America. Cambridge: Cambridge University Press. https://doi.org/10.1017/CBO9781316257289.

Tancara Castillo, C. (2020). 'Clausura del año escolar sin plan de emergencia fue un fracaso para la educación', *Página Siete*. 25 December. Available at: www.paginasiete.bo/especial02/2020/12/25/clausura-del-ano-escolar-sin-plan-de-emergencia-fue-un-fracaso-para-la-educacion-279022.html (accessed 3 May 2022).

Toledo Orozco, Z. (2022). 'Informal Gold Miners, State Fragmentation, and Resource Governance in Bolivia and Peru'. Latin American Politics and Society, 64(2): 45–66. https://doi.org/10.1017/lap.2022.5.

Touchton, M., F.M. Knaul, H. Arreola-Ornelas, T. Porteny, M. Sánchez, O. Méndez, M. Faganello, V. Edelson, B. Gygi, C. Hummel, S. Otero, J. Insua, E. Undurraga, and J.A. Rosado (2021). 'A Partisan Pandemic: State Government Public Health Policies to Combat COVID-19 in Brazil'. BMJ Global Health, 6(6): e005223. https://doi.org/10.1136/bmjgh-2021-005223.

Trigo, M.S., and A. Kurmanaev (2020). 'Bolivia esta bloqueada, los manifestantes obstruyen el acceso a las ciudades', *New York Times*. 7 August. Available at: www.nytimes.com/es/2020/08/07/espanol/america-latina/bloqueos-bolivia.html (accessed 3 May 2022).

Vargas Maldonado, A.C. (1998). 'La burocracia boliviana y sus transformaciones: Entre la lógica clientelar y la lógica racional'. Temas Sociales, 20: 189–193.

Velasco Guachalla, V.X., C. Hummel, S. Handlin, and A.E. Smith (2021). 'Latin America Erupts: When Does Competitive Authoritarianism Take Root?'. Journal of Democracy, 32(3): 63–77. https://doi.org/10.1353/jod.2021.0034.

Velasco Guachalla, V.X., C. Hummel, J. Nelson-Nuñez, and C. Boulding (2021a). 'Compounding Crises: Bolivia in 2020'. Revista de Ciencia Politica, 41(2): 211–237. http://dx.doi.org/10.4067/S0718-090X2021005000116.

Velasco Guachalla, V.X., C. Hummel, J. Nelson-Nuñez, and C. Boulding (2021b). 'Legitimacy and Policy during Crises: Subnational COVID-19 Responses in Bolivia'. Perspectives on Politics, 20(2): 528–546. https://doi.org/10.1017/S1537592721001183.

Wolff, J. (2020). 'The Turbulent End of an Era in Bolivia: Contested Elections, the Ouster of Evo Morales, and the Beginning of a Transition Towards an Uncertain Future'. Revista de Ciencia Política, 40(2): 163–186.

World Bank (2021). 'World Development Indicators: Population, Total'. Available at: https://data.worldbank.org/indicator/SP.POP.TOTL?locations=BO (accessed 3 May 2022).

Zechmeister, E.J., and N. Lupu (eds) (2019). Pulse of Democracy. Nashville, TN: LAPOP. Available at: www.vanderbilt.edu/lapop/ab2018/2018-19_AmericasBarometer_Regional_Report_10.13.19.pdf (accessed 5 May 2022).

Ziaja, S., J. Grävingholt, and M. Kreibaum (2019). 'Constellations of Fragility: An Empirical Typology of States'. Studies in Comparative International Development, 54(2): 299–321. https://doi.org/10.1007/s12116-019-09284-3.

Zuazo, M., J.P. Faguet, and G. Bonifaz (2012). Descentralización y democratización en Bolivia: La historia del Estado débil, la sociedad rebelde y el anhelo de democracia. Bonn: Friedrich-Ebert-Stiftung.

7

The Devasting Effects of the COVID-19 Pandemic on Peru

The Undermining Role of Vertical Health Policies in Health Systems

Camila Gianella

7.1 Introduction

At a global level, there is a growing consensus regarding the critical role of the state's capacity to guarantee resilient health systems able to effectively respond to health emergencies, such as the one generated by the COVID-19 pandemic. Less consensus exists around what features of the state are critical in explaining the performance and outcomes of the conditions when dealing with the pandemic.

For example, emerging evidence shows that although a country's income level relates to the state's capacity to face crises like the one generated by COVID-19, this is not the only factor or the most prominent (Pitterle and Lennart Niermann 2021).

Latin America offers an excellent example of this. The region has been hit hard by the pandemic. In recent years, most countries in the region have become recognized as middle-income countries after decades of being classified as poor. Yet the devastating impact of the pandemic revealed the extent of structural problems, such as unequal wealth distribution, low levels of investment in public services, and labour informality, which have contributed to the spreading of the disease and limited the recovery in economic activity. The COVID-19 pandemic has prompted the most significant gross domestic product (GDP) contraction in the past 100 years and triggered a decline in employment not seen in the past seven decades, with the regional informal sector experiencing the most significant job destruction (ECLAC 2021).

Within Latin America, the case of Peru has been particularly striking. The country has shown more significant weakness than countries of similar income when responding to the crisis generated by the pandemic. This, in turn, has contributed to the 213,000 COVID-19 deaths in a population of less than 33 million (Our World in Data 2021).

Camila Gianella, *The Devasting Effects of the COVID-19 Pandemic on Peru*. In: *How States Respond to Crisis*.
Edited by: Rachel M. Gisselquist and Andrea Vaccaro, Oxford University Press. © UNU-WIDER (2025).
DOI: 10.1093/9780198907237.003.0007

Before the pandemic, this upper-middle-income country was regarded as a capable state. Peru had experienced 18 years of sustained growth at rates above the Latin American average. In addition, the country had an unusually low debt of 26 per cent of its GDP and had managed to control inflation (at less than 2 per cent). In recognition of its macroeconomic performance, the International Monetary Fund referred to Peru as a rising star (Montenegro 2020; ProInversión 2019). Besides macroeconomic indicators, Peru was on track to fulfilling the Sustainable Development Goals (SDGs) and was making good progress on improving health coverage.

Also, the Peruvian government had the authority and legitimacy to adopt mandatory social isolation to stop the spread of COVID-19. Unlike other Latin American countries severely affected by the pandemic, such as Brazil or Nicaragua (as addressed in Jarquín 2022), authorities in Peru did not deny the threat of the pandemic. They ordered a state of emergency that was supported by the majority of the population. In March 2020, when former president Martín Vizcarra adopted the general lockdown, the presidential approval rating grew from 52 per cent to 87 per cent.

Compared with other countries in the region, Peru's ability to deliver sustained macroeconomic performance and progress towards international development goals suggests a comparatively 'capable' state. We would expect such a state to also engineer an effective pandemic response. It is a puzzle, then, that it did not.

Using one core health programme—maternal health—labelled as successful for the reduction of maternal mortality since 2000 (UNFPA 2017; WHO 2019), this chapter argues that in contrast to what is described in Asante (2022), in Peru, previous public health programmes have not contributed to building the health system's 'residual capacity'. The focus on maternal mortality is not a random choice. The literature has already described the fact that this indicator is sensitive to the health system's capacity to provide quality health services at the primary level and refer to complex care. Besides, maternal mortality is sensitive to social inequity and socioeconomic marginalization (Physicians for Human Rights 2007; Pinzón-Flórez et al. 2017; Thaddeus and Maine 1994). Since the mid-1990s, Peruvian authorities have invested in and rolled out various programmes, strategies, and national plans to prevent and reduce maternal deaths, including activities to decrease domiciliary deliveries and improve health services' accessibility and quality of care (Del Carpio 2013; Ministerio de Salud 2009).

An increase in maternal mortality during the COVID-19 pandemic has been reported in other countries; the more concerning reports come from low- and middle-income countries (i.e. countries that already carry the majority of the global burden of maternal mortality) (Chmielewska et al. 2021). The achievements of Peru in the last years should, in theory, have prevented the dramatic increase in maternal deaths observed in 2020 and 2021. Before the pandemic, Peru had managed to reduce the maternal mortality ratio from 144 to 88 per 100,000 live births (a decline that kept pace up until the year 2019) and expand coverage of maternal care services, reaching 94 per cent of births attended by skilled professionals at a health facility. The country also had in place a national network for the surveillance of maternal mortality; this network provides weekly updates to characterize the maternal mortality profile in the 24 regions (Carrillo-Larco et al. 2022). In other words, Peru was in a good place to design interventions to address maternal mortality, according to subnational patterns, by age or specific causes. However, during the first year of the pandemic, it increased by 50 per cent (Carrillo-Larco et al. 2022).

Before the COVID-19 pandemic, scholars pointed to the risks of oversimplifying global indicators in implementing the Millennium Development Goals and designing the SDGs. For scholars such as Merry (2016), the emergence of numeric targets reflects a global trend where quantification of governance is perceived as the goal standard. Evidence-based governance represents the 'indicator culture' (Merry 2016) where indicators become the governance technology. However, by translating social phenomena into measurable outcomes, indicators can redefine concepts intended to measure and set policy priorities, including at the national level (Fukuda-Parr et al. 2014).

The power of the indicators has been reinforced by the 'measurement obsession' in global development (Fukuda-Parr and McNeill 2019; Fukuda-Parr et al. 2014), which emphasizes the prioritization of vertical programmes that rely heavily on technical solutions, avoiding ideas of social justice and neglecting the need for social change and the strengthening of national institutions (Birn and Nervi 2019; Fukuda-Parr et al. 2014).

In addition to concerns regarding the risks of the oversimplification of 'indicator culture', another corpus of the literature has stressed the need to understand how evidence-based governance is implemented and what is telling about the relations between the different layers of the state, and between the different layers of the state and the citizens. Authors such as Gupta (2012) have referred to targets being decided from above without consultation with the implementers about their feasibility and desirability as structural violence. For this author, this type of violence is systematically produced by the frictions between the agendas, ministries/offices, levels, and spaces that make up the state (Gupta 2012). This violence is also exercised by domination (Auyero 2009), which works by yielding to the power of more powerful others at the different levels of the implementation of the policies. The authority of powerful agents surrounds implementers of the policies. Citizens targeted by social programmes are also surrounded by the rules of the 'experts' who decide the policies and by the power of implementers (Cookson 2018). This dynamic provides inaccurate information regarding the services that the population needs, undermining the state's real ability to provide, as well as the capacity to make the state accountable for neglecting population needs.

I argue that the poor performance of the Peruvian state during the COVID-19 pandemic, including the increase in maternal deaths, is an expression of 'structural violence' (Gupta 2012), which is rooted in the adoption of evidence-based governance detached from structural reforms to reduce inequities. The adoption of evidence-based governance by the health system in Peru and, more broadly, Latin America is related to the period of neoliberal macroeconomic reforms adopted at the end of the 1980s and the beginning of the 1990s, with a typical pattern of policies enshrined in the so-called Washington Consensus characterized by a targeting approach, the shrinking of the state, and the prioritization of cost-effectiveness analysis in designing policy.

The health system, particularly maternal health services, offers an excellent case to analyse this structural violence. Health systems are core social institutions (Freedman 2006; Yamin and Norheim 2010) similar to the judicial or democratic political systems. In this sense, health systems are providers of health and healthcare and a vital part of the social fabric—structures where societal values and norms are communicated and reinforced. These societal values and standards influence how health systems design and assess health policies and interventions. Thus, selecting criteria and indicators to evaluate health systems' and interventions' performance and results is contentious and embedded in normative judgements and moral considerations that are not value neutral and often not explicitly presented by the literature. In the case of maternal health, the indicator of maternal deaths, while valuable in providing information about a particular phenomenon, does not provide a complete picture of the underlying determinants of health that could contribute to the maternal deaths, such as access to safe and potable drinking water and adequate sanitation facilities, hospitals, trained health workers, and essential drugs. The literature has shown how the lack of availability can influence the decision to seek care when health facilities are so scarce that distance is a discouraging factor. The lack of availability and geographic accessibility can make travel to a health facility long, producing delays in arriving to treatment (Physicians for Human Rights 2007; Thaddeus and Maine 1994).

The chapter is organized as follows: first, it describes the state of maternal mortality in Peru during the COVID-19 response through 2020 and 2021. This description includes the policies and programmes deployed to address maternal mortality during those years. Second, it analyses the policy's efforts in targeting maternal health and maternal mortality. Section 7.4 presents final remarks.

7.2 COVID-19 and maternal healthcare services

On 15 March 2020, with 28 confirmed cases and no reported deaths, the Peruvian government issued Supreme Decree 044-2020-PCM, declaring a national state of emergency. Early on, the government implemented a series of extreme measures based on recommendations of the World Health Organization (WHO), such as closing borders, restricting freedom of movement nationwide, banning crowds, closing schools, universities, and churches, and generally restricting all non-essential activities and services, such as outpatient care (including immunization, prenatal, obstetric, contraception, paediatric, adult, nutrition, and health promotion activities). As a result, 8,723 primary health centres closed down outpatient services for more than three months.

Also in March 2020, the Peruvian state ordered health workers with comorbidities to take health leave and work remotely (DU 026-20). To address the human resources shortage within and increasing demand for COVID-19 services, Peruvian health authorities reorganized and reassigned the available health workforce to cover COVID-19 services. New staff were hired to work exclusively in these services (Murillo-Peña et al. 2021).

However, these measures were not enough to respond to the needs created by the pandemic. Peru had the highest COVID-19 mortality rate among health workers of any country globally. This rate began to decrease once vaccination for health workers was provided during the first quarter of 2021 (Mayta Tristan 2021). Despite this, by mid-2021, many health workers remained on leave—and the proportion was higher in rural areas (see Tables 7.1 and 7.2 describing the situation of health workers on leave).

Within a context of rapidly increasing numbers of COVID-19 cases and deaths, a shortage of health workers, and restrictions on the availability and accessibility of maternal health services, Peruvian health authorities ordered some measures aimed at attending to the non-COVID-19-related health needs of the population, without any study of their feasibility. In the case of maternal health, in April 2020, the Ministry of Health (MoH) issued Directiva Sanitaria 094-MINSA/2020 DGIESP to guarantee antenatal, perinatal, and postpartum care access during the COVID-19 emergency and Directiva Sanitaria 097-MINSA/2020 DGIESP, establishing the procedures to be followed to attend to the health needs of pregnant women and newborns who were at risk from or who tested positive for COVID-19. Both regulations included monitoring strategies via mobile phones and video calls.

It was not clear how these directives were to be implemented. The orders were not accompanied by concrete measures ordering the opening of non-emergency maternal care services or hiring new personnel. Moreover, assuming the close-down of maternal health services, some national programmes, such as Juntos (the conditional cash transfer programme), stopped collecting and reporting data on maternal health.

Another measure announced in April 2020 was 'telemedicine' as a means to protect health workers and guarantee access to health services. But the measure did not take into consideration the fact that 8 out of 10 primary care centres in Peru do not have internet access (Seinfeld et al. 2021); besides, while 84.4 per cent of poor households have access to a mobile phone, only 7.1 per cent have access to the internet (Mesa de Concertación Para la Lucha Contra la Pobreza 2020).

Table 7.1 Health workers on health leave (DU 026-20)

	2020								2021								
	May	**Jun**	**Jul**	**Aug**	**Sep**	**Oct**	**Nov**	**Dec**	**Jan**	**Feb**	**Mar**	**Apr**	**May**	**Jun**	**Jul**	**Aug**	**Sep**
% MoH and regional govern-ment health workers on leave	5.0	9.6	9.6	9.7	8.9	8.7	8.6	8.5	8.1	8.4	7.8	7.5	6.9	6.8	6.8	6.7	6.5
Peru	12,879	24,671	24,672	25,027	22,894	22,352	22,243	21,888	20,931	21,722	20,146	19,392	17,765	17,634	17,463	17,170	16,784
Rural	12,113	23,445	23,446	23,832	21,696	21,150	21,059	20,716	19,833	20,616	19,160	18,435	16,916	16,798	16,665	16,410	16,061
Urban	766	1,226	1,226	1,195	1,198	1,202	1,184	1,172	1,098	1,106	986	957	849	836	798	760	723

Note: N = 257,566.
Source: Author's construction based on data obtained privately from the MoH.

Table 7.2 Percentage of health workers (MoH and regional government) on health leave

Profession	2020								2021								
	May	Jun	Jul	Aug	Sep	Oct	Nov	Dec	Jan	Feb	Mar	Apr	May	Jun	Jul	Aug	Sep
Medical doctors	5.25	9.82	9.83	10.17	9.20	8.95	8.93	8.81	8.47	8.23	7.79	7.25	5.62	5.43	5.54	5.34	5.23
Nurses	4.10	8.52	8.52	8.66	8.16	8.14	8.14	8.01	7.64	8.21	7.59	7.25	6.26	6.22	6.14	6.01	5.87
Midwives	4.28	8.16	8.16	8.27	7.43	7.06	6.97	6.80	6.58	6.37	5.77	5.42	4.72	4.67	4.59	4.59	4.43

Source: Author's construction based on data obtained privately from the MoH.

Thus, this measure was not helpful in addressing the demand for maternal health services at primary healthcare centres. Research performed with health personnel from sexual and reproductive health services in Lima during the pandemic found that one outstanding feature of the MoH COVID-19 response, described by health workers, was the lack of planning. There were no clear indications on how, under these new circumstances, non-COVID-19 health services should be organized, how patients' follow-up should take place, or how patients' access would be guaranteed to their regular drugs or other supplies (Pesantes and Cortez 2021).

To respond to this situation, health workers on leave implemented strategies to follow up with their patients using their mobile phones. Personal phones were used to send patients reminders of their appointments or information regarding where to go for the delivery. This demonstrates that health workers did not receive the equipment or financial resources required to follow up their patients remotely as ordered by Directiva Sanitaria 094-MINSA/2020 DGIESP and Directiva Sanitaria 097-MINSA/2020 DGIESP. In addition, formal procedures were not adapted. Pharmacies required the physical prescription of medicines (from contraceptives to iron), making it impossible for health workers working remotely to prescribe any medication to their patients.

The poor implementation of policy measures such as Directiva Sanitaria 094-MINSA/2020 DGIESP and Directiva Sanitaria 097-MINSA/2020 DGIESP happened despite the efforts made by lower-level officials who were, for many reasons including lack of material conditions, incapable of implementing the 'desires' of the high-ranking officials who had planned a response without undertaking any feasibility analysis. As a result, 34.4 per cent of maternal deaths in 2020 occurred without any antenatal control; in 2020 and 2021 together this figure reached 41.2 per cent. By contrast, in 2019 it was 29.9 per cent (Centro Nacional de Epidemiología, Prevención y Control de Enfermedades 2021).

By June 2020, the available data already showed an increase in maternal deaths (Centro Nacional de Epidemiología, Prevención y Control de Enfermedades 2020). However, no measures were taken to amend the shortfalls of the previous orders. Pregnancy was not considered a risk factor in the COVID-19 clinical guidelines and regulations issued by the MoH. Moreover, despite the increase in maternal deaths and the information on the lack of health personnel (see Tables 7.1 and 7.2), there were no specific or emergency measures to address maternal mortality as part of the COVID-19 response, or even to supervise the implementation of Directiva Sanitaria 094-MINSA/2020 DGIESP and Directiva Sanitaria 097-MINSA/2020 DGIESP.

Despite maternal deaths increasing by 45.4 per cent in 2020, pregnant women were not prioritized for vaccination—that is, they were not considered among the at-risk groups. Only in June 2021, when immunization by age groups was already on track, were women at 28 or more weeks of pregnancy prioritized for vaccination. In August 2021, this changed to 12 weeks of pregnancy.

Besides, some hospitals became COVID-19 hospitals (i.e. they stopped providing care to those with other health conditions, including antenatal control and deliveries); others refused to care for anyone suspected of having COVID-19. All this created geographical and economic barriers (due to the cost of transport) to access to healthcare, thereby producing delays in the receipt of timely care, including in the case of obstetric emergencies. The majority of maternal deaths took place in a health facility during 2020 and 2021 and the number of institutional maternal deaths increased from that in previous years (83.21 per cent against 75.5 per cent in 2020 and 74.5 per cent in 2019). For these women, reaching a health facility was not enough to save their lives.

That a lack of planning contributed to preventable deaths is illustrated in the case of Mrs NB, a 32-year-old woman who died on 29 April 2021 after delivering a stillborn baby. Mrs NB lived with her husband and daughter in a rural community in Rio Negro, Satipo, Junín, where they grow and trade pineapples. According to official data, around 30 per cent of Rio Negro's population lives in poverty. In this district of 34,427 inhabitants, 1,043 families belong to the Junto conditional cash transfer programme.

Despite a public health post 4 kilometres away from the community, Mrs NB's family and neighbours prefer to travel 50 kilometres to Pichanaki to seek healthcare. Even if they have to pay for the services and the transport, Pichanaki offers better services. During her pregnancy, Mrs NB went to her antenatal care; all was normal. At the health post, they ordered some tests and referred her to Satipo, a town two hours away. Even if she had to pay, she preferred to travel to Pichanaki, which was closer.

Two days before her death, she started to experience fever and headaches. These are emergency symptoms during pregnancy. However, Mrs NB and her husband thought first of COVID-19, went for a private test, and got a negative result. After this, they thought that the symptoms were related to the imminent delivery (she was around 39 weeks). Mrs NB and her husband decided to travel to Pichanaki to seek healthcare. Even though their relatives supported them to cover the transport costs, it was not easy to find private transport to take them to Pichanaki. April was among the worst months of the COVID-19 pandemic in Peru. When Mrs NB arrived at Pichanaki, the hospital was 'full'. Although her case was an obstetric emergency, the staff told Mrs NB's husband to take her to La Merced, 73 kilometres away from Pichanaki. With their resources, Mrs NB and her husband travelled to seek healthcare. At La Merced, the staff told Mrs NB's husband that she had delivered a stillborn baby; after some hours, he was informed that his wife had had COVID-19 and died. They told him that Mrs NB's symptoms (headache and fever) were COVID-19 symptoms. Besides her, no one in the family had reported any

COVID-19 symptoms.[1] If pregnant women, such as Mrs NB, had been prioritized along with the first group vaccinated, she would have had the chance to get at least one shot of the vaccine.

Mrs NB's case also shows the lack of referral capacity of primary health services in Peru. In Peru, antenatal care coverage is not linked to the timely referral of emergencies. As Mrs NB's case shows, even in cases where the pregnant woman visits a health centre for antenatal care, in obstetric emergencies the woman and her family have to deal with the costs of the referral, as well as with the bureaucracy.

7.3 Maternal mortality

In contrast to other Latin American countries, and despite limited attempts to implement redistributive policies within the welfare system, Peru has kept the neoliberal core of the welfare model (Minteguiaga and Ubasart-González 2021), maintaining a segmented welfare system that institutionally separates social insurance and social assistance programmes. The health system, as part of the welfare system, maintains a tripartite segmentation: public (social assistance programmes), social insurance, and private (Cotlear et al. 2015), and health policies, such as the maternal health programme, have retained core components of the neoliberal approach.

The first is the 'targeting' approach; Peruvian health policies designed since the 1990s have centralized this feature. One example of the targeting system is the conditional cash transfer schemes implemented across the region. These schemes were framed as policy tools to reduce poverty and expand access to nutrition, education, and healthcare to marginalized groups who could not afford or access market-based services (Cookson 2018). With some variations, conditional cash transfer programmes use the census to identify eligible households; some of them, as in the case of the Peruvian version, use two-step identification: the government first recognizes the poorest districts and then, within the community, the families. The programmes involve the payment of a small sum of money and incentive contingent on the fulfilment of certain programmatic goals, such as school attendance, use of health services, and pregnant women's attendance at prenatal care (controls).

The Peruvian version of a conditional cash transfer scheme, which includes maternal health, is Juntos. This programme, created in 2005, targeted women to increase the demand and use of health services, especially maternal and child healthcare.

[1] Interview with Mrs NB's husband, 1 November 2021, Rio Negro, Satipo, Junín.

Juntos presents an excellent example of the limits and problems of the targeting approach and how structural violence and domination are exercised. The programme goals were designed without public debate and are the same, independent of the context and challenge implementers face. Women are subject to domination by the programme implementers, arbitrarily creating shadow conditionalities (such as participating in workshops, growing a garden, using a smokeless stove, or participating in other social programmes) that women perceive as mandatory (Cookson 2018; Huber et al. 2009). Moreover, the programme is rooted in the idea of health status as, primarily, an outcome of individual decisions and therefore in the need to make poor people co-responsible for their health, without reflection on whether a mother's poverty should be taken as evidence that she acts irresponsibly (Cookson 2018) or about the social determinants of health. This approach is blind to any reflection and debate regarding histories of exclusion and violence and the need for social change.

A second component is the promotion of vertical programmes linked to specific outcomes. In Peru, from 2007, as part of national budget reform, the Ministry of Economy and Finance (MEF) introduced new payment mechanisms to encourage the more efficient allocation of resources across national health strategies. In particular, the Budgeting for Results Programmes (Presupuestos por Resultados, PpRs), defined as a public management strategy that links resource allocation to products and measurable results for the population (OECD 2017), switched from budget lines (human resources, goods and services, etc.) to a productivity-based approach. In the case of health, interventions are selected based on health priorities that are closely linked to goal and target commitments by the Peruvian state at the international level.

While some studies have found some positive impacts of PpRs in terms of expenditure and increases in coverage, there are also some risks linked to this tool. PpRs are established for specific health problems or population groups. Their use therefore risks failing to address questions of the total financial resources needed for the health sector (OECD 2017). PpRs also do not consider institutional strengthening within the health sector. Besides, the core of PpRs (policy to be implemented at the national level) overlooks critical state dimensions, such as state capacity and legitimacy (see Chapter 1 in this volume), that affect the policy implementation and therefore its effectiveness. Despite significant disparities within the national territory of health facilities accessibility and the availability of human resources, as well as in the use of healthcare, PpRs consider the same set of indicators to the whole territory, assuming that the same intervention, despite critical contextual factors, should have the same output.

The implementation of PpRs has implied that national health strategies come under the guidance of the MEF. The predominance of the MEF in policy-making began in the 1990s when Alberto Fujimori called on a group of economists to implement a set of neoliberal reforms. The success of these reforms, framed as 'technical and independent', in controlling hyperinflation contributed to consolidating the power of the technocrats of the MEF in policy design through different governments (Dargent 2011). This explains the maintenance of the neoliberal core of the welfare model in Peru.

A third central component is the over-focus on coverage. Healthcare coverage has become the leading indicator of the healthcare system's performance, neglecting supervision, quality, and other critical components of health services (Gianella and Yamin 2018).

A fourth component is the shrinking of public services and promoting of private sector participation in healthcare provision. One indicator of this is the low level of investment in public health services. While it is true that, in general, Latin American countries report public health expenditure below the Pan American Health Organization (PAHO) recommendation of 6 per cent of GDP (CEPAL 2021), Peru's public health expenditure has remained one of the lowest in the region (CEPAL 2021; Du Bois et al. 2004). Moreover, despite significant advances in universal health coverage in Peru in the last decade, increasing from 64 per cent of Peruvians with some health insurance in 2010 to 95 per cent in 2020 (SUSALUD 2021), out-of-pocket expenditure remains high and has even increased in recent years (Kanavos et al. 2019). Studies have found that Peruvian households are at higher risk of incurring catastrophic health expenditure (CHE)—that is, when families use more than 40 per cent of non-food expenditure to pay for medical care—than those in other Latin American countries (OECD 2017).

The shrinking of public services has allowed the maintenance of a highly fragmented health system in terms of its organization and structure that constrains the state's capacity to deliver high-quality healthcare for all; the fragmentation of the Peruvian health system is expressed in its various funding sources, diversity of insurance schemes with varying coverage, and multiple health service delivery channels. One key characteristic of the Peruvian health system, specifically of Peru's insurance schemes, is the relationship between income level, access to formal employment, and health plan coverage (healthcare basket). In contrast to what has happened in other Latin American countries—like Colombia, where health reforms have transitioned into the unification of public health plans—in Peru, EsSalud (a scheme that provides healthcare, as well as pension and welfare coverage, financed through payroll discounts among those in formal employment and public sources) offers more services to its insurers than the Seguro Integral de Salud (SIS), which is funded through general taxes and primarily targets those in poverty to provide free healthcare for those with certain conditions.

These components have contributed to creating a health system that reports a high level of insurance coverage but has poor conditions for the provision of care. By January 2020, according to the MoH, 77.8 per cent of first-level healthcare services had inadequate capacity, expressed in the precariousness of the infrastructure and obsolete, inoperative, or defective equipment (ComexPerú 2020). By the beginning of 2021, this had reached 97 per cent of first-level healthcare services and 100 per cent in 5 out of 25 regions (Callao, Lambayeque, Loreto, Madre de Dios, and Ucayali). Before the pandemic, Peru had 29 intensive care beds per million inhabitants, below the ratio in other countries in the region, such as Brazil (which had 206), Colombia (105), Chile (73), and Ecuador (69) (Comité de Alto Nivel sobre el COVID-19 2021).

This fragmentation creates significant barriers to accessing critical services, such as the COVID-19 vaccines. Even though vaccines were purchased with public funds, the National COVID-19 Vaccination Plan stated that vaccines would be distributed through the various public health service delivery channels. As a result, during March and April 2021, the vaccination of the elderly was highly fragmented, with massive inequities in access. EsSalud began with vaccination of those who were insured by the scheme, offering at-home vaccination. SIS began later, and those insured under that scheme had to travel to vaccination centres: no options were provided to those without the capability or mobility to do so. Vaccination centres were also segmented by type of insurance. In May, a new vaccination plan was adopted; from then on, all vaccination centres were for the whole population, independently of insurance.

In the case of maternal mortality, before the COVID-19 pandemic the leading causes of maternal mortality in Peru were hypertension induced by pregnancy (related to eclampsia and pre-eclampsia) and abortion complications; in the case of pregnancy-related death, the causes were suicide, cancer, and respiratory tract infections (Centro Nacional de Epidemiología, Prevención y Control de Enfermedades 2020; Gil 2018). As mentioned above, Peru had reported a decrease in maternal mortality before the pandemic—of 72 per cent between 1990 and 2015—and was considered on track to achieve SDG target 3.1 (reduce the global maternal mortality ratio). However, maternal mortality had been unevenly distributed across the country. The Amazon regions of Ucayali, Amazonas, Madre de Dios, and Loreto report maternal mortality ratios (MMRs) that are far above the national ratios and the SDG goal of an MMR of under 70 maternal deaths per 100,000 live births (167.8, 157.5, 151.8, and 133.8, respectively) (Gil 2018).

Regarding the most recent policy and programmes designed to address maternal mortality, one of the programmes that played a central role in the reforms of the Peruvian health sector in 2021 was the Programme to Support Health Sector Reform (Programa de Apoyo a la Reforma del Sector Salud, PARSalud I and II). The programme started in 1999 with a World Bank and International Development Bank (IDB) loan. After 2002, the scope of the programme was narrowed to focus to a considerable extent on maternal and child health and the reduction of maternal mortality to improve the overall health sector (Physicians for Human Rights 2007). PARSalud specifically targets the regions with the worst health outcomes.

PARSalud's strategy covers two areas where improvements were crucial to reducing maternal mortality. The first consisted of promoting greater access to perinatal care. The second was to improve maternal healthcare services' quality through investment in infrastructure and equipment, staff training, a system of referrals and counter-referrals, and the implementation of protocols to ensure proper case management (e.g. the use of oxytocin to prevent postpartum haemorrhage).

Programme evaluations have shown positive outcomes in the coverage of skilled birth attendance, the coverage of a ferrous sulphate supplement, delivery of corticoids to women in the case of premature birth, and the use of magnesium sulphate in cases of hypertension induced by pregnancy.

Since 2008, there has been a PpR for maternal and neonatal health that shares outputs with PARSalud. Some evidence exists of the impact of the fiscal programme on maternal and neonatal health, as in the case of PARSalud's positive impacts, such as an increase (at a higher rate among women living in rural areas) in the percentage of institutional deliveries performed by skilled health workers (medical doctor, midwife, and nurse) (OECD 2017).

Peru's primary and comprehensive emergency obstetric care (EmOC) services remain a challenge. An assessment of basic emergency obstetric and newborn services (FONE 1) showed that none of the 619 health facilities assessed had reached 100 per cent resolution capacity for prenatal care (comprehensive care that seeks the participation of the pregnant woman, couple, and family in preparation for institutional childbirth, puerperium, and care of the newborn); that is, they did not have the professionals, equipment, instruments, or medicines required for antenatal care. The same assessment showed that only one centre was in the '90 per cent or more' resolution capacity range for hypertension induced by pregnancy, eclampsia, and pre-eclampsia (Instituto Nacional de Estadística e Informática 2016).

In the case of complex EmOC, such as severe pregnancy-induced hypertension and eclampsia, which involves specialized management of complications in general intensive care, of the 45 hospitals (13 of them located in Metropolitan Lima and 2 in Callao) that should have the capacity to provide this level of care (FONE 2), none reached the '90 per cent or more' range of resolution capacity. Five, all located in Metropolitan Lima, reached 'from 70 per cent to 79 per cent' of resolution capacity.

Moreover, human resources are also insufficient. In a 2021 publication, the Colegio de Obstetras del Perú (Peruvian Professional Association of Obstetricians) stated that the number of midwives working in public health services before the pandemic (around 17,000) was already insufficient to cover population needs.

Besides, as Mrs NB's case shows, women cannot access adequate care without a referral. Even if Mrs NB had attended her antenatal controls at the health post closer to her home, and even though she was insured, the health post and her insurance (SIS) were unable to provide Mrs NB with the conditions for the referral: there were no emergency services and Mrs NB and her family were forced to search and pay for private transport to reach a health centre that could provide EmOC.

7.4 The perfect storm

Why is it that a state like Peru, dedicated to fulfilling development goals and with sustained good macroeconomic performance, appears to be incapable of dealing with the COVID-19 pandemic? This puzzle cannot be addressed detached from a recognition of the approach that Peruvian health policies have adopted since the 1990s. The over-focus on certain numeric indicators as a means to assess the outcomes of prioritized vertical programmes, neglecting supervision, quality, and other critical components of health services such as out-of-pocket expenditure or the assessment of total financial resources needed for the health sector, has undermined the capacity of these programmes to build up residual capacity within the health system. In the case of maternal health, the national information system provides information on key maternal health indicators such as the increase in maternal deaths and the decrease in the number of routine antenatal care consultations. The weakness of the health system has made it impossible to rapidly restructure and remotely deliver regular care to pregnant women.

This weakness has been built and sustained by the different layers of the Peruvian state, which, adopting mainstream evidence-based governance, designed and implemented a set of reforms and programmes aimed at improving performance against certain numeric targets without a deeper analysis of the structural conditions that allow and reinforce health inequities. The narrow approach has shown significant weaknesses in the health system that have been actively ignored by the Peruvian state. Improvements against some targeted indicators, such as the MMR, have not been linked to improvements in the whole health system and have contributed to providing an inaccurate image of the Peruvian health system. Despite considerable progress towards achieving the SDGs, including targeting health and wellbeing (SDG 3), by March 2020 the Peruvian health system was in crisis: underfunded with poor resolutive capacity. This lack of ability reflected how the Peruvian state has been functioning and the structural violence the state has been exercising across its different areas of responsibility. In this chapter, I have referred to certain vertical programmes with targets that local-level public servants have had to fulfil without thinking about their working conditions or about quality. The indicator has become the goal, and the implementers of the policies, at different levels, work to reach the targets even if this implies forcing subordinates to walk for many hours to get to some villages, sacrificing the quality of care, forcing poor women to travel for many hours to reach a health post, or blaming poor women for their health status or 'risks'. National strategies, such as PpRs, have been designed and implemented regardless of state effectiveness. State capacity has been dangerously overlooked.

By 2020, there was a corpus of literature showing the dramatic limitations of evidence-based governance in social policies, including health (Cookson 2018; Ewig 2012; Gianella Malca 2019; Huber et al. 2009; Petrera and Jiménez 2018; Physicians for Human Rights 2007; Yon 2017). Reports on the Peruvian health system showed a significant weakness (Instituto Nacional de Estadística e Informática 2016; Ministerio de Salud 2021; OECD 2017), revealing that good performance against the prioritized indicators does not indicate a robust health system. Moreover, a year of good performance in certain key programmes and indicators does not guarantee building a health system's 'residual capacity'. The over-focus on certain indicators, and the active ignoring of the underlying determinants of health, have contributed to the deaths of many.

Debates on post-COVID-19 recovery should consider a redesign of the tools used to assess health system performance and should take seriously the criticisms already raised of the weaknesses and risks of focusing too exclusively on indicators such as the SDGs in health systems design. As Gisselquist and Vaccaro suggest in Chapter 1, health outcomes are related to critical state dimensions. Peru shows that overlooking these dimensions by health policies contributes to creating an incorrect view of the health system's capacity to provide healthcare.

References

Asante, K.T. (2022). 'Residual Capacity and the Political Economy of Pandemic Response in Ghana'. WIDER Working Paper 2022/175-4. Helsinki: UNU-WIDER. https://doi.org/10.35188/UNU-WIDER/2022/175-4.

Auyero, J. (2009). *Flammable Environmental Suffering in an Argentine Shantytown*. Oxford: Oxford University Press.

Birn, A.-E., and L. Nervi (2019). 'What Matters in Health (Care) Universes: Delusions, Dilutions, and Ways towards Universal Health Justice'. *Globalization and Health*, 15(S1). https://doi.org/10.1186/s12992-019-0521-7.

Carrillo-Larco, R.M., W.C. Guzman-Vilca, F. Leon-Velarde, A. Bernabe-Ortiz, M.M. Jimenez, M.E. Penny, C. Gianella, M. Leguía, P. Tsukayama, S.M. Hartinger, A.G. Lescano, M.S. Cuba-Fuentes, Y. Cutipé, F. Diez-Canseco, W. Mendoza, C. Ugarte-Gil, A. Valdivia-Gago, C. Zavaleta-Cortijo, and J.J. Miranda (2022). 'Peru: Progress in Health and Sciences in 200 Years of Independence'. *The Lancet Regional Health: Americas*, 7: 100148. https://doi.org/10.1016/j.lana.2021.100148.

Centro Nacional de Epidemiología, Prevención y Control de Enfermedades (2020). 'Muerte Materna'. Lima: Ministerio de Salud. Available at: www.dge.gob.pe/portal/docs/tools/teleconferencia/2020/SE412020/04.pdf (accessed 10 October 2021).

Centro Nacional de Epidemiología, Prevención y Control de Enfermedades (2021). 'Muerte Materna'. Lima: Ministerio de Salud.

CEPAL (Comision Economica Para America Latina y el Caribe) (2021). *Lineamientos y propuestas para un plan de autosuficiencia sanitaria para América Latina y el Caribe.* Santiago: CEPAL.

Chmielewska, B., I. Barratt, R. Townsend, E. Kalafat, J. Van der Meulen, I. Gurol-Urganci, P. O'Brien, E. Morris, T. Draycott, S. Thangaratinam, K. Le Doare, S. Ladhani, P. von Dadelszen, L. Magee, and A. Khalil (2021). 'Effects of the COVID-19 Pandemic on Maternal and Perinatal Outcomes: A Systematic Review and Meta-Analysis'. *The Lancet Global Health*, 9(6): e759–772. https://doi.org/10.1016/S2214-109X(21)00079-6.

Colegio de Obstetras del Perú (2021). '3123 Obstetras Se Infectaron de Covid-19 y 41 Han Fallecido'. Press release. Available at: https://colegiodeobstetras.pe/2021/02/nota_de_prensa_3123_obstetras_se_infectaron_de_covid_19_y_41_han_fallecido (accessed 20 July 2021).

ComexPerú (2020). '¿Cómo empieza el sectro salud en 2020? Infraestructura y equipamiento'. Semanario 1017 (21 January).

Comité de Alto Nivel sobre el COVID-19 (2021). *Informe sobre las causas del elevado número de muertes por la pandemia del COVID-19 en el Perú.* Lima: Consejo Nacional de Ciencia, Tecnología e Innovación.

Cookson, T.P (2018). *Unjust Conditions: Women's Work and the Hidden Cost of Cash Transfer Programs.* Oakland, CA: University of California Press. https://doi.org/10.1515/9780520969520.

Cotlear, D., O. Gómez-Dantés, F. Knaul, R. Atun, I.C.H.C. Barreto, O. Cetrángolo, M. Cueto, P. Francke, P. Frenz, R. Guerrero, R. Lozano, R. Marten, and R. Sáenz (2015). 'Overcoming Social Segregation in Health Care in Latin America'. *The Lancet*, 385(9974): 1248–1259. https://doi.org/10.1016/S0140-6736(14)61647-0.

Dargent, E. (2011). 'Agents or Actors? Assessing the Autonomy of Economic Technocrats in Colombia and Peru'. *Comparative Politics*, 43(3): 313–332. https://doi.org/10.5129/001041511795274913.

Del Carpio, L. (2013). 'Situación de la mortalidad materna en el Perú, 2000–2012'. *Revista Peruana de Medicina Experimental y Salud Pública*, 30(3): 461–464. https://doi.org/10.17843/rpmesp.2013.303.284.

Du Bois Freund, F., J.F. Chávez, and A. Cusato Novelli (2004). *Programas sociales, salud y educación en el Perú: Un balance de las polóticas sociales.* Lima: Instituto Peruano de Economía Social de Mercado (IPESM).

ECLAC (Economic Commission for Latin America and the Caribbean) (2021). *Economic Survey of Latin America and the Caribbean, 2021 (LC/PUB.2021/10-P/Rev.1).* Santiago de Chile: ECLAC. https://doi.org/10.1057/978-1-349-95121-5_3136-1.

Ewig, C. (2012). *Neoliberalismo de la segundo ola: Género, raza y reforma del sector salud en el Perú.* Lima: Instituto de Estudios Peruanos.

Freedman, L. (2006). 'Achieving the MDGs: Health Systems as Core Social Institutions'. *Development*, 48(1): 19–24. https://doi.org/10.1057/palgrave.development.1100107.

Fukuda-Parr, S., and D. McNeill (2019). 'Knowledge and Politics in Setting and Measuring the SDGs: Introduction to Special Issue'. *Global Policy*, 10(S1): 5–15. https://doi.org/10.1111/1758-5899.12604.

Fukuda-Parr, S., A.E. Yamin, and J. Greenstein (2014). 'The Power of Numbers: A Critical Review of Millennium Development Goal Targets for Human Development and Human Rights'. *Journal of Human Development and Capabilities*, 15(2–3): 105–117. https://doi.org/10.1080/19452829.2013.864622.

Gianella, C. and A. Yamin (2018). 'Struggle and Resistance: Using International Bodies to Advance Sexual and Reproductive Rights in Peru'. *Berkeley Journal of Gender, Law, and Justice*, 33(1): 41–73.

Gianella Malca, C. (2019). 'Exploración de las barreras para el acceso oportuno al diagnóstico y tratamiento del cáncer de cuello uterino y de mama en el Perú y su relación con la inversión pública'. In R. López Linares, C.G. Malca, and E. Meza Cornejo (eds), *La Otra Lucha Contra el Cáncer: Justicia Fiscal por la Salud de las Mujeres*. Lima: Oxfam, pp. 17–48.

Gil, F. (2018). 'Situación Epidemiológica de la muerte materna en el Perú'. CMI Brief 2021:2. Bergen: Chr. Michelsen Institute.

Gupta, A. (2012). *Red Tape: Bureaucracy, Structural Violence, and Poverty in India*. Durham, NC: Duke University Press. https://doi.org/10.1215/9780822394709.

Huber, L., P. Zárate, A. Durand, Ó. Madalengoitia, and J. Morel (2009). *Programa Juntos: Certezas y malentendidos en torno a las transferencias condicionadas, estudio de caso de seis distritos rurales del Perú*. Lima: Instituto de Estudios Peruanos.

Instituto Nacional de Estadística e Informática (2016). *Establecimientos de Salud con Funciones Obstétricas y Neonatales, 2013 y 2015*. Lima: Instituto Nacional de Estadística e Informática.

Jarquín, M.C. (2022). 'COVID-19 and the State: Nicaragua Case Study'. WIDER Working Paper 2022/172-3. Helsinki: UNU-WIDER. https://doi.org/10.35188/UNU-WIDER/2022/172-3.

Kanavos, P., G. Colville Parkin, K. Bregtje, and J. Gill (2019). *Latin America Healthcare System Overview: A Comparative Analysis of Fiscal Space in Healthcare*. London: LSE Consulting, London School of Economics and Political Science.

Mayta Tristan (2021, 23 April, 20:50). 'Actualización de la vigilancia de hospitalización por covid-19 en médicos peruanos del @CMP_PERU Luego de dos semanas del primer reporte continúa reducción de ocupación hospitalaria y nuevos ingresos 80,2 per cent médicos vacunas 1a dosis, 67,5 per cent 2 dosis Sinopharm #LasVacunasuncionan'. Twitter post (accessed 23 April 2021).

Merry, S.E. (2016). *The Seductions of Quantification: Measuring Human Rights, Gender Violence, and Sex Trafficking*. Chicago, IL: The University of Chicago Press. https://doi.org/10.7208/chicago/9780226261317.001.0001.

Mesa de Concertación Para la Lucha Contra la Pobreza (2020). *Informe Nacional sobre el impacto del COVID-19 en las dimensiones económica, social y en salud en el Perú (al mes de mayo, 2020)*. Lima: Mesa de Concertación para la lucha contra la pobreza.

Ministerio de Salud (2009). *Plan estratégico nacional para la reducción de la mortalidad materna y perinatal 2009–2015*. Lima: Ministerio de Salud.

Ministerio de Salud (2021). *Diagnóstico de brechas de infraestructura y equipamiento del sector salud*. Lima: Ministerio de Salud.

Minteguiaga, S.E., and G. Ubasart-González (2021). 'Reviewing Exclusionary Welfare Regimes: Andean Countries (Bolivia, Ecuador, and Peru)'. In N. Sátyro, E. Del Pino, and C. Midaglia (eds), *Latin American Social Policy Developments in the Twenty-First Century*. Cham: Palgrave Macmillan, 101–133. https://doi.org/10.1007/978-3-030-61270-2_4.

Montenegro, J.A. (2020). 'Perú: El potencial y la oportunidad de su economía'. CNN, 13 March.

Murillo-Peña, J.P., P.J. Mendoza-Arana, L.R. Rojas-Mezarina, L.A. Huamán-Angulo, F. Peralta Quispe, P.A. Riega-López, M.L. Chilca Alva, J. Silva Valencia, C.M. Ugarte Taboada, J.C. Loayza Altamirano, W. Pérez Lázaro, M. Moscoso Porras, A. Cabana Peceros, and S.A. Escobar Agreda (2021). 'Cambios en la densidad de recursos humanos en salud durante la epidemia de COVID-19 en el Perú, abril–agosto 2020'. *Anales de la Facultad de Medicina*, 82(1): 5–12. http://dx.doi.org/10.15381/anales.v82i1.20822.

OECD (2017). *OECD Reviews of Health Systems: Peru 2017*. Paris: OECD.

Our World in Data (2021). 'Peru: Coronavirus Pandemic Country Profile'. Available at: https://ourworldindata.org/coronavirus/country/peru#what-is-the-cumulative-number-of-confirmed-deaths (accessed 29 October 2021).

Pesantes, M.A., and L. Cortez (2021). 'Ensuring Sexual and Reproductive Healthcare Services amidst a Pandemic: Experiences from the Health Workers in Lima, Peru'. Unpublished manuscript.

Petrera, M., and E. Jiménez (2018). 'Determinants of Out-of-Pocket Spending on Health among the Poor Population Served by Public Health Services in Peru, 2010–2011'. *Revista panamericana de salud publica: Pan American Journal of Public Health*, 42: e20.

Physicians for Human Rights (2007). *Deadly Delays: Maternal Mortality in Peru*. New York: Physicians for Human Rights.

Pinzón-Flórez, C.E., J.A. Fernandez-Niño, L.M. Cardenas-Cardenas, D.M. Díaz-Quijano, M. Ruiz-Rodriguez, L. Reveiz, and A. Arredondo-López (2017). 'Generation and Evaluation of an Indicator of the Health System's Performance in Maternal and Reproductive Health in Colombia: An Ecological Study'. *PLoS One*, 12(8): e0180857. https://doi.org/10.1371/journal.pone.0180857.

Pitterle, I., and L. Lennart Niermann (2021). 'The COVID-19 Crisis: What Explains Cross-Country Differences in the Pandemic's Short-Term Economic Impact?' Working Paper 174. New York: United Nations Department of Economic and Social Affairs (UNDESA).

ProInversión (2019). 'Resultados macroeconómicos'. Available at: www.investinperu.pe/modulos/JER/PlantillaStandard.aspx?ARE=0&PFL=0&JER=5651 (accessed 30 August 2020).

Seinfeld, J., O. Ugarte, C. Amaro, O. Salomón, and A. Dancuart (2021). *Cambios en el sistema de salud centrados en el ciudadano*. Lima: CIES (Consorcio de investigación económica y social).

SUSALUD (2021). *Informe técnico análisis e identificación de las personas no aseguradas en salud a nivel nacional*. Lima: SUSALUD (Superintendencia Nacional de Salud).

Thaddeus, S., and D. Maine (1994). 'Too Far to Walk: Maternal Mortality in Context'. *Social Science & Medicine*, 38(8): 1091–1110. https://doi.org/10.1016/0277-9536(94)90226-7.

UNFPA (2017). *Regiones con altas tasas de mortalidad materna enfrentan serios desafíos para asegurar la calidad en la atención de la salud materna*. Lima: UNFPA.

WHO (World Health Organization) (2019). *Trends in Maternal Mortality 2000 to 2017: Estimates by WHO, UNICEF, UNFPA, World Bank Group and the United Nations Population Division*. Geneva: WHO.

Yamin, A.E., and O.F. Norheim (2014). 'Taking Equality Seriously: Applying Human Rights Frameworks to Priority Setting in Health'. *Human Rights Quarterly*, 36(2): 296–324. https://doi.org/10.1353/hrq.2014.0027.

Yon, C. (2017). 'La interculturalidad realmente existente en salud'. *Revista Argumentos*, 11(3): 36–41.

8
Nicaragua's Puzzling Pandemic Response

Mateo Jarquín

8.1 Introduction

Nicaragua's COVID-19 experience was unique. Unlike most of its Latin American peers, Nicaraguan authorities eschewed lockdowns and other common strategies to mitigate spread; their containment policies were among the world's weakest. Nicaragua is the poorest country in Central America, itself a lower-income subregion of Latin America, and scores relatively low on indexes of state effectiveness. Still, the public health measures that Nicaragua implemented in response to the pandemic—as well as fiscal policies to alleviate socioeconomic consequences—were weak even by comparison with countries with similar health infrastructures (Gisselquist and Vaccaro 2021). Even more unusual was the reported health impact: according to official statistics, Nicaragua experienced many fewer infections and fatalities than its neighbours, despite the hands-off public health response. For example, Guatemala—a developing country that experienced 'typical' health outcomes (Gisselquist and Vaccaro 2021)—has roughly 2.5 times the number of inhabitants but reported approximately 28 times as many cases and 37 times as many deaths in the first year of the pandemic (see Table 8.6). In the second half of the first year (October 2020–March 2021), the Nicaraguan health ministry (MINSA) reported, with mechanical stability and precision, exactly one COVID-19-related death per week (Confidencial 2021a).

The second part of the puzzle is easy to explain: local and international public health experts widely acknowledge that the Nicaraguan government has brazenly withheld or manipulated information on health outcomes (Huete-Pérez et al. 2021; Pearson et al. 2021; Vannini 2021), dramatically downplaying cases and deaths for various reasons outlined in this chapter (Human Rights Watch 2021). But questions remain about the first part of the puzzle: why did the government in Managua decide to forgo containment and economic support policies in the first instance? The unusual Nicaraguan response to the pandemic, which saw government officials actively promote mass agglomerations of people at non-essential events such as political rallies and music festivals, prompted headlines around the world condemning it as 'reckless', 'bizarre', and 'disrespectful of Nicaraguans' human rights (Amnesty International 2020; Human Rights Watch 2020; Washington Post Editorial Board 2020). Public health scholars and other social scientists

Mateo Jarquín, *Nicaragua's Puzzling Pandemic Response*. In: *How States Respond to Crisis*.
Edited by: Rachel M. Gisselquist and Andrea Vaccaro, Oxford University Press.
DOI: 10.1093/9780198907237.003.0008

were left scratching their heads; absent an obvious explanation for why the country would reject international recommendations and buck the trend established by neighbouring governments, some analysts suggested that President Daniel Ortega and other members of the state elite had behaved in an 'irrational' fashion (Pearson et al. 2020). Indeed, most scholars expect that governments will seek to leverage the state's capacity, authority, and legitimacy (measures of a state's effectiveness) in order to protect citizens' lives. It follows, then, that most countries should have responded to an exogenous shock such as the coronavirus pandemic by enacting policies designed to reduce infections, hospitalizations, and deaths (Fukuyama 2020).

However, scholars also hold that effective state institutions are beneficial because they can help bring about economic growth and social stability; we therefore expect strong institutionality to mitigate other potential problems caused by an external shock, such as economic dislocation and social conflict. Therefore, theories of governance and the state leave open the possibility that policy responses to the COVID-19 pandemic could be optimized towards outcomes beyond the realm of public health. They also acknowledge that state capacities—in this case, the robustness of a state health system—do not by themselves determine pandemic response; existing research shows that state resources are mobilized in different ways and to different ends depending on the leadership in place (Enriquez et al. 2020; Fukuyama 2020). Therefore, analyses of COVID-19 and the state in the Global South should examine all dimensions of state effectiveness while also considering the specific context in which governmental policy decisions are made (paying special attention to the unique interests and worldviews of top leaders in charge at the time of the pandemic).

A close analysis of the Nicaraguan case, one that explores how the COVID-19 challenge overlapped with an existing political and economic crisis, can explain the country's outlier response to the pandemic. When Nicaragua's first cases were reported in March 2020, the country was in the midst of a severe economic recession born from a political crisis that began two years earlier. In the spring of 2018, an avalanche of street protests against the authoritarian rule of President Daniel Ortega—in power since 2007—disrupted the normal functioning of society and called into question the government's legitimacy (its right to continue ruling) and authority (its ability to exercise power to, among other things, bring about order and security) (The Economist 2018b). While security forces came close to losing territorial control in only a few isolated instances, many observers expected the ruling Sandinista National Liberation Front (FSLN) to either collapse under domestic and international pressure or accede to protesters' demands to hold democratic elections (The Economist 2018a). The Ortega government only regained its footing after ordering a violent crackdown—one which claimed at least 300 lives and prompted strong criticism from international human rights bodies—that further polarized society and led more actors in Nicaragua and beyond to question the government's continued hold on power (IAHCR 2018). Ortega and his wife, Vice President Rosario Murillo, argued that domestic and international criticism formed part of deliberate attempts to delegitimize their family's rule and bring about a 'coup' (Fernando Álvarez 2018). When the World Health Organization (WHO) declared a global pandemic, government elites in Nicaragua had to reckon not only with problems of state capacity (the number of beds, doctors, medical equipment, etc.) but also vulnerabilities in terms of state legitimacy and authority.

The government's lack of transparency admittedly makes it difficult to document policy-makers' motives and reasoning as they navigated the pandemic. But limited official communiqués and leaked government documents provide important clues. Restricted or distorted information also complicates the assessment of public health impacts. Reporting from independent medical associations and other Nicaraguan civil society actors, when juxtaposed with official statistics, provides some insights; international observers, including multilateral public health institutions and human rights organizations, help to round out the picture. But absent information that is comparable in its completeness to that provided by other countries, definitive conclusions about the health impact of COVID-19 on Nicaragua, let alone cross-country comparisons, are unsustainable at this time. This analysis focuses on the period between March 2020 (when the first infections were reported in Nicaragua) and March 2021 (when the first vaccines arrived). For reasons discussed below, it became even more difficult to obtain credible death and case statistics after March 2021.

This chapter argues that, rather than optimizing for fewer cases and deaths (as many studies would assume), the authoritarian government of President Daniel Ortega instead attuned its pandemic response to other political and economic variables. *Al pueblo de Nicaragua y al mundo*, a May 2020 White Paper from Ortega's office, declared that Nicaragua would 'seek a balance between public health and a healthy economy' (Secretaría Privada para Políticas Nacionales 2020). In practice, the government response leaned towards the latter. In the context of pre-existing political instability that threatened the regime's legitimacy and survival, policy-makers were especially interested in safeguarding macroeconomic indicators and fomenting a sense of normalcy and continuity among the populace. For related reasons, they demonized calls for quarantines (suggesting that those measures would disrupt growth and normalcy) and severely restricted public health information. Independent monitoring by Nicaraguan civil society, along with excess death statistics (the country ranked third worst in the world as of August 2020), suggests that health outcomes were, at minimum, far worse than the government reported (*Financial Times* coronavirus tracker; NPR 2021). At the same time, the Nicaraguan economy performed better (measured by the annual GDP growth rate) than the Latin American average in 2020, though the extent to which lockdowns, or the lack thereof, explain this performance gap is still unclear.

Furthermore, by the end of the period covered in this chapter, ruling elites implemented new laws in the context of the pandemic that further criminalized political and civil society leaders who had called for international sanctions, a democratic transition, or the FSLN's removal from power. After one year of pandemic, in other words, President Daniel Ortega's regime looked more consolidated than it did prior to it.

Although the impact of COVID-19 on Nicaraguan society is currently difficult to measure, its government's outlier policy response makes the country uniquely valuable for debates on why some states were more effective than others in responding to the pandemic. A close analysis of the case highlights well-known challenges to state-centred, comparative analysis; for example, countries' tendency to underreport public health outcomes is an important theme here. But the Nicaraguan case also raises wider questions about how to frame and approach individual country studies. In Nicaragua, government and leadership mattered more than state resources or capacities; the latter created the context and imposed constraints, but the former ultimately determined the policy response. To understand the connection between the two requires that we look beyond state capacity and ask how state elites perceived the ways in which the pandemic might affect state legitimacy and authority. In adopting a leadership lens to understand the state–pandemic nexus in Nicaragua, this chapter also engages the topics of denialism and regime type, exploring how these concepts can be constructively employed to analyse and classify cases.

8.2 The initial response: quasi-denialism

According to most democracy indexes, Nicaragua is a fully consolidated authoritarian regime, and ranks among the least democratic countries in the western hemisphere (Economist Intelligence Unit 2021). The regime type deepens the puzzle of the Nicaraguan response to the pandemic. In comparing policy responses between democracies and non-democracies, some initial studies noted that the latter were quicker to impose quarantines, lockdowns, and other restrictions in order reduce infections, prevent hospitalizations, and therefore save lives (Cheibub et al. 2020). Authoritarian governments, the thinking goes, may have been more willing than democratic systems to assume certain political costs—namely, the curtailment of citizens' basic civil rights—associated with drastic mitigation policies. In controlling all branches of the Nicaraguan government, President Ortega and Vice President Murillo had wide latitude to act as they deemed fit; in fact, scholars have argued that Nicaragua's pandemic response—in its lack of transparency or accountability, and in the disproportionately controlling role played by the presidential couple—further underscored the authoritarian character of the country's political regime (Thaler 2021). And yet, despite facing few checks against their ability to act upon policy preferences, Ortega and Murillo decided against restricting gatherings or movement of citizens. In fact, in the first month of the pandemic Nicaraguan authorities adopted a quasi-denialist stance, assuring citizens that the virus was not likely to cause widespread infections or hospitalizations. Extraordinary measures, they suggested, were thus uncalled for and life should go on as usual. Understanding this unique initial response requires a brief analysis of the political context in Nicaragua.

A pre-existing political and economic crisis, dating back to the spring of 2018, 'conditioned' the ways in which state and society responded to the arrival of COVID-19 three years later (Jarquín and Martí i Puig 2021). After arriving at the presidency through free elections in 2007, President Ortega gradually consolidated control over the judicial and legislative branches of government, as well as key institutions including the country's security forces. The FSLN, by then completely hegemonized by the Ortega family, was able to achieve stable authoritarian rule by manipulating elections, repressing dissent, reaching corporatist agreements with key nonstate actors—namely, the business elite and the Catholic Church—and offering social peace and consistent economic growth to the population at large (Thaler 2017). In April 2018, however, latent resentments over the Ortega family's political project exploded in the form of massive street demonstrations. Over a period of roughly six weeks, protesters vandalized government propaganda and erected roadblocks across the country in a bid to force Ortega to the negotiating table, disrupting the state's ability to provide order and stability. A resultant anti-government coalition—composed of civil society, student movements, and Ortega's erstwhile allies in the Church and private sector—demanded the president's resignation or, at minimum, early elections with full democratic guarantees. In a sultanistic regime where the lines between public and private (and party and state) are blurred (López Baltodano 2020; Stuenkel and Feldmann 2017), to satisfy those demands likely would have entailed a significant revision of the present state formation. In response to this broad-based questioning of their legitimacy, Ortega and Murillo denied the anti-government coalition's self-identification as a peaceful, pro-democracy movement. Instead, they suggested that the Nicaraguan government was the victim of an 'attempted coup attempt' supported by hostile outside actors, including the government of the United States. The FSLN regained full territorial control only after launching a campaign of police and paramilitary violence that killed hundreds, displaced thousands, and engendered sanctions from the international community. The repression further polarized Nicaraguan society and, combined with other disruptions caused by street protests, contributed to a severe economic recession in 2018. But it also ensured the survival of current state elites, who in July 2018 had claimed victory by assuring Nicaraguans and international onlookers that 'normalcy' had been restored (Jarquín and Thaler 2020).

When WHO officials declared a global pandemic on 11 March 2020 and urged governments to take corresponding measures, the Nicaraguan leadership reacted as if it were carrying forward earlier efforts to neutralize political dynamics that had called their government's legitimacy and future into question. Namely, they denied the nature of the threat, downplayed its severity, and generally worked to ensure that fears associated with COVID-19 did not cause panic or loss of confidence in state institutions. Within days of the WHO declaration, all of Nicaragua's Central American neighbours announced strict lockdowns and closed borders. Meanwhile, Nicaraguan health minister Carolina Dávila promised that Nicaragua would do neither of those things (Confidencial 2020). Rather than closing schools or encouraging Nicaraguans to stay at home, Vice President Murillo called on citizens to attend a mass rally on 15 March, titled 'Love in the Times of COVID-19', where they would march in solidarity with other nations affected by the virus (Times of Israel 2020). In other words, Nicaraguan officials did not deny that the pandemic was real; they only denied that it would affect Nicaragua the way it affected other countries (one prominent FSLN radio host told listeners that COVID-19 was a disease of 'rich and bourgeois' countries, not poor ones) (El País 2020). In fact, even as authorities swore off typical mitigation strategies (Huete-Pérez and Hildebrand 2020), leaked health ministry documents showed that officials had taken the threat seriously since January 2020, quietly making limited interventions: preparing hospitals for eventual outbreaks, screening foreign visitors at borders, and creating a system of door-to-door, in-person visits to trace the virus (Ministerio de Salud 2020). The subtle implementation of these policies is difficult to reconcile with authorities' decision not to make them public, instead expressing an official discourse suffused with elements of denialism.

During the first month of the pandemic, Nicaraguan state elites gave little indication as to why they were not implementing health measures widely adopted across Latin America and strongly recommended by international organizations. With a gross national income per capita of US$1,850 in 2020 (the Latin American average is US$7,612), Nicaragua had relatively few resources to mobilize towards pandemic response (World Bank 2020b). Measured in terms of physicians and hospital beds per 1,000 people, the country also lags behind the regional average when it comes to health coverage (World Bank 2020c, d). However, Nicaragua is not the only country with scarce resources and low capacity. Central American neighbours El Salvador, Guatemala, and Honduras all spend less on healthcare systems (as a percentage of GDP) that cover even less of their respective populations (World Bank 2022). Still, only Nicaragua decided against major mitigation strategies.

Compounding the confusion was the fact that Nicaragua was among the last countries in the western hemisphere to report a confirmed case and one of the last to acknowledge community transmission. After one month, the MINSA had confirmed only 9 cases (1.34 per million inhabitants), whereas neighbouring

Honduras and Costa Rica had confirmed 419 (39.05 per million) and 626 (115.78 per million), respectively (Our World in Data 2021).

Some sympathetic voices celebrated that Nicaragua had the lowest infection rate in the hemisphere (Perry 2020); but the Nicaraguan government refused to disclose how many tests it had conducted, making it impossible to verify the real extent of the spread.[1] Furthermore, journalistic investigations found indications of widespread community transmission (such as unusual numbers of hospitalizations and burials), as well as evidence that doctors and public health officials were being punished for encouraging the population to self-quarantine. As the founder and president of the Nicaraguan Academy of Sciences put it, the country lacked 'credible public data to understand the degree to which COVID-19 had spread in the country' (Huete-Pérez 2020), a claimed echoed by officials from the Pan American Health Organization (PAHO), who charged Nicaragua with failing to provide accurate data and implementing 'inadequate' prevention and control policies (France 24 2020).

These inconsistencies led to the creation of the so-called Citizens' Observatory (Observatorio Ciudadano)—a conglomerate of public health experts, doctors, and civil society actors—which went directly to hospitals to attempt an unofficial account of the pandemic's reach. One month after the WHO declaration, Observatorio Ciudadano reported that the number of infections was perhaps 20 times what the government claimed. The gap would persist as the months went by (see Tables 8.3 and 8.4).

The disconnect between official and unofficial counts heightened the sense of uncertainty and further polarized Nicaraguan politics. Many opposition voices accused the government of punishing the population through its unorthodox pandemic response, a view which some scholars shared: the Ortega government's policies and lack of transparency were, one analyst argued, 'consistent with and a continuation of the crimes against humanity committed in 2018 and 2019' (Cupples 2020, 323).

Throughout the pandemic's turbid first few weeks, President Daniel Ortega was entirely absent. Perhaps hoping to avoid alarming the population, he went more than a month without making statements of any kind about the virus. When he finally delivered a televised speech on 15 April 2020, he hinted for the first time at an official explanation for why the government had decided against lockdowns, quarantines, or stay-at-home orders: 'Nicaraguans haven't stopped working', the leader explained, 'because if they stop working the country will die' (El 19 Digital 2020). Ortega was apparently alluding to a wider trade-off facing countries across the world, especially in developing regions: between protecting

[1] Our World in Data reports no data on the number of tests realized in Nicaragua. See also Huete-Pérez (2020).

lives and protecting economic livelihoods. Authorities would flesh out this simple explanation in subsequent weeks, though questions would remain.

8.3 A Swedish model for poor countries?

In another televised speech on the 1 May holiday, President Ortega reiterated these arguments. Calls to stay at home, he once again suggested, threatened to 'destroy' an economy driven primarily by the informal sector. This time, however, the Nicaraguan head of state expanded upon another theme: the pandemic's intersection with the country's pre-existing political crisis. Specifically, he claimed that those groups calling for quarantines and physical distancing were the same ones that had allegedly attempted a 'coup' against his government in 2018. He told Nicaraguans that bad-faith opposition groups, disguised as medical professionals and civil society organizations, were seeking to exploit the pandemic in order to undermine the stability and order that the regime had achieved at great cost (Luna 2020). Both of these implied policy logics—one preoccupied with employment and economic growth, the other concerned with the threat that the pandemic posed to state authority and legitimacy—were made explicit in a White Paper published by the Nicaraguan presidency on 15 May 2020.

The 73-page document, titled *To the Nicaraguan People and the World: A Report on COVID-19 and a Singular Strategy*, addressed international criticism by formalizing the argument that quarantines and stay-at-home orders were inappropriate in the context of the second-poorest country in Latin America and the Caribbean: 'The policy is based on the fact that 40 per cent of the population lives in rural areas and 80 per cent of urban workers belong to the informal sector' (Secretaría Privada para Políticas Nacionales 2020: 3). On the one hand, the document defended the government's public health choices by pointing to particularities inherent to the Nicaraguan case. Its 'singular' approach of eschewing lockdowns was allegedly justified, for example, because the country's 'Family and Community Health Model'—a framework that taps local and municipal networks in order to target and expand state interventions in public health—made it better prepared to weather the pandemic than other countries with similar income levels. On the other hand, the White Paper made a more generalizing, abstract argument about economic costs associated with lockdowns. The authors noted that the United Nations Economic Commission for Latin America (ECLA) projected that the region—where most countries acted swiftly to close borders and prevent mass gatherings—would experience its worst GDP contraction since the 2008 global financial crisis. Interruptions to economic activity caused by quarantines, the document implied, were the main culprit: 'In the face of such unfavorable scenarios at the regional and global levels, the Government of Reconciliation and National Unity (GRUN) has not declared a quarantine or closed the economy ... Nicaragua will seek a balance between public health and a healthy economy' (Secretaría Privada para Políticas Nacionales 2020: 16). The authors also claimed that major interventions of this sort would not do much, in any event, to prevent stresses on the health system; this idea was consistent with claims from Nicaraguan scientists that the government was seemingly pursuing a 'herd immunity' strategy (Huete-Pérez et al. 2021). Despite arguing that Nicaragua's response was 'singular', and even though it rejected a 'one-size-fits-all' approach to the pandemic, the document also invited other developing countries to emulate Nicaragua's hands-off approach given the economic trade-offs. In doing so, the White Paper compared the Nicaraguan response to that of Sweden, a high-income European country with a robust state health infrastructure that also imposed fewer physical distancing measures than its peers: 'Nicaragua and Sweden represent alternatives to the total "lockdown" of a developing country and developed country, respectively ... Nicaragua is the same example as Sweden, but among developing countries' (Secretaría Privada para Políticas Nacionales 2020: 12–13).

Additionally, the White Paper fleshed out Ortega's arguments regarding the country's unique political context. First, it acknowledged that Nicaragua—unlike its Central American neighbours and the Latin America region more generally—was already experiencing an economic recession when the virus hit in 2020, largely as a result of the 2018 political crisis. Having achieved an annual GDP growth rate higher than 4 per cent for eight years in a row, the Nicaraguan economy contracted by over 3 per cent in 2018 and 2019 (see Figure 8.1).

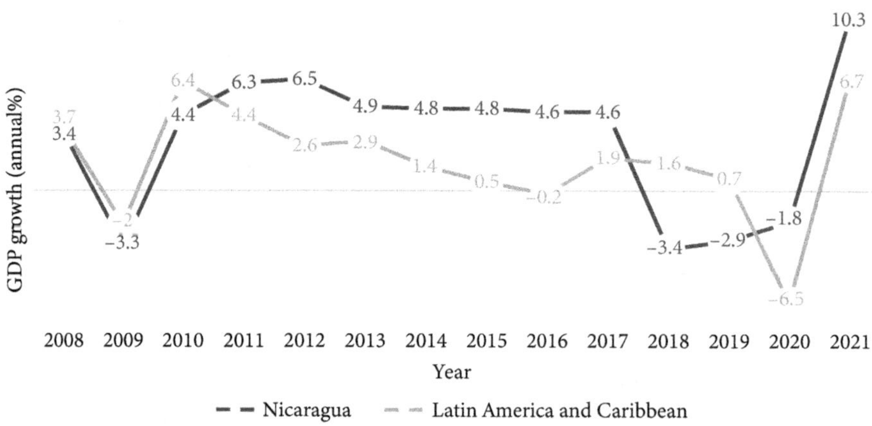

Figure 8.1 GDP growth (annual %), Nicaragua versus Latin America and Caribbean, 2008–2021.

Source: Reproduced from World Bank (2020a) under CC BY 4.0 licence https://creativecommons.org/licenses/by/4.0.

The economic costs of lockdowns, authorities believed, were even less acceptable in this scenario. Second, the White Paper argued that criticism of the government's pandemic response, both at home and abroad, was politically motivated:

> With the ongoing COVID-19 pandemic, the coup-plotting opposition of Nicaragua and its sponsors among US covert operations agencies have lashed out with a massive disinformation campaign; following their old habit of lying daily to the Nicaraguan people in an attempt to undermine confidence in the government; they have seen in the pandemic a great opportunity to terrorize and disinform the population ... They criticize the government for not establishing quarantines, closing borders, prohibiting the entry of foreigners to national territory, or closing public schools and universities, all with the purpose of weakening the economy. (Secretaría Privada para Políticas Nacionales 2020: 45)

The White Paper clarified much of the logic behind Nicaragua's outlier response to the pandemic, but several questions remained unanswered. For example, the document did not explain why the presidency had waited until the end of May, over two months after the pandemic had been declared, before explaining its 'singular' policies to the population in any detail. Nor did the White Paper address the lack of widespread, easily accessible testing; nothing in the document suggested that testing or contract tracing were contradictory to the overall strategy of keeping the country open for business. Finally, while it commented on why the government had not decreed lockdowns, closed schools, or restricted economic activities, it did not explain why officials had actively promoted non-essential gatherings such as sporting events, festivals, and political rallies.

In retrospect, President Ortega and his inner circle—in having a quasi-denialist initial reaction to the pandemic—seem to have been constrained by the cognitive framework they previously adopted in response to the 2018 political crisis, characterized by an impulse to insist on normalcy and continuity, even as severe locations were taking place (Jarquín and Martí i Puig 2021). Thus, officials initially told Nicaraguans that COVID-19 posed no threat; they also censored citizens calling for quarantines and mask wearing, accusing some of deliberately attempting to sow panic in the population (Parkin Daniels 2021). Most of this denialist impulse subsided over time, as official sources of authority started encouraging citizens to wear masks indoors and increase handwashing.

Regardless, the government never stopped policing information regarding infections, hospitalizations, deaths, and tests realized—an issue the White Paper danced around. Responding to claims that officials had drastically distorted information to minimize the death toll, the document simply stated that the number of deceased due to viral disease was, prima facie, not unusual. It omitted mention of the strikingly low number of reported infections compared with Nicaragua's Central American neighbours (see Tables 8.1 and 8.2).

Table 8.1 Total COVID-19 cases and deaths (cumulative, per million inhabitants) by the time of White Paper publication: 12 March 2020 to 25 May 2020

Country	Confirmed cases	Confirmed deaths
Costa Rica	185.05	1.95
El Salvador	304.21	5.37
Guatemala	206.03	3.23
Honduras	416.28	18.09
Nicaragua	41.63	2.54

Source: Author's construction based on Our World in Data/Johns Hopkins University CSSE COVID-19 data (Our World in Data 2021).

Table 8.2 Total COVID-19 cases and deaths (cumulative, total) by the time of White Paper publication: 12 March 2020 to 25 May 2020

Country	Confirmed cases	Confirmed deaths
Costa Rica	951	10
El Salvador	1983	35
Guatemala	3,760	59
Honduras	4,189	182
Nicaragua	279	17

Source: Author's construction based on Our World in Data/Johns Hopkins University CSSE COVID-19 data (Our World in Data 2021).

By the date of the document's release, the Nicaraguan health ministry had acknowledged only 17 COVID-19-related deaths; by contrast, the Observatorio Ciudadano's unofficial count—by that point cited in international coverage in parallel to official statistics—reported 598 'suspected' COVID-19 deaths (see Table 8.3).

The wide gap between official and unofficial statistics persisted throughout the year covered by this analysis (see Table 8.4), as did the enormous gap between reported health outcomes in Nicaragua compared with its Central American neighbours (see Tables 8.5 and 8.6), which reported over 15 times as many COVID-19-related deaths per million inhabitants on average. Independent investigations by Nicaraguan journalists proved how the Nicaraguan government had massaged the data. Based on leaked data from the Nicaraguan health ministry, one investigation found that thousands of deceased patients, having tested positive for COVID-19 during hospitalization, were listed on their death certificates as having died of other causes (most often atypical pneumonia or hypertension) (Miranda and Salazar 2021). An investigation by *The Lancet*, based on interviews with

Table 8.3 Total COVID-19 deaths (cumulative, total) by the time of White Paper publication: 12 March 2020 to 25 May 2020

Official confirmed deaths (MINSA)	**17**
Unofficial count of 'suspected' COVID-19 deaths (Observatorio Ciudadano)	598

Source: Author's construction based on Our World in Data/Johns Hopkins University CSSE COVID-19 data (official confirmed deaths) (Our World in Data 2021) and Observatorio Ciudadano COVID-19 en Nicaragua data (unofficial count) (Observatorio Ciudadano multiple dates).

Table 8.4 Total COVID-19 cases and deaths (cumulative, total) after one year: 12 March 2020 to 10 March 2021

	Cases	**Deaths**
Official confirmed cases (MINSA)	6,537	175
Unofficial count of 'suspected' cases and deaths (Observatorio Ciudadano)	13,237	3,002

Source: Author's construction based on Our World in Data/Johns Hopkins University CSSE COVID-19 data (official confirmed cases) (Our World in Data 2021) and Observatorio Ciudadano COVID-19 en Nicaragua data (unofficial count) (Observatorio Ciudadano multiple dates).

Nicaraguan physicians, corroborated claims that doctors had been fired or otherwise sanctioned for speaking publicly about the virus and pressured to misreport any deaths resulting from COVID-19; some even reported 'having been pressured into denying patients oxygen' in order to suppress evidence of COVID-19 (Parkin Daniels 2021).

We can only speculate as to why the government chose to restrict information on public health outcomes to such a degree. Transparent information might have evidenced an official resignation to high death rates, generating popular discontent and political pushback that would have undermined the entire strategy of maintaining a sense of normalcy and stability; emphasizing the economic costs of lockdowns was politically more viable (Valenzuela-Stookey 2020). There was also a strong precedent for this behaviour in Nicaraguan institutions in recent years, where centralism, insularism, and data manipulation are observable features of a health system defined by 'strong partisan interference and corruption in the health sector' (Sotelo and Vargas 2020).

Although some puzzles remained, the White Paper demonstrated that the state response was not irrational. In flouting most recommendations from the

Table 8.5 Total COVID-19 cases and deaths (cumulative, per million inhabitants) after one year: 12 March 2020 to 11 March 2021

Country	Confirmed cases	Confirmed deaths
Costa Rica	40,441.69	554.19
El Salvador	9,482.86	296.85
Guatemala	9,925.72	357.87
Honduras	17,532.26	428.40
Nicaragua	975.33	26.11

Source: Author's construction based on Our World in Data/Johns Hopkins University CSSE COVID-19 data (Our World in Data 2021).

Table 8.6 Total COVID-19 cases and deaths (cumulative, total) after one year: 12 March 2020 to 11 March 2021

Country	Confirmed cases	Confirmed deaths
Costa Rica	207,832	2,848
El Salvador	61,814	1,935
Guatemala	181,143	6,531
Honduras	176,427	4,311
Nicaragua	6,537	175

Source: Author's construction based on Our World in Data/Johns Hopkins University CSSE COVID-19 data (Our World in Data 2021).

WHO and PAHO, ruling elites followed a discernible strategy—'a strategy of balance between the pandemic and the economy, fighting vigorously against the coronavirus and COVID-19 without closing our economy'—that optimized for economic growth while neutralizing the risk that the pandemic would create political dynamics that might generate new calls for regime change. Even though its policies contradicted assumptions that states would mobilize resources to prevent infection and therefore reduce lives, and although policy-makers evinced an unusual resignation to deaths and infections, Nicaragua's outlier response was not necessarily incompatible with prevailing theories of governance, as the next section discusses.

8.4 Health, political, and economic impacts (and problems of interpretation)

It is difficult to measure the 'success' or 'failure' of state responses to an external shock like the COVID-19 pandemic, given the heterogenous nature of a challenge that entailed public health crises, global economic shock, political shifts, and general insecurity and uncertainty (Brück et al. 2020). Models that predict state responses to the pandemic based on indexes of authority, legitimacy, and capacity must acknowledge that said responses may be unevenly spread across those different dimensions. In the Nicaraguan case, a unique political context informed state elites' perception of the principal risks posed by the pandemic and determined which consequences (economic growth vs. hospitalizations, for example) received the greatest emphasis. Unconventional policies—eschewing lockdowns and keeping the economy open in lieu of economic support policies—were born, specifically, from the calculation that pandemic-related disruptions to daily life and economic activity would fuel opposition claims that state elites lacked the legitimacy or authority to continue governing. Assessing the relative success of those policies is further complicated by the lack of credible data, comparable to that which we have for other countries, on public health impacts in Nicaragua; it is difficult, in other words, to say whether the country fared worse or better than, say, neighbouring Honduras. Nonetheless, a government leadership approach to the state–pandemic nexus in the Nicaraguan case—aside from providing a fuller explanation of the country's unorthodox pandemic policies—points to wider insights on how to approach the comparative study of state responses to the COVID-19 pandemic in the Global South.

The Nicaraguan economy outperformed both its Central American neighbours and the Latin American average in 2020 and 2021. A quick glance at annual GDP growth rates since the global financial crisis tells a simple story (see Figure 8.1). After plummeting alongside the Latin American average in 2008/2009, the Nicaraguan economy tracked the regional average for the subsequent decade, growing at a better-than-average pace. In 2018, disruptions caused by protests and regime repression saw the Nicaraguan GDP growth rate abruptly crash, falling well below the regional average. While the Nicaraguan economy still contracted in 2020, it managed a soft landing compared to what most Latin American economies underwent during the COVID-19 pandemic. Nicaragua subsequently experienced a strong recovery in 2021. However, questions remain about the role that pandemic-related policies played in this outcome; some recent research, for example, casts doubt on the health–economy binary upon which the Ortega government premised its decision against lockdowns (McKee and Stuckler 2020). Nicaragua may have taken advantage of lockdowns in neighbouring countries to increase its own agricultural and manufacturing exports (Cota 2021). But future research will have to consider whether the decision to keep the economy open was a wise investment in terms of GDP growth or productivity in the long run. Furthermore, any potential economic benefits must be measured against the human cost.

Unfortunately, it is unusually difficult to calculate the human cost in the Nicaraguan case. During the pandemic's initial stages, many scholars warned that by avoiding major distancing measures or lockdowns, Nicaragua courted the prospect of catastrophically high rates of infections and deaths compared with other Latin American countries. In retrospect, some characterized Nicaragua's pandemic response as 'disastrous' (Schwartz and Thaler 2022). Such a decisive assessment is difficult to sustain given the incompleteness of the data currently available. Comparisons across countries are not possible because the data for Nicaragua, whether the heavily distorted official statistics or unofficial estimates by Observatorio Ciudadano, are not directly comparable with the official statistics provided by other countries.

Nevertheless, the available evidence does allow us to conclude that, at minimum, the public health impacts were far worse than what the government acknowledged. According to a *Financial Times* analysis, only two countries in the world (Ecuador and Mexico) fared worse than Nicaragua in terms of excess deaths (Confidencial 2021b). Based on excess data statistics, one study found that only Tajikistan undercounted COVID-19 deaths on a greater scale than Nicaragua (Karlinsky and Kobak 2021). However, Nicaragua suddenly stopped reporting excess death statistics in August 2020, limiting the viability of cross-country comparisons based on that measure.[2] Assessments must also consider that, in any event, not all outcomes were determined by state policies; in the absence of major quarantine policies, nonstate actors (such as business organizations, medical associations, and human rights groups) launched campaigns during peak outbreaks calling on citizens to stay at home. Observatorio Ciudadano, without which we would have very little information on the health impacts in Nicaragua, was part of this nonstate response to the pandemic.

Given such incomplete information, only the architects of the Nicaraguan experiment remain in a position to judge whether they successfully achieved the 'balance' between public health and economic growth that they had sought. Over the course of the pandemic's first year, international observers took note of the fact that striking numbers of FSLN party members, including at least 12 senior officials, were dying of pulmonary illnesses (Robles 2020). On 13 April 2021, Paul Oquist—cabinet official, top Ortega advisor, and purported author of the May 2020 White Paper—died after experiencing COVID-19-related symptoms, though his government did not register his death as COVID-19-related (Miranda 2021).

While public health and economic impacts are difficult to determine, state elites seemingly found more unambiguous success in satisfying the political logic of their pandemic response. Two years before COVID-19 particles arrived in Nicaragua, ruling elites were in a tenuous position; they faced widespread street protests, a relatively unified opposition, and doubts about the FSLN's ability to maintain control. Over time, however, Ortega and his inner circle were able to reverse this adverse scenario. During the pandemic, the National Assembly,

[2] Our World in Data reports no data on excess deaths in Nicaragua after August 2020.

directly controlled by Ortega and Murillo, implemented new laws that further criminalized civil society and arrested dozens of critics. In a scenario where many Nicaraguans were afraid to congregate for fear of contracting the virus, the government faced a diminished risk of street protests. Importantly, fragmented anti-government actors failed to turn Ortega's unusual pandemic response into a rallying cry for opposition unity, nor did they seize the opportunity to present themselves as a coherent governing alternative to the current regime. As a result, the FSLN government was more strongly consolidated after a year of global pandemic than it was before, though only time will tell if these policies contributed to political stability in the long run (Jarquín and Martí i Puig 2021).

The Nicaraguan case points to challenges, both old and new, to cross-country analyses of how states and societies responded to the coronavirus pandemic. The underreporting of infections and deaths, for instance, is a widespread problem that complicates comparisons between countries; the Ortega government is an extreme example in this regard. But Nicaragua also stands out because it is a case where government and leadership clearly mattered more than state capacity in determining the policy response. Most studies on the Nicaraguan case have reached similar conclusions (Schwartz and Thaler 2022). The primacy of the leadership variable also fits with wider research on the Latin America region, where state responses—in terms of containment strategies and economic support policies—varied widely during the first year of the pandemic. As one analysis noted, the biggest determinant of health outcomes was not inequality, informality, state effectiveness, or levels of social trust. Instead, the most salient factor 'has turned out to be leadership' (Enriquez et al. 2020).

This is not to suggest that state effectiveness *ex ante* was irrelevant. State capacity constrained the Ortega government's policy options. First, their pandemic White Paper noted how the country's low-income status made lockdown-based containment strategies unsustainable, suggesting that they might have pursued another policy path under different economic circumstances. Second, having just undergone an experience (the 2018 political crisis) where state authority had been significantly compromised, policy-makers seemingly felt compelled to pursue policies that would prioritize the ability to provide order and stability. Finally, it can also be inferred that the state's relatively low levels of legitimacy—its ability to acquire the consent of the population to govern—also shaped government leaders' behaviour. In a country lacking separation of powers, elected officials, or other ingrained accountability mechanisms, Nicaragua's presidential couple had unconstrained decision-making authority. And in pursuing policies that clearly contradicted international health recommendations, they were not inhibited by semi-autonomous government agencies led by scientists or medical experts; the presidency could control all aspects of the public health response in minute detail.

In summary, it is difficult to imagine Ortega's unorthodox pandemic leadership in a scenario where the Nicaraguan state enjoyed greater capacity, legitimacy, and authority, and where power was distributed more equally around the political arena.

In analysing the state–pandemic nexus in Nicaragua through a leadership lens, this chapter has also engaged with ongoing debates about the relevance of regime type to responses to the COVID-19 crisis. In the case of the Ortega government, authoritarianism matters—though not in any mechanistic way. In Nicaragua, the interests and capacities of the state are not easily distinguished from the interests and resources of a small ruling elite. Moreover, the government's personalistic and dynastic qualities—unique in the western hemisphere—mean that levels of accountability and transparency are especially low, even when compared with those of other non-democracies. In its quasi-denialist initial response, and its refusal to provide credible information throughout the pandemic, the government was following precedents established during the earlier consolidation of an authoritarian regime (Thaler 2021). Prior to the pandemic, scholars had also found that the country's health infrastructure was heavily 'politicised' (Vargas-Palacios et al. 2018). However, deeply consolidated authoritarianism in no way precluded a response that followed international health recommendations; non-democratic regimes in Cuba and Venezuela (Nicaragua's closest partners) implemented major mitigation strategies in line with, or at times surpassing, those seen in Latin American democracies.

This analysis of Nicaragua also raises questions about how we taxonomize state responses to the pandemic. Scholars have typically grouped Nicaragua under the 'denialist' category of countries (Buben and Kouba 2020). In one sense, denialism is an apt and revealing label: in the way that they downplayed the pandemic's severity and shrugged off international criticism, Ortega and Murillo behaved similarly to other world leaders, such as Alexander Lukashenko (Belarus) and Jair Bolsonaro (Brazil), frequently seen as being denialist in their response. In some ways, Nicaragua's presidential couple went further: they criminalized the efforts of citizens and the medical community to disseminate information and advice regarding the virus. At the same time, the denialist tag obscures two key facts. First, the Nicaraguan government's official discourse on the virus shifted significantly over time, abandoning outright scepticism about COVID-19 after the first two months of the pandemic. Second, there is no evidence that top policy-makers denied the reality of the COVID-19 pandemic, or that they were indifferent to its impact on Nicaraguan society. In fact, as the above analysis has demonstrated, they were highly alarmed and implemented a discernible strategy, albeit one that marked a striking departure from international recommendations and privileged economic outcomes over public health priorities.

8.5 Conclusion

This chapter contextualized two major outliers regarding Nicaragua's experience during the COVID-19 pandemic. First, it showed that the country's spectacularly low rates of death and infection were the result, as one study put it, of 'purposeful misdiagnosis or underreporting' (Karlinsky and Kobak 2021). Second, it argued that Nicaraguan leaders' decision to forgo quarantines and other recommended mitigation policies was part of a rational strategy to prioritize economic growth and a sense of normalcy over public health. These leaders made assessments that were unique to Nicaragua's political context but also specific to their position within it. They judged that the most severe risk associated with the pandemic was the possibility of disruptions that would enable calls for regime change by anti-government actors at home and abroad. They also reasoned that lockdowns would stunt the economic growth necessary to maintain the social stability that, in turn, underpins the Ortega-Murillo family's dynastic authoritarian project. Another set of Nicaraguan state elites, working with the same state capacities and limitations, would likely have arrived at a different calculus. Therefore, a complete understanding of Nicaragua's pandemic response requires consideration not only of the state but also of elite government ideas and interests.

The Nicaraguan case is especially challenging to analyse. The lack of minimally credible information about cases and deaths frustrates any assessment of public health impacts. Ahead of elections in November 2021, regime officials cracked down on civil society groups including Observatorio Ciudadano, compounding the problem of data availability. Additionally, the Nicaragua case is challenging simply because the policies its government implemented were so controversial. In responding to COVID-19, President Daniel Ortega—who had recently been accused by the Inter-American Commission on Human Rights (IACHR) of committing 'crimes against humanity' during repression of protests in 2018—ignored advice from international medical authorities, criminalized civil society public health initiatives, and grossly manipulated information about the virus and its spread. Few scholars would condone any of these policies; this fact has naturally driven many observers towards a critical stance. Indeed, this chapter has been critical of the Nicaraguan approach to the pandemic: it argued that the regime's authoritarian nature was a decisive factor, it cited evidence that authorities had lied about cases and deaths, and it called into question some of the reasoning behind the government's decision to eschew lockdowns and other mitigation strategies. However, in the interest of providing a complete explanation of Nicaragua's pandemic response, it sought to take said reasoning—expressed in official communiqués and speeches—as seriously as possible.

Importantly, the arguments in this chapter should be read with the understanding that the health, economic, and political consequences of COVID-19, and the Ortega government's unorthodox countermeasures, are likely to shift over time. Many of the puzzles surrounding Nicaragua's outlier case will only become solvable with the perspective afforded by hindsight.

References

Amnesty International (2020). 'Nicaragua: Government Increases Risk of COVID-19 Infection in a Country Already Devastated by Two Years of Crisis'. Amnesty International News, 16 April.

Brück, T., N. Ferguson, P. Justino, and W. Stojetz (2020). 'Trust in the Time of Corona'. WIDER Working Paper 82/2020. Helsinki: UNU-WIDER. https://doi.org/10.1177/0141076820956802.

Buben, R., and K. Kouba (2020). 'The Causes of Disease Impact Denialism in Nicaragua's Response to COVID-19'. *Bulletin of Latin American Research*, 39(1): 103–107. https://doi.org/10.1111/blar.13176.

Cheibub, J.A., J.Y. Hong, and A. Przeworski (2020). 'Rights and Deaths: Government Reactions to the Pandemic'. Working paper, SSRN. https://doi.org/10.2139/ssrn.3645410.

Confidencial (2020). 'Gobierno: "Nicaragua no ha establecido ni hará cuarentena por coronavirus"'. *Confidencial*, 28 February.

Confidencial (2021a). 'MINSA cumple un año reportando un solo muerto seminal por cOVID-19'. *Confidencial*, 7 October.

Confidencial (2021b). 'Nicaragua ocupa el tercer lugar en el mundo de sobremortalidad atribuible a la COVID-19'. *Confidencial*, 7 April.

Cota, I. (2021). 'La economía da alas a Daniel Ortega en Nicaragua'. *El País*, 5 November.

Cupples, J. (2020). 'Love in the Time of COVID-19: Or, Nicaragua, the Strange Country Where Children Still Go to School'. *Journal of Latin American Geography*, 19(3): 323–333. https://doi.org/10.1353/lag.2020.0056.

The Economist (2018a). 'Time Is Running Out for Nicaragua's President Daniel Ortega'. *The Economist*, 9 June.

The Economist (2018b). 'The Violent End of Daniel Ortega's Decade of Quiet'. *The Economist*, 28 April.

Economist Intelligence Unit (2021). *Democracy Index 2020: In Sickness and in Health?* London: Economist Intelligence Unit.

El 19 Digital (2020). 'Discurso del presidente de Nicaragua, Comandante Daniel Ortega'. *El 19 Digital*, 15 April.

El País (2020). 'Nicaragua: COVID-19 es un "virus de ricos y burgueses"'. *El País* (Uruguay), 6 April.

Enriquez, D., S. Rojas Cabal, and M.A. Centeno (2020). 'Latin America's COVID-19 Nightmare: Lessons from the World's Hardest-Hit Region'. *Foreign Affairs*, 1 September.

Fernando Álvarez, C. (2018). 'Así se vivió y se derrotó el golpe de Estado en Nicaragua'. *El 19 Digital*, 30 December.

France 24 (2020). 'Nicaragua incumple su obligación de reporter casos y muertes por COVID-19, dice OPS'. France 24, 19 May.

Fukuyama, F. (2020). 'The Pandemic and Political Order: It Takes a State'. *Foreign Affairs*, July/August.

Gisselquist, R.M., and A. Vaccaro (2021). 'Covid-19 and the State'. WIDER Working Paper 2021/80. Helsinki: UNU-WIDER. https://doi.org/10.35188/UNU-WIDER/2021/018-4.

Huete-Pérez, J.A. (2020). 'La peligrosa fase de transmisión comunitaria del COVID-19 sin planes de mitigación'. *Confidencial*, 13 April.

Huete-Pérez, J.A., C. Cabezas-Robelo, L. Páiz-Medina, C.A. Hernández Álvarez, C. Quant-Durán, and J.H. McKerrow. (2021). 'First Report on Prevalence of SARS-CoV-2 Infection among Health-Care Workers in Nicaragua'. *PLoS One*, 16(1): e0246084. https://doi.org/10.1371/journal.pone.0246084.

Huete-Pérez, J.A., and J. Hildebrand (2020). 'Nicaragua's COVID-19 Crisis Demands a Response'. *Science*, 369(6502): 385. https://doi.org/10.1126/science.abd4975.

Human Rights Watch (2020). 'Nicaragua: Reckless COVID-19 Response'. Human Rights Watch, 10 April.

Human Rights Watch (2021). *World Report 2021. Nicaragua: Events of 2020*. New York: Human Rights Watch.

IACHR (2018). *Final Report on the Acts of Violence that Occurred between April 18 and May 30, 2018*. Washington, DC: Inter-American Commission on Human Rights (IAHCR).

Jarquín, M., and S. Martí I Puig (2021). 'Nicaragua: Denying the Health Crisis and the Political Crisis'. In M. Fernandez and C. Machado (eds), *COVID-19's Political Challenges in Latin America*. Cham: Springer, pp. 35–45. https://doi.org/10.1007/978-3-030-77602-2_4.

Jarquín, M., and K. Thaler (2020). 'Two Years after Nicaragua's Mass Uprising, Why Is Daniel Ortega Still in Power?'. *The Washington Post*, 1 May.

Karlinksy, A., and D. Kobak (2021). 'Tracking Excess Mortality across Countries during the COVID-19 Pandemic with the World Mortality Dataset'. *eLife*, 30 June. https://doi.org/10.1101/2021.01.27.21250604.

López Baltodano, U. (2020). 'Del sultanismo a la democracia: El régimen político de Nicaragua'. In A. Cortés Ramos, U. López Baltodano, and L. Moncada Bellorin (eds), *Anhelos de un nuevo horizonte: Aportes para la construcción de una Nicaragua democrática*. San José, Costa Rica: FLACSO, pp. 135–174.

Luna, Y. (2020). 'Ortega lanza ataque frontal contra la campaña para prevenir el COVID-19'. *Confidencial*, 1 May.

Mckee, M., and D. Stuckler (2020). 'If the World Fails to Protect the Economy, COVID-19 Will Damage Health Not Just Now but Also in the Future'. *Nature Medicine*, 26(5): 640–642. https://doi.org/10.1038/s41591-020-0863-y.

Ministerio de Salud (2020). *Protocolo de Preparación y Respuesta ante el Riesgo de Introducción de Virus Coronavirus (COVID-19)*. Managua: Ministerio de Salud de Nicaragua.

Miranda, W. (2021). 'Fallece con síntomas de covid-19 uno de los principales asesores de Daniel Ortega en Nicaragua'. *El País*, 13 April.

Miranda, W., and M. Salazar (2021). 'Así se oculta la muerte por la COVID-19 en Nicaragua'. *Divergentes*, 12 January.

NPR (2021). 'Citizens Work to Expose COVID's Real Toll in Nicaragua as Leaders Claim Success'. NPR (National Public Radio), 12 May.

Observatorio Ciudadano (multiple dates). 'Notas de prensa e informes semanales'. Available at: https://observatorioni.org/informes-notas-y-semanales (accessed 21 April 2022).

Our World in Data (2021). 'COVID-19 Data Explorer: Cumulative Confirmed COVID-19 Cases per Million People'. Available at: https://ourworldindata.org/explorers/coronavirus-data-explorer?time=2020-03-16..2021-03-15&facet=none&pickerSort=desc&pic

kerMetric=location&Metric=Confirmed+cases&Interval=Cumulative&Relative+to+Population=true&Color+by+test+positivity=false&country=NIC~GTM (accessed 21 April 2022).

Parkin Daniels, J. (2021). 'Nicaraguan Health-Care Workers under Attack'. *The Lancet World Report*, 398(10311): 1555–1556. https://doi.org/10.1016/S0140-6736(21)02378-3.

Pearson, A.A., A.M. Prado, and F.D. Colburn (2020). 'Nicaragua's Surprising Response to COVID-19'. *Journal of Global Health*, 10(1): 010371. https://doi.org/10.7189/jogh.10.010371.

Pearson, A.A., A.M. Prado, and F.D. Colburn (2021). 'The Puzzle of COVID-19 in Central America and Panama'. *Journal of Global Health*, 11: 03077. https://doi.org/10.7189/jogh.11.03077.

Perry, J. (2020). 'Nicaragua's Response to COVID-19'. *The Lancet Global Health*, 8(7): E899. https://doi.org/10.1016/S2214-109X(20)30220-5.

Robles, F. (2020). 'Nicaragua's Ruling Sandinistas Fall Victim to COVID-19, Highlighting Disease's Spread'. *The New York Times*, 18 July.

Schwartz, R., and K.M. Thaler (2022). 'Nicaragua: Populist Performance and Authoritarian Practice during COVID-19'. In L. Renno and N. Ringe (eds), *Populists and the Pandemic: How Populists around the World Responded to COVID-19*. London: Routledge, pp. 184–195.

Secretaría Privada para Políticas Nacionales (2020). *Al pueblo de Nicaragua y al mundo: Informe sobre el COVID-19 y una estrategia singular*. White Paper, 25 May. Managua: Secretaría Privada para Políticas Nacionales, Presidencia de la República.

Sotelo, G., and E. Vargas (2020). 'Políticas de salud en Nicaragua'. In A. Cortés Ramos, U. López Baltodano, and L. Moncada Bellorin (eds), *Anhelos de un nuevo horizonte: Aportes para la construcción de una Nicaragua democrática*. San José, Costa Rica: FLACSO, 413–422.

Stuenkel, O., and A. Feldmann (2017). 'The Unchecked Demise of Nicaraguan Democracy'. Carnegie Endowment for International Peace, 16 November.

Thaler, K.M. (2017). 'Nicaragua: A Return to Caudillismo'. *Journal of Democracy*, 28(2): 157–169. https://doi.org/10.1353/jod.2017.0032.

Thaler, K.M. (2021). 'Nicaragua and COVID-19: Authoritarian Indifference'. In J. Nederveen Pieterse, H. Lim, and H. Khondker (eds), *COVID-19 and Governance: Crisis Reveals*. Abingdon: Routledge, pp. 229–241.

Times of Israel (2020). 'Quarantine Shmuarantine: Nicaragua Holds Mass March against Virus'. *Times of Israel*, 15 March.

Valenzuela-Stookey, Q. (2020). 'Deciphering Nicaragua's Tepid COVID Response'. NACLA (North American Congress on Latin America), 17 June.

Vannini, M. (2021). *Love in Time of COVID 19: Pandemic, Repression, and Access to Information in Nicaragua*. COVID-19 Reports on Latin American and the Caribbean 65. Monitoring COVID-19 in Latin America and the Caribbean.

Vargas-Palacios, E., R. Pineda, and E. Galán-Rodas (2018). 'The Politicised and Crumbling Nicaraguan Health System'. *The Lancet*, 392(10165): 2694–2695. https://doi.org/10.1016/S0140-6736(18)32990-8.

Washington Post Editorial Board (2020). 'In a Pandemic, Nicaragua's President Refuses to Put His People First'. *The Washington Post*, 8 August.

World Bank (2020a). 'Data: GDP Growth (Annual %)'. Washington, DC: World Bank.

World Bank (2020b). 'Data: GNI Per Capita, Atlas Method (Current US$)'. Washington, DC: World Bank.
World Bank (2020c). 'Data: Hospital Beds (Per 1,000 People)'. Washington, DC: World Bank.
World Bank (2020d). 'Data: Physicians (Per 1,000 People)'. Washington, DC: World Bank.
World Bank (2022). 'Data: Current Health Expenditure (% of GDP)'. Washington, DC: World Bank.

Index

Tables and figures are indicated by an italic *t* and *f*, following the paragraph number.

For the benefit of digital users, indexed terms that span two pages (e.g., 52–53) may, on occasion, appear on only one of those pages.